Taming
YOUR PRIVATE
TH●UGHTS

Also by Jay Dennis and Marilyn Jeffcoat

The Prayer Experiment

The Prayer Experiment Manual

Taming
YOUR PRIVATE
TH⬡UGHTS

YOU CAN STOP SIN WHERE IT STARTS

Jay Dennis & Marilyn Jeffcoat
AUTHORS OF *THE PRAYER EXPERIMENT*

ZONDERVAN™

GRAND RAPIDS, MICHIGAN 49530

ZONDERVAN™

Taming Your Private Thoughts
Copyright © 2002 by Jay Dennis and Marilyn Jeffcoat

Requests for information should be addressed to:

Zondervan, *Grand Rapids, Michigan 49530*

Library of Congress Cataloging-in-Publication Data

Dennis, Jay, 1959-
    Taming your private thoughts : you can stop sin where it starts / Jay Dennis and
Marilyn Jeffcoat.
       p. cm.
    Includes bibliographical references.
    ISBN 0-310-23811-0
    1. Thought and thinking — Religious aspects — Christianity. 2. Temptation. 3. Sin.
I. Jeffcoat, Marilyn. II. Title.
    BV4598.4 .D46 2002
    241'.3 — dc21   2001005897

This edition printed on acid-free paper.

Interior design by Todd Sprague

Printed in the United States of America

02 03 04 05 06 07 / ❖ DC/ 10 9 8 7 6 5 4 3 2

Dedication

By Jay ...

I lovingly dedicate this book to my children, Will and Emily. You make me proud every day that I am your dad. Mom and I bless you. You are both such winners!

By Marilyn ...

I dedicate this book to my precious husband, Jon. Sweetheart, you certainly have had your hands full trying to tame me! Thanks for not giving up on me, for loving me unconditionally over the years, for consistently modeling unselfish servanthood, for encouraging me always to obey God's call upon my life, and for courageously wanting always to push the faith envelope together. There's no other guy like you. I love, cherish, respect, and really like you.

Contents

Acknowledgments

From Jay . . .

I wish to acknowledge the following people whose presence in my life have made this book possible. Thank you to. . .

- my loving wife and best friend, Angie. Your understanding of all of the demands in my life goes way beyond anything I could ever hope. About the time I think I could not possibly love you more, my heart grows.
- my writing partner, Marilyn. Your commitment to excellence and your genuine Christianity make being your partner a real privilege.
- the people of First Baptist Church at the Mall in Lakeland, Florida. Your never learning to say *No* to God is a constant joy to me.
- the staff team of First Baptist Church at the Mall. You amaze me to what degree you will go to in order to make a difference in our world.
- my parents, Bill and Donna Dennis. You never stopped believing in me.
- my prayer warrior, Jan Hunter. The hours you spend on your knees for me has made all the difference.
- my cherished friends in the ministry—T. W. Wilson, who is now in heaven, Billy Kim, Jimmy Draper, Jay Strack, Ken Alford, John Sullivan, Kelvin Mosely, and a host of others—who have extended Christ's love to me.

From Marilyn . . .

I acknowledge that. . .

- I have the greatest family in the world! Thank you, Jon, James, Mom, Dad, Sandy, Dot, and Cyndi for all the years and the many ways you have patiently and lovingly supported me as I did my ministry thing. I dearly love you all. "Boo," you have been nothing but a blessing to your dad and me. Thanks for your humor, love, unselfishness, helpfulness, and always being willing to risk it all for Christ's sake. You are the creative effort of which I am most proud!
- Without Jay Dennis, I could not have written this book. Little brother, our relationship has truly been iron sharpening iron and an incredible God-adventure.

- I am extraordinarily blessed to have the most wonderful friends—Sue, Pat, Ragan, Cindy, Tim, Teresa, Larry, Ginger, and Rick—who love me in spite of my being way behind in reciprocating dinner invitations! Cindy and Sue, your prayers and love keep me going.
- Without the anointed preaching and godly example of five pastors—Charlie Graves, Wilson Nelson, Jim Henry, Jimmy Knott, and Jay Dennis—my thoughts would have never been tamed and my spiritual growth severely stunted.
- Without the creative way in which The First Academy approached their staff expectations of me and God's leading Linda Knott to be my coteacher, I could not have had the freedom to pursue a writing ministry while I was on staff there.

I continually thank God for you all.

From Jay and Marilyn . . .

We wish to thank . . .

- Paul Engle, senior acquisitions editor at Zondervan, who has been a model of Christ-like mentoring and a good friend.
- Stan Gundry and the rest of the Zondervan team, whose excellence in publishing is only surpassed by the excellence of their consistent, godly lives.
- those who allowed us to share their stories for the encouragement of others and to glorify God for what he has done in their lives.
- the professional counselors—Glenda Hill, Dwight Bain, Patricia Maclay, and David Clarke—who allowed us to interview them and provided expert assistance with this manuscript.
- Martin Culpepper, who is more than our agent—a true friend and constant encourager to push the envelope for God.

Introduction

BE REAL. WOULD YOU WANT people to know your thoughts—*all* your thoughts? Of course you wouldn't. You want to protect your privacy.

But there is more to it, isn't there? While you may look as if you have it all together on the outside, you would be mortified if the people you see everyday really knew what went on inside of your heart and mind. In fact, either before or when you sit down to have a heart-to-heart conversation with God, there is usually a lot that you feel you need to clean up on the inside to get things right again. Unconfessed sin, anger, hurt, bitterness, fear, anxiety, stress, depression, or maybe guilt keep you from knowing the fullness of the Christian experience.

Think with me for a moment. Can you recall when your thought life changed from innocence to guilt, from unsoiled to tainted, from pure to worldly? The purpose of this book is to cause you to "S.T.O.P." (an acrostic that will mean more to you when you get into the last section of this book) and think about those things and maybe some other things you have not thought about in years. As you read these chapters, you will have the chance to get into other people's heads through the case studies and biblical stories. Perhaps in doing so you will see yourself and how you think about things more clearly.

As Jay and I worked on this book, we both by necessity had to "live it" for what turned out to be a l-o-n-g year! It was tough. For me, that meant a difficult journey of unpacking a lot of issues in my life that had been neatly stored away for decades. But I was serious about God's exposing—and then helping me deal with—anything in my life and in my thinking that might be a hindrance to the total enjoyment of my relationship with him. Reluctantly, I asked God to allow me to recall when and how in my childhood and adolescence the purity of my thought life was gradually stripped away. And then, fearfully, I asked him to expose as much of the sin and wrong thinking of my adulthood that he thought I was strong enough to bear.

Well, I should have known better! Jay and I learned well through the testing and writing of our last book, *The Prayer Experiment*, that we'd better be careful what we pray for—and this experience proved no different. For both of us the fiery furnace of trials, Satan's assault on the thought life, and surprise adverse circumstances were more like constant companions rather than the occasional drop-by visitors. Often it felt as if we were being put through the spin cycle—and our Enemy had an endless supply of quarters! It became painfully obvious that Satan did not want us dealing with that which can set us free.

In spite of that, both of us found great freedom in the process! And God did not abandon us at any time to work things out on our own. I found it liberating when God allowed me to trace the roots of my thought struggles to a fantasy life fostered by a teen-magazine crushes and overexposure to adult-themed television. As I carefully considered all that God was allowing me to recall, I realized that those things probably had as much impact on me as all the good parenting and church upbringing with which I was blessed. As character-shaping as the strong Christian influence on my life was, the introduction of one inappropriate way of thinking on top of another was just as strong—if not more so.

For decades this battle between wrong and right thinking raged inside of me—even while I was in full-time vocational ministry. Countless times in my past I have thought that others would be shocked or disappointed if they knew what I was really thinking, because I have often struggled with a thought life that was, at times, out of control and, at best, only partially controlled by the Holy Spirit. Often I had wished there was a way to successfully stop the seemingly uncontrollable unhealthy thoughts that bombarded my mind.

By God's grace over recent years, I have been blessed to see God do a huge work in my life—a major overhaul. The person I presently am only vaguely resembles the person I used to be. I am so grateful for the reality of the growth of the "fruit of the Spirit" (Galatians 5:22–23) in me. And then this book—which meant further painful thought- and life-tweaking—allowed more reclamation of my mind by the Holy Spirit. But don't get me wrong, the thought battle is not over for me! In fact, it is never over for believers. Every Christian who is striving to live a godly life must daily engage the enemy, Satan, who seeks to destroy all that God has accomplished in and through his or her life.

A word about the unique writing partnership with which I am blessed. God, in his immeasurable goodness and grace, allows all of us, as his adopted children in Christ, to enjoy Family—that is, "Family of God"—privileges. For me, one of the greatest Family blessings I have enjoyed in my Christian journey is my Father's introducing into my life other believers who have become like brothers and sisters to me. So, a few years ago God led Jay to my office door at First Baptist Church in Orlando to see if I would be interested in writing with him.

Jay has become a cherished brother in Christ. He has also become my pastor. When Jay first contacted me about writing with him, my husband and I visited Jay's church in Lakeland to see if he was "the real deal." We found then—and every day since—that he *is* the real deal. Since that first visit, we have rarely missed a Sunday of driving an hour each way from Orlando to Lakeland to hear Jay preach and to worship God with his congregation.

From the beginning and then consistently throughout our writing relationship, I have seen one of the most believable Christians I have ever encountered. This man does not deviate from trying to obey God in all things. The verse that immediately comes to mind when I think of Jay is Matthew 5:8: "Blessed are the pure in heart, for they will see God."

Because of what I have observed in his credibility and in his professional abilities, I felt Jay's was the perfect voice for our book. You will notice that we have chosen to write this book in Jay's first-person-singular voice. Our desire was to facilitate ease in reading and to present our ideas from a seasoned pastoral perspective. The ideas presented are a blending of our perspectives, which are born out of the decades of ministry experience that we both have had.

Some of the subject matter with which we deal is a little more "delicate in nature" than most Sunday sermons my preacher-partner delivers or I generally discuss in a seminary setting. But there is no way to deal with thought-life issues without discussing some private matters. Jay and I believe these to be important Family matters that we must confront as the sensitive-to-the-true-needs-of-people church and as growing Christians.

Our writing partnership has proven ideal for this particular project. For example, there were a number of interviews with females that I conducted for this book instead of Jay, because he—as a male and a pastor—felt it inappropriate for him to discuss what were often intimate details concerning these women's personal lives, and vice versa was true as well. Our teaming not only allows us to protect our integrity but also bolster our effectiveness. We have been blessed to see how God uses us as members of the body of Christ to help and complement each other. Partnering together we can offer not only a sometimes-radically-different male and female viewpoint, but also different life, ministry, and theological perspectives. We have sought to blend our contributions together in what we pray is one well-orbed voice.

Does the S.T.O.P. method that we introduce in this book really work for nipping sin in the bud? Yes. Yes! Jay and I both have made it a part of our lives as we individually have dealt with wrong or sinful thinking. We have seen it help those with whom we counsel and those whom we teach. In addition, we have been pleased that every counselor with whom we have shared this method has agreed that it can make a huge difference in the way people think and live.

Are you ready to S.T.O.P. those thoughts that constantly disrupt your fellowship with God, that have a stronghold on your life, or that keep you feeling defeated? If so, then it is high time you start *Taming Your Private Thoughts!*

MARILYN JEFFCOAT

Part One

Charting Sin's Beginning

Each one is tempted when, by his own evil desire, he is dragged away and enticed. Then, after desire has conceived, it gives birth to sin; and sin, when it is full-grown, gives birth to death.

Don't be deceived, my dear brothers.

JAMES 1:14–16

It Began Just as a Thought

NEVER HAVE I FELT MORE UNDONE. Hot streams of tears cascaded down my cheeks as I sobbed. I repeatedly cried aloud, "Oh, my God, what have I done, what have I done!" Each mile that I drove, I became more consumed with sheer panic coupled with overwhelming remorse and unbridled anger at myself for allowing this to happen. Unable to drive any farther, I found myself slamming on the brakes and pulling over because I was feeling physically ill from the gut-wrenching pain.

The place where I stopped my car is the place to which I regularly retreat for solitude and quiet time with God. It is the idyllic location where I run after work and unload the day's burdens on an understanding heavenly Father. It is also the beautiful setting where I regularly lead a men's discipleship group in the challenge to embrace uncompromising devotion to the Lord. Now, from the perspective of where I was crouched beside my car, my favorite place—where so many things in my mind had been settled—seemed foreign and anything but peaceful. I could not believe I was there and in this horrible mess.

When I was finally able to stumble back into the car, I turned off the engine and just sat there in the darkness. All I could hear was my rapid breathing and pounding heart. *Okay, let me think. I have to pull myself together. What am I going to say? The first question she is going to ask me is "Why, Jay?"*—a question I now am forced to stop and ask myself.

We had often talked about how we didn't have to worry about this happening to us. Now, here I was being faced with sharing something that would break her heart into a thousand pieces. This is the woman who was there for me during the sacrificial seminary years when I was preoccupied with graduate and postgraduate courses. She is the one who stood beside me through unbelievably tough church situations where most people would have said, "I didn't sign up for this." What a fool I have been! I just crushed her trust and communicated by my actions that "I don't love you like you think I do." *Oh, God, I have given up all we had taken years to build... and for what? An adrenalin rush? A testosterone thrill? A short-lived pleasure? An adolescent fling?* I now realize—all too late—that I got major ripped-off in that exchange.

Things will never again be the same. How will I tell my son ... my daughter? How can I possibly look into the eyes of that young man who implicitly trusts his dad and say, "Son, Dad has been unfaithful to your mother. Life as we have known it has ended." How can I peer into the loving eyes of a young lady who has put her dad on a high pedestal and say, "Honey, Dad has made a selfish choice that is going to change our family's future."

What about the people I serve as pastor, who look to me as their spiritual leader? Will their view of God—and Christian leaders—be forever altered? Will the people that came to Christ under my ministry someway feel that their decision wasn't valid? Will those I baptized or married feel like it wasn't God-blessed? I'm through! I'm done! It's all over! I've thrown everything away! What took many years to build was torn down by one choice ... one disastrous choice. There's no rewind button on this one.

But there is a S.T.O.P. play. I cannot tell you the pleasure—and relief—it gives me to tell you that none of this has happened. I have often used such mental rehearsals of potential consequences as a deterrent to dwelling or acting on sinful thoughts. Such a painful exercise has often served as a powerful reminder to me that I never want to go there. It's not worth it. Unfortunately, I have known too many

Christian men and women who either did not adequately rehearse the consequences of potential sinful choices—or simply chose to act in spite of their better judgment.

How Could a Man of God Do That?

It began just as a thought—and then a fantasy. Jack thought he could handle indulging in a mental fantasy world. After all, his marriage was shaky—it had been for years—and he craved the intimacy and excitement he lacked with his wife. In interviewing him for this book, Jack painfully recounted how at first it was "just thoughts" that he let linger. While this caused him feelings of great guilt, he began to desire stimulation beyond what his mind alone could supply.

Jack began watching inappropriate shows and movies on television—sometimes peering at the scrambled images of cable premium channels to which he did not subscribe. This initially did the trick in satisfying the growing sexual appetite in him. During this time, Jack and his wife were living separate lives—under the same roof. For a long time they had been functioning—and growing—apart. A sexual relationship between the two of them had been nonexistent for years.

> The mind of man is the battleground on which every moral and spiritual battle is fought.
>
> —J. Oswald Sanders[1]

One day a young woman came to see Jack for marriage counseling. Up to this point in his ministry, this seasoned pastor had consistently followed all appropriate counseling guidelines. This session, however, proved to be a turning point by opening up a world of fantasy that he did not know existed. A shift happened as a result of a decisive session that day: Jack was introduced to the Internet as a vehicle for sexual exploration in a way that enticed him to check it out for himself.

Concerning this turning point, Jack explains, "At first it was simple. I had never been unfaithful in the entire sixteen years of marriage—not even remotely close. I swore I would never be. I discovered I could see pictures on the Internet, and no one would ever know. It was terribly wrong, and I cannot believe I let it happen." He soon became involved in cybersex via Internet chat rooms. This led to telephone calls to cyber-partners and ultimately to a rendezvous with a woman he had met online.

Jack was serving as the president of a denominational conference when he met this woman in another city. They ended up committing adultery. Jack says, "There was no excuse for it. It was wrong and it was sin. We both knew it!" But they kept on meeting each week—on his golf days and any other time he could possibly arrange in his schedule.

Eventually Jack's wife found out about the affair. Soon his church leadership was informed of the double life Jack had been leading. He lost his pastorate, his marriage, and his family. Jack now looks back with remorse over losing everything. "I walked away with nothing. Everything in my life was gone. I lost everything of value to me. I was unemployed. I became completely broke with no job, no skills, and no reputation. Calamity after calamity came. I felt all alone. I would not pray, because I knew God would not listen. I talked to no one. There were only one or two people I ever saw. I continued in the relationship I was in. I did not try to hide it. I made foolish decisions on top of the ones I had already made. Sin is very blinding." Jack's thought life became master of his real life—and his world was never the same.[2]

Thought Genesis

"In the beginning was . . . a thought." Everything begins with a thought. God thought it. God spoke it. It happened: The world came into being. The book of Genesis is replete with accounts of beginnings: the beginning of creation, the beginning of humankind, the beginning of humankind's fall into sin, the beginning of the redemptive process for humankind, the beginning of the Israelite nation. In fact, the first phrase in the Hebrew text of Genesis 1:1 is *bereshith*—"in the beginning"— which is also the Hebrew title[3] of the book.[4] God thought and acted on his thoughts. Man and woman thought and acted on their thoughts.

In fact, everything we see and everything that happens began with someone having had a thought and then acting on it. The Empire State

Building and the Golden Gate Bridge didn't "just happen." The Super Bowl and U.S. Open don't "just happen." Planners and dreamers, promoters and builders have creative thoughts and act on those thoughts. A what-if, an imagine-that, an I-wonder-about-this begins the process and ultimately compels the thought-meister to act.

Think about it. Thoughts have produced . . .

- the Seven Wonders of the Ancient World, as well as Hiroshima.
- a cure for polio, as well as World Trade Center Towers and Pentagon terrorist attacks.
- Beethoven's *Fifth Symphony*, as well as crack cocaine.
- communism's fall, as well as Bosnia's ethnic cleansing.
- Dr. DeBakey's heart-bypass surgery, as well as Dr. Kevorkian's death machine.

Psychologists say that ten thousand thoughts go through the human mind in one day. That is 3,500,000,000 thoughts a year![5] Someone has said that every kidnapping was once one of those thoughts, and every extramarital affair was first a fantasy.[6] Within our thoughts resides the capacity for good or evil, for help or hurt, for positive or negative actions, for trusting or doubting. How we respond to life events and possibilities has its genesis in our thought life. We are bombarded with sounds and sights that plant thoughts within our mind—to which I will refer as "thought plants."

That to which we are exposed often dictates what we think about. "Left on their own," our thoughts have a tendency toward that which is wrong instead of heading in the direction of what is right. Sinful thoughts are just one step removed from sinful actions. The book of Proverbs asserts, "For as he thinks within himself, so he is"

> Within our thoughts resides the capacity for good or evil, for help or hurt, for positive or negative actions, for trusting or doubting.

(Proverbs 23:7 NASB). Control your thought life, and you control your actions.

How does the sin problem begin in the life of an individual? Is there a prescribed formula for how a typical person falls into sin? No, it's different for each one of us. There seems to be, however, a diabolical, unique design based on what will most likely tempt each one of us personally to give in to sin. The Garden of Eden account (Genesis 3) illustrates a broad pattern of the temptation-sin process. Satan used a "thought plant" to tempt the world's first female, Eve. She spotted in the middle of the garden a tree, the Tree of the Knowledge of Good and Evil—a thought plant. Satan would use this off-limits, stay-away-from-it-or-else, super-desirable-but-totally-forbidden fruit tree to plant the thought of sinning against God.

How did the tempter operate? He insinuated that Eve was missing out on so much because of God. He implied that God was not good, that God's Word was not totally true. These are the thought plants planted by Satan, seeded in the mind of Eve—and which, by the way, he continues to plant in our minds today:

Thought Plant #1:	"You're free to do as you please." *"You will surely not die" (v. 4).*
Thought Plant #2:	"No one has a right to tell you what to do." *"Indeed, God has said, 'You shall not eat of any tree of the Garden'?" (v. 1 NASB).*
Thought Plant #3:	"Let me show you another way to think about it." *"Did God REALLY say that?" (v. 1).*
Thought Plant #4:	"God doesn't want you to have any fun." *"For God knows that when you eat of it your eyes will be opened, and you will be like God, knowing good and evil" (v. 5).*

While we will not be confronted by a talking snake today, we will encounter a smooth-talking, deadly-as-a-snake enemy. Satan continues to employ this method effectively. So we need to be alert and recognize his *modus operandi* with the following two steps.

1. The seed of the sin problem is planted in our thoughts. Utilizing the power of suggestions, Satan plants thoughts that are often unrelenting and enticing, seductive and captivating:

   - "Go ahead, everybody else does it."
   - "If it feels good, do it."
   - "Nobody else has to know."
   - "You deserve it."
   - "One time won't hurt."
   - "You can't live your life based on an outdated book."
   - "You can sin and get by with it."

2. If these thoughts are allowed to become runaway—unchecked and uncontrolled—they will eventually lead to sinful actions. Then it is not a matter of if, but when.

How alluring! In a variety of beautiful shapes, sizes, and colors, the new genus of "thought plants" has its roots in the old ones. Old and new bear definite similarities. They still need to be fed in order to grow and flourish. Their fruit, while tantalizing, is still forbidden and deadly. The garden of our minds can become overgrown with these more-vociferous-than-Kudzu Satan-thought plants that can choke out God-thought plants if left unattended.

Eve Bit the Apple and They Both Bit the Dust

Genesis offers so few details of what transpired between that first husband and wife in the Garden of Eden as they contemplated sin. In our off-the-wall way of reenacting the sequence of events in our minds, Marilyn and I have imagined what might have transpired if the Eden scene were somehow scripted for twenty-first-century television instead of the Hebrew Pentateuch.

It was an ordinary day in Paradise. Adam and Eve rode together in their Bronco SUV for their morning commute in to the office, where they both worked for the Big Boss. Traffic was moving as slow as snails on the freeway, plus this idiotic mule-of-a-driver had just cut him off—all of which made Adam consider inventing road rage as a solution for dealing with this early morning vehicular challenge. Eve was oblivious to it all as she read the day's newspaper and listened to a favorite CD.

The couple did not talk to each other until they reached the parking garage of 100 Garden Office Tower. As they grabbed their briefcases, they kissed each other on the cheek and said, "See ya later." And off they went into separate directions. Adam dashed for the elevator as Eve stopped by the coffee shop for a bagel and latte.

Once in his corner office, Adam began checking his e-mail and voice mail. Within minutes he was responding to two messages from L. E. Fante. Upon reaching Mr. Fante, Adam was reminded of a luncheon meeting at the Oasis Country Club for the purpose of planning this year's charity rodeo.

As Eve settled at her desk, she began syncing her pocket PC with her desktop computer. After retrieving today's appointments and downloading some must-read periodicals, she began the arduous task of doing the layout for this month's issue of Better Homes and Gardens. *While she was playing phone-tag with one of her photo journalists, Ima Swann, she began surfing the Net. During this process Eve ran across a new site:* Apples R Us. *Listed on their homepage were many products they carry, including apple pie, apple muffins, apple butter, apple sauce, apple cobbler, apple cider, Apple Jacks, apple preserves, apple fritters, Apple computers, and Apple Surprise.*

Interested in Apple Surprise, she clicked on the product icon for a description of this item. Instead seeing of a product description, she was linked to a chat room with a visitor, with the screen name "Lou C. Furr," who was already present and who immediately addressed Eve.

```
Lou: "Hello, Eve."
Eve: "Hello."
Lou: "I am glad you entered this chat room.
      I have been wanting to meet you ever
      since you and your husband moved into
      Garden Estates."
Eve: "Are you a neighbor of ours?"
Lou: "I have a place there, but I come and
      go a lot. I am what you might call a
      traveling salesman."
Eve: "What do you sell? Apple products?"
Lou: "Actually. I represent an organization
      called God-Makers."
```

Eve: "What! I only know of one God. Are
there others?"

Lou: "Well, there certainly can be. You
seem like a smart young woman who
would know a good opportunity when she
saw one. Would you care to join me for
lunch today at Applebee's and learn
all I can do to improve your life?"

Eve: "That sounds intriguing! Oh . . . why
not. It looks like I have some white
space around 12:30. Would that work
for you? At which restaurant location
would you like to meet? "

Lou: "Twelve-thirty works for me as well. I
will meet you near the hostess stand
at the Applebee's on Knowledge Tree
Avenue South."

Eve: "Great. See you there."

Eve signed off her computer and buzzed Adam's office. Adam was out
of his office gathering information for the next day's meeting with the Man
Upstairs. Eve left a voice mail for her husband informing him of her luncheon engagement and inviting him to join her. Running late for his lunch date,
Adam neglected to check his messages when he returned to the office. He
dashed out of the office with no knowledge of Eve's invitation.

Around noon, Eve tried to reach Adam again. Unsuccessful, she left a
voice message on his cell phone and then left work to drive to Applebee's,
where Lou was already waiting on her.

Lou: "Hello, Eve. I am Lou C. Furr."

Eve: "It's a pleasure to meet you. Am I running late?"

Lou: "Oh, no. You are right on time. In fact,
they just told me that they have our table
ready."

Eve followed Lou to a table under a lovely tree on the patio. Lou
informed Eve that he would like to take the liberty to order for them both.
Soon the server arrived to take their order and shortly returned with their
drinks. A consummate pitchman, Lou enthralled his dining companion as
they leisurely ate their lunch with his dazzling ideas of how she could be

promoted beyond her present position and enjoy the good life as she expanded her mind—and her capabilities. This sounded almost too good to be true; yet Satan assured her that she had been previously misinformed about territorial limitations that would keep her from pursuing this advancement.

Lou: "Eve, are you ready for this new venture?"
Eve: "Uh, I guess ... but I sure wish Adam were here to hear all of this. Can he be brought in on this deal, too?"
Lou: "Of course. I will leave the necessary paperwork for him as well. Now, why don't you sign this contract? And we'll seal the deal with some of this spectacular dessert."

With those words, Satan pointed to their server who was approaching with a flaming dessert of an array of fruit with a delicious, shiny apple at its center.

Eve: "Oh, I mustn't eat that. It is beautiful, and I would love to have some ... but I am on a restricted diet."
Lou: "Don't be silly. You simply must try a taste of it. Surely one little bite of the apple won't hurt you...."

Bedazzled

"I think you're hot, baby," Elliot, the office nerd in the sell-your-soul-to-the-devil-for-seven-lousy-wishes movie *Bedazzled* says to the devil when he meets her. She coyly responds, "You have no idea." Like Eve in the Garden, this naïve character has no idea with whom he is dealing. When Elliot meets this devil-with-the-red-dress-on, he is totally captivated by her provocative presence and ideas. The geek guy is immediately propositioned by Ms. Luciferess, who says she will change his life and grant him seven wishes—for a price. Contract negotiations are followed by Elliot's ordering the usual: riches, power, fame, sensitivity, athletic prowess, and, of course, the woman of his dreams. Elliot learns quickly the lesson "Be careful what you wish for" when he is double-crossed after every wish by this snake of a woman.

Every word that flows out of this Satan-in-stilettos's mouth is a lie. When she whispers promises of love, happiness, and wealth, what this conniving devil really means is hate, sadness, and despair. While this remake of a 1967 comedy by the same title is fictitious, the plot rings true to what each of us experiences when we encounter Satan and are seduced by his enticing offer to make our wishes come true.

Many of us make deals with the devil without even knowing it. For many of us our Top Seven Wishes might be similar to those of Elliot.

1. I wish I had a million dollars.
2. I wish I were powerful.
3. I wish I were pretty and thin, handsome and fit.
4. I wish I were younger.
5. I wish I had certain possessions.
6. I wish I were smarter.
7. I wish I were truly happy.

We are compelled to answer what cost we are willing to pay in order to have our worldly wishes satisfied. Like Elliot we can be easily deceived by the enticement of something better, something beautiful, something else, something more, something beyond. We often find out too late that not everything is as it appears—not everything that glitters is gold, not everything shiny is precious.

Snake Charmer

Daily Telegraph
Tuesday, 23 September, 1997
Snake Charmers Arrested

TWO Indian snake charmers were arrested in New Delhi after threatening a woman with their serpents and stealing a gold ring from her.

Scores of snake charmers roam the streets of the Indian capital, performing for tourists. Venom from the captive snakes is removed by their handlers but some of the snake charmers still try to intimidate people into giving them money.

For generations they have intrigued and enthralled, giving children their first introduction to snakes. But today, Indian snake charmers are a community fighting to keep their tradition alive. The saffron-clad, mysterious-eyed charmers are being ordered to free their snakes and to look for alternative ways to earn a living. Invoking the 1972 Wildlife Protection Act, which makes it illegal to capture snakes, wildlife activists and the municipal authorities in India have begun raiding snake charmers' homes, forcing open their battered baskets and freeing reptiles into the wild.

Wildlife activists complain that cobras used by snake charmers are forced to bite on a piece of cloth, which is then jerked out of their mouths, ripping their teeth out. This can often lead to septicaemia in the snakes, resulting in a slow and painful death over three or four months. Meanwhile, snakes like the King Cobra and the Python are on the list of endangered species.

Snake charmer Durga Nath says snakes are treated like family members, and even worshipped. "We go to the jungles and also to the fields and catch these snakes. We keep them at our houses. We rear and train them. Then, we perform on city roads. For a certain period we keep these snakes and, after that, we free them." Many believe snake charmers, as synonymous with India as the Taj Mahal, are a part of the country's heritage and should not be wiped out.[7]

Tales and scenes of snake charmers can be captivating. I cannot imagine what would cause an individual to brave planned encounters—and interactions—with these deadly creatures. On the other hand, I must admit that I am a huge fan of Steve Irwin, Australia's "Crocodile Hunter." I sit in awe of him as he defies danger by wrestling crocodiles, climbing trees to play with orangutans, or picking up the most venomous snakes known on earth and treating them as trusted friends.

> Satan's venomous words often blind us to the reality of the consequences of sin.

In one episode, Irwin was in Africa hunting for cobras and found the dreaded Red Spitting Cobra. Steve was wearing sunglasses—something he normally doesn't sport—which I soon discovered were not for the purpose of blocking UV rays, but for protecting his eyes from the cobra's venom. This venom, which the cobra will aim at a person's face, can be accurately sprayed up to eight feet and cause blindness.[8] The reptile effectively uses that which comes out of his mouth to blind the unsuspecting victim before he inflicts his deadly blow. The "Crocodile Hunter" ended up needing those glasses, as the red cobra was soon "on target" for his eyes.

How like our enemy! Satan's venomous words often blind us to the reality and consequences of sin. While snake charmers still exist in the world, we dare not forget that Eve was charmed by a snake—and we can be, too!

I Thought It Was Just a King Snake!

Palm Beach Gardens, Florida—Mike Kiekenapp was mimicking what he thought was a harmless King Snake when the reptile suddenly bit the 15-year-old on his outstretched tongue. What the Howell Watkins Middle School eighth-grader didn't realize was that the 2-foot-long snake he scooped up in his front yard the day before was a poisonous coral snake—with cobra-like venom. Kiekanapp was showing the snake to friends when it bit him. He then jumped on his bike and raced a quarter-mile to his home. The family called 911. When Palm Beach Gardens paramedic Tony Vazquez and his fellow firefighters arrived at 5 P.M. Friday, Mike was going downhill fast.

"Upon arrival [Rescue 61] found a 15-year-old male patient vomiting, drooling, diaphoretic [sweating profusely], extremely anxious, with bite marks to the patient's tongue," Vazquez's report said. Thirteen minutes later, Kiekenapp was rushed into St. Mary's Medical Center, where he was given anti-venom to neutralize the poison as a tube was put down his throat to retain an airway because his tongue was rapidly swelling. He spent several days in critical condition on a respirator because his swelled throat interfered with the breathing, said his mother, Dorothy. Doctors told her he would have died without prompt medical care, she said. "On Saturday and Sunday, his face really blew up," his mother said. "He looked like the Pillsbury Doughboy."[9]

Fortunately, Mike survived this ordeal. He reminds me of a lot of people today who are playing with—toying with—temptation. Similar to the way someone can mistake a coral snake for a king snake, people can easily be deceived into thinking that they can handle dangerous— or deadly—temptation without being bitten. It's not only dangerous to attempt to get close to one of those disguised coral snakes that can be found everywhere. It's equally dangerous when we're tempted to think, "I can handle it." Think about these examples:

- David, as he looked lustfully on Bathsheba, must have thought, "I can handle it."
- The teenager, curious about astrology and the occult, who occasionally dabbled in it but is now "in deep," must have thought, "I can handle it."
- The famous, young Hollywood actor who has repeatedly gotten arrested for drug use and parole violations must have thought that first time he snorted cocaine, "I can handle it."
- The man who loses everything on a get-rich-quick scheme must have thought, "I can handle it."
- Ananias and Sapphira, who became enamored with money, must have thought, "We can handle it."
- The national Christian radio personality who resigned from his ministry after having admitted to having an "inappropriate relationship" with a woman not his wife[10] must have thought, "I can handle it."
- The person who would not deal with grief and who now is struggling with major depression must have thought, "I can handle it."
- A once shoe-in for the Hall of Fame, former baseball player who lost it all because he gambled on a game, must have thought, "I can handle it."
- Peter, who was filled with self-confidence as he walked by the fire to warm himself prior to denying Jesus three times, must have thought, "I can handle them."
- The individual who has allowed a misunderstanding to break a relationship and is now unforgiving and bitter must have thought about unresolved hurt feelings, "I can handle it."

- The former denominational leader who used his position to pad his own pocket as he carried on marital infidelity must have thought, "I can handle it."
- The lonely wife who began flirting with a guy at her office and who, after agreeing to meet him for drinks after work, found herself in a motel room alone with him must have thought, "I can handle this."

They are all coral snakes, whose venom poisons life but who were mistaken for a harmless king snake. The fifteen-year-old bitten by the coral snake recovered; some who handle these symbolic coral snakes never recover.

You Can't Compare Apples and Oranges

I tend to perceive situations in life one way while my wife, Angie, thinks quite another way. At times the results have been hilarious, but at other times it has gotten me into a heap of trouble. I guess that stuff about men being from Mars and women being from Venus is true. I must admit that I am having a hard enough time just getting a heavenly perspective on earth, much less trying to understand the other planetary languages of the opposite sex! It's an age-old problem. Men and women are different in every fiber of their being—and they are as tough to compare as apples and oranges. On one hand it's "Viva la Difference!" and on the other hand it's "I'll-Never-Ever-Understand-a la Difference!"

Not long ago, I thought I would do something that would earn me brownie points with my wife. I volunteered to go to the grocery store, one of the chores I most despise. Skeptical about my being able to properly execute this duty but really needing my help because she was in a time crunch, my wife reluctantly gave me her list. Off I went on my mission!

After arriving at the grocery store and filling my basket with all those things that my wife must have inadvertently left off the list—like Gummie Bears, Cheez Wiz, sugar-drenched cereal, and powdered doughnut holes[11]—I noticed that Angie had listed "Jello" as an item, but she had not specified the flavor. My daughter, Emily, was with me, and she suggested that her mom probably needed strawberry Jello. Sounded good to me. So, I had Emily push the cart and go out for a long pass, and in I tossed some strawberry Jello for a touchdown—and some strange looks on the faces of other more sedate shoppers!

As I proudly returned home with mission accomplished, I was feeling a bit cocky about what I had done for my wife. But that was not my worst mistake. I mentioned to Angie that she had not bothered to tell me exactly what kind of Jello she wanted. And that is when the battle between Mr. Adam Apple and Mrs. Eve Orange ensued.

> Ang:"Oh, YES, I DID tell you."
> Jay: "Oh, no, you DIDN'T."
> Ang:"Oh, yes, I did, DEAR, but you weren't listening."
> Jay: "Well, HONEY, thanks for thanking me for going to the store for you!"

Gone was the joy of doing something nice for my beloved. (By the way, I *did* get the right kind, but who's belaboring the point?) I just turned and muttered, "I'm going into the other room to catch up on some pouting." Chalk it up to how we think—differently!

My wife, and I suppose this goes for all women, has the uncanny ability to do a zillion things at once. She can talk on the phone, prepare a meal, write a letter, and take care of our children's urgent needs at the same time. Not me, man! I can't even talk on the phone and flip channels on the TV at the same time. (You know those homes that have phones in the bathrooms? Obviously this was designed with women—definitely not men—in mind. We would most certainly end up flushing the receiver!)

Men and women are simply wired differently by divine design. To which my writing partner is shaking her head and saying, "Amen!" We have illustrated this by comparing apples and oranges.

Yet while men and women differ in so many ways, we are very much alike in one particular area: We are equally vulnerable to Satan's deceiving us and tempting us to sin. Our thought lives—although they may be focused on quite diverse things—can be uniformly damning to our lives and witness as Christians. The enemy's modus operandi is planting thoughts that will appeal not only to the sexes but to what will most entice us as individuals to sin. Temptations are not one-size-fits-all but are tailor-made to fit each of us.

I am not tempted to drink, so Satan doesn't even bother to try and plant the thought in my mind to go to the local Beverage Castle to stock up on six-packs. I am, however, tempted to lose my temper while driving. So guess what? Often I'm confronted with drivers who do not possess my gift of wisdom behind the wheel—thus putting my Christian mindset to test. Inevitably I will get behind someone going ten miles per hour in a no-passing-zone while the speed limit is forty-five.

I remember one Sunday morning as I drove from my house to church, I found myself behind a slowpoke and couldn't pass him. I'm embarrassed to tell you that I prayed—aloud, with the emphasis on "loud"—he would turn into the Presbyterian church between my house and First Baptist rather than driving all the way to our church. Praise God, he did! Less than an hour later, as I was preaching in church, I was telling people how they should live consistent lives before the Lord. As I was bringing home the point, a sick feeling in the pit of my soul began gnawing at me. It was, no doubt, the Holy Spirit saying "There's something wrong with this picture."

Men	Women
Black and Decker power tools	Creative Memories photo alb
Deer camp	Bridal and baby showers
Levis and a flannel shirt	Laura Ashley prints
Remote control	Off-limits purse
Barry Bonds	Oprah Winfrey
Directions-allergic	Back-seat driver
Pumping iron	Jenny Craig
Saturday afternoon football games	Shop till you drop
Toilet seat left up	Hair in the shower drain
Fix it	Feel it
Bob Villa	Martha Stewart
"Yep, nope, huh, uh-huh"	"Share with me all the detai
Pout	Tears
"I'll be home soon!"	"I have nothing to wear!"
Golf weekends	In-home shopping partie:
Commitmentaphobia	Insectaphobia

Whatever your vulnerabilities, you can be sure that's where Satan will attempt to landscape your mind with seemingly beautiful and luscious thought plants. He will purposefully place exquisite wrong-thought specimens in the garden of your mind, for he knows that every temptation comes to us via our thoughts.[12] Today we are still overgrown with plants from the cuttings of Eden's inviting, but forbidden, vegetation.

"Hangest thou in there, oh, baby!!"

Now a word of encouragement for you: There may be times as you are reading the first eight chapters of *Taming Your Private Thoughts* that feelings of discouragement or defeat surface. You may find yourself thinking, "Yes! That's the kind of problem with which I continually struggle and have had no permanent success in dealing with. When are you going to tell me how to stop this?" Well, as the little sign next to my computer reads, "Hangest thou in there, oh, baby!!" There is hope revealed and explained in the last four chapters. Let me caution you, however, not to give into the temptation to jump ahead to the ending. Make yourself deal with the tough issues concerning sinful thoughts first. Then you can better understand and appreciate God's wonderful help.

A sin flow-chart—depicting the process of sin—taken from James 1:14–16 will be introduced in chapters 1–8. This will give you a visual reminder of the process that will be explained in each chapter.

The first step in the sin process is *temptation*. "But each one is tempted . . ." (James 1:14). *Each one* speaks of the common struggle with temptation that we all share and the predictable way in which sin occurs. This is Step 1 in what happens in the life of every person who gives into sinful thoughts. You will soon see that each step in this sin flow-chart takes us further away from God.

Step 1.
TEMPTATION
"But each one is tempted . . ."

Unless the sin progression is stopped, it will continue on to the next step, which is . . .

2

Flirting with Desire

Sweaty palms. Fluttering eyelids. Nervous laughter. Irregular breathing. Body language that says, "I'm interested." Flirtation in progress. Then, when there's enough courage, the pick-up line: "Excuse me. Do you have a Band-Aid? I skinned my knee when I fell for you." Okay, I admit that the line is not original and just a bit corny. Give me a break. I am more than a couple of decades out of practice. Remember, I'm a long-time-happily-married-guy-with-eyes/pick-up-lines-only-for-my-mate.

But if I were to advise a single male on the art of flirtation with a Christian female, I might offer these sure-to-get-her-attention pick-up lines:

"Pardon me, but I believe one of your ribs belongs to me."
"Do you believe in divine appointments?"
"Is it a sin that you stole my heart?"
"God told me to come talk to you."
"Nice Bible."

Flirtation must be governed. A guy can be labeled "a player" if he hits on every woman who crosses his path. A woman can be labeled "a tease" if she is too approachable to too many. Married men and women can be labeled "unfaithful" if they continue to strut their stuff, roll their eyes, whisper sweet nothings, or give off an air of "I'm available" after they've said their "I do's" to someone else. Inappropriate flirting with the opposite sex is wrong. So is flirting with wrong thoughts.

Satan is a seduction artist who hits on everyone—male and female, married and single, young and old alike—and has a perfect 1000 batting average. He hits in all places—in the car, at work, at home, and even at church. He hits at all times—when we expect it and especially when we don't. Satan has perfected his craft over years of experience with people. After all these centuries, we are still naïve about this temptation gigolo. Be certain: Satan's pick-up lines are smooth—and they work:

"Come on. It's just innocent fun."
"It can't be wrong if it feels so right."
"You deserve more than this."
"Try it. You won't be sorry."
"Just this once."
"Got nerve?"
"Do it NOW."

I Only Read It for the Articles

I remember well the first time I looked at a *Playboy* magazine. I was in the fourth or fifth grade, and a classmate introduced me to this magazine that apparently was a part of his father's stash. It was after school, and we were hanging out at his house. He had hidden the magazine behind some junk in a field close to his house. No one could see us. No one knew what we were doing. There, behind that trash pile, my thought life was introduced to trashy images that could never be erased.

Playboy, the world's number-one men's magazine with a monthly circulation of more than three million U.S. readers,[1] has enticed many young—and old—males to take a look. While men jokingly comment, "I only read it for the articles," I want to say, "Yeah, right. Then you would keep purchasing the magazine if Hefner replaced the bunny centerfold and photos with human-interest stories, news briefs, and business analyses?"

But lest I seem biased, let's consider torrid-variety romance novels. Guys aren't the only ones hooked on trashy reading material. Fifty-three percent of all mass-market paperback books sold in this country are romance novels. Approximately nineteen publishing houses produce romance novels. In 1996, 2020 romance novels were released, with 182 million copies sold in that same year. Sold in over one hundred foreign markets and translated into more than twenty-five languages, romances generate approximately one billion dollars per year in sales and earn more money in the United States than baseball![2]

It's not just the stats, but my observations have led me to believe that we have a new national pastime. I am talking about the saintly grandmother-types who swap grocery bags full of paperbacks. After observing this on a number of occasions and being brought up-to-speed on what these women were doing by my perceptive wife, I decided I would interrupt—just for the fun of it—a deal going down.

"Good morning, ladies! I see you are trading bags of books again. That's great! I love to see people enjoy reading. I am a bookaholic, too. Can I get in on one of your exchanges?" I teasingly inquired.

"Uh, er, um, Pastor, I am not sure that you would enjoy reading what we like to read. These are women's books," the veteran swapper explained.

"Oh, well, then maybe I need to get some of your books for my wife. She loves to read as well. Who are your favorite Christian women writers?" I coyly asked.

"Actually, Pastor, these are not exactly 'Christian' books, although they aren't exactly un-Christian either. They are romance stories. You know we widows are very lonely, and we like to read these just to pass our time."

"Romance stories? Let me see. . ." I said, feigning shock as I reached in and pulled out one of the books that would rival a "girlie magazine" for its provocative cover. As I flipped through a few of the pages in this book, I began reading aloud some of the torrid copy.

Quickly I was stopped by the other woman, who begged me to stop. "Pastor, pl-l-e-ease don't read any more. It's not proper. You've got to understand. We're older women. That stuff doesn't mean anything to us. You are a younger man, and it's not right for you to read that sort of stuff."

Well, they *were* right. It wasn't right for me to read that stuff—nor was it right for them. But something tells me I probably got that message across. I don't think there will be any more trashy-romances-swapping at the church for these two—at least, when the preacher's in town! Now, to turn my attention to *The National Enquirer* discussion at the women's group. . . (Not really. I'm just kidding.)

While I joke about these things, there is a serious epidemic of acceptable-but-harmful entertainment habits that are impacting the minds of Christians who do not recognize the inherent dangers of their reading, viewing, and listening practices. Do any of the justifications sound familiar?

- "I only went to that R-rated movie because my favorite actor was in it."
- "I only watch MTV because I like to watch certain entertainers perform their hits."
- "I only watch that soap opera because I've been keeping up with the story line since high school days, and its characters seem like old friends."
- "I only go to the clubs because I am lonely and want to meet people."
- "I only listen to that music because I like the beat, plus I don't pay any attention to the lyrics."
- "I only watch that questionable sitcom to relax and shut out the world after a hard day's work."

So what's the problem with these forms of entertainment if the person's intentions are innocent? Even if people don't think they are being affected by these activities, these images, words, and sounds can open a gate to the mind. Once an impure thought makes its way through the mind-gate, unless that thought is stopped, the next step is fantasizing over these thoughts. Fertile soil in which sin can easily grow has been created by such thought-pollution.

The Lord warned the first son, Cain: "If you do what is right, will you not be accepted? But if you do not do what is right, sin is crouching at your door; it desires to have you, but you must master it" (Genesis 4:7). These words apply to each one of us. Our minds are the door-keepers—the gate-keepers—to what we eventually do.

- Cain killed his brother ... as a jealous thought was allowed through the gate (Genesis 4:8).
- Lot's wife looked back at Sodom ... as a disobedient thought was allowed through the gate (Genesis 19:26).
- Samson lost his life and testimony ... as a lustful thought was allowed through the gate (Judges 16:16–20).
- Ananias and Sapphira lied to God ... as a greedy thought was allowed through the gate (Acts 5:1–10).
- Peter denied Christ ... as a prideful thought was allowed through the gate (John 18:25–27).
- Demas backslid ... as a worldly thought was allowed through the gate (2 Timothy 4:10).
- Euodia and Syntyche caused division in the church ... as a discordant thought was allowed through the gate (Philippians 4:2–3).

Not only were these thoughts allowed through the gate, but once they gained entry they were not stopped until they had done their damage. We must control what we let in and what we allow to stay in our thought life.

Camp-Out on Fantasy Island

"De plane! De plane!" Tattoo (Hervé Villechaize) exclaimed as the newest arrivals approached Fantasy Island. Soon the suave and genteel Mr. Roarke (Ricardo Montalban) appeared to greet his guests and welcome them to their new tropical paradise home-away-from-home. This rather predictable story line in most of the 130 episodes of this 1978–1984 series[3] usually involved a paying guest realizing his or her favorite fantasy with a twist of mystery and romance thrown in for good measure. Mr. Roarke would sagely and sympathetically guide guests who, once their fantasies had been realized, ultimately had to deal with the consequences of their fantasies-brought-to-life.

> Our minds are the door-keepers— the gate-keepers— to what we eventually do.

The show's popularity was due—at least in part—to the viewing audience's vicariously enjoying the living-out of unrealized fantasies. We all harbor fantasies in our minds that, if let out of port to sail, freely might carry us to destinations so off-course from our normal ports-of-call that it would be hard for us to return home. Given the opportunity to camp out on Fantasy Island, many of us would sign up, make the nonrefundable deposit, buy the camping gear and wardrobe, and calendar the vacation time from reality. We long to be transported from the world in which we live, work, and meet obligations to another world, a place where the illusive dream tantalizes and, like the mythological siren, beckons us out to sea.

I am no stranger to fantasy. Given a stressful week with never-ending obligations, appointments on top of appointments, insurmountable staff concerns, no-win-high-stress counseling situations, and the always-to-be-prepared next sermon, I am a prime candidate for calling Mr. Roarke about an escape package to Fantasy Island.

For me, my cherished fantasy would involve an escape from all professional responsibilities—totally being away from phones, fax machines, as well as laptop, pocket, and personal computers. I would jump on a Harley and ride up Highway 1 from Newport Beach (California) as far north as I could go. I would eat when hungry, get a room when sleepy, and pull up on the beach as often as I wanted to listen to the Pacific waves. Dressed in my most worn jeans, my old leather bomber jacket, and my black Justin boots, with my hair growing as long as my adventure lasted, I would listen over and over again to the Eagles song "Peaceful Easy Feeling."

When Marilyn and I met to work on this chapter at our favorite writing spot, the conference room of First Baptist/Orlando[4], I shared with her my version of a fantasy escape. She said, "I guess that might work for you—and maybe our guy readers. But I have found what would be every woman's fantasy." Well, that got my attention! She reached into her briefcase and retrieved a newspaper. "Read and learn!" she declared as she shoved this newspaper under my nose.

Circled was an article about The Hotel Hershey's $7 million spa that recently opened in Hershey, Pennsylvania. Featuring treatments such as chocolate baths and fondue wraps, the spa spoils guests while paying tribute to Milton Hershey's legacy. Guests relax in whirlpool baths containing Hershey's unsweetened cocoa powder mixed with instant nonfat dry milk or enjoy a cocoa butter scrub. It's all part of the spa's pitch that guests can have their chocolate—and benefit from it, too.[5] With a gleam in her eye, Marilyn said, "You can have your old Harley. Just give me Hershey."

I guess we all fantasize in different ways and to different extremes. Fantasies can be healthy forms of release or unhealthy lust-in-the-making. While I might have fleeting fantasies of playing running back for the Tampa Bay Bucaneers, and those underdeveloped fantasies give me a moment or two of reprise on a Sunday afternoon, I can have other fantasies that would be harmful to me, my relationship to the Lord, and my relationships to others. If I fantasized about wealth and power to the point that my fantasies turned to covetousness and schemes to acquire, I could frivolously spend my time and misdirect my energies to the pursuit of these goals, rather than doing those things to which I am called.

Fantasies can be dangerous. The raunchy reality Fox series, *Temptation Island*, capitalized on just that. Viewers were invited to hold their breath as they watched four unmarried but supposedly committed couples travel to the Caribbean to test the strength of their relationships. On the island of Belize, the couples were separated from their partners—until the final day of their stay—and introduced to sexy singles who attempted to seduce them into tawdry sexual activity. Note: This was the first prime-time television series in which all of the participants were required to be tested for sexually transmitted diseases before they were approved for the show. The show's producers knew well that fantasies—entertained and lived out—can be dangerous.

The mind, so we often think, is an island—deserted, unknown, and remote. Too often we allow the mind to become a Fantasy Island when we allow inappropriate thoughts to enter and stay. We wrongly assume that we can entertain fantasies and no one will get hurt—no one ever has to know. How wrong! The apostle Paul addressed the danger of this kind of reasoning: "Do not think about how to gratify the desires of the sinful nature" (Romans 13:14).

> Satan is a great travel agent who is always ready to assist us in leaving God-thoughts and traveling to Fantasy Island.

Satan is a great travel agent who is always ready to assist us in leaving God-thoughts and traveling to Fantasy Island—the out-of-the-bounds-of-God's-will places in the thought life. Once there we can easily be diverted to a side trip to Temptation Island—the place in our thought life that cries out for us to go "where the action is."

Flirting with Disaster

Flirting with Disaster is more than a Ben Stiller movie title. It also well describes many of the thoughts we have—whose downward progression spells disaster. Flirting with thoughts has been around since the beginning—since the time the serpent flirted and toyed with Eve's thoughts (Genesis 3:1–6). As in the Garden of Eden, flirtation with sinful ideas can lead to disastrous consequences.

The Internet offers how-to-flirt websites, online flirting manuals, and tips for cyber-flirting. In addition to web help, there are a number of books on the subject, including *101 Ways to Flirt* and *How To Attract Anyone, Anytime, Anyplace: The Smart Guide to Flirting*. While I am not advocating the use of any of these helps, I do want to make the point: Flirting is serious business.

Too often I have counseled those who have experienced the tragic results of cyber-flirting. Marriage upon marriage is being destroyed from this supposedly "innocent" flirting.

- Cyber-flirt, victim marriage #1: A young married lady involved in a church ministry began chatting with a man who became more than a fantasy to her when she left her husband for her unseen online lover.
- Cyber-flirt, victim marriage #2: An active church member was devastated when his wife—who had begun chatting with a man in another state—moved out because their marriage was no longer exciting.
- Cyber-flirt, victim marriage #3: Another professing Christian man discovered his wife was having an online affair. Soon thereafter his wife left him for her cyber-lover.
- Cyber-flirt, victim marriage #4: A woman sought counseling after she became enamored with chatting over the Internet with two men she had never met. She arranged to meet both of these men, and fortunately, after meeting them, she ended the relationships. Unfortunately, her husband—upon discovering what she had done—demanded a divorce.

The opportunity for sin begins by flirting in the mind with thoughts that lie outside the boundaries of God's will. It is important to remember: Flirting is a "thought-thing" before it becomes a "realized-thing."

"But each one is tempted when, by his own evil desire, he is dragged away and enticed" (James 1:14). Reflecting on this biblical truth, Edmund Hiebert writes, "Temptation has its source not in the outer lure but in the inner lust."[6] The order of committing a sin isn't usually slam, bam, committing a sin, and then thinking about it. Rather, it usually begins with our thinking about it before committing the sin. Jesus said, "For out of the heart come evil thoughts, murder, adultery, sexual immorality, theft, false testimony, slander" (Matthew 15:19). The biblical word "heart" is often associated with the mind—and that's precisely where the trouble begins.

In *The Genius of Temptation*, Michelle McKinney Hammond writes, "These things of the world go in through our eyes and ears, lodge in our hearts, and come back out of our mouths. Once repeated, they're filed in our minds, where they settle comfortably into our subconscious. And each of these things waits for the right moment to rise up and superimpose itself over a thought that has left a convenient space to accommodate it. The next step we take is to put that thought into action."[7] We must not allow ourselves to be led on by the googoo-eyed thrill of flirting with improper thinking. Satan loves to set a trap for our thought lives in this way. Wrong thoughts send out an invitation to disaster. At the core of sin is a thought that has gotten off-track from God's will.

> We must not allow ourselves to be led on by the googoo-eyed thrill of flirting with improper thinking.

Off-track Thoughts

Shortly after we wrote the first chapter of this book, I heard the song "A Fine Line," the first track on a Hootie & the Blowfish CD. The lyrics of the song reminded me of the opening paragraphs of this book, in which I wrote about my rehearsal of the consequences of moral failure. "A Fine Line" tells of a man who has pulled his car off the pavement on the curve of a highway to figure out where he's headed in life. He has a wife and two kids, as well as another woman in another city who is now pregnant with his child. There seems to be no escape: everyone involved is going to wind up with a broken heart.

How did this guy get so off-track with his life? The song comments that there's a fine line between right and wrong, and this guy has been crossing over that border too long. Many of us, too, get off track with our lives. When we look in life's rearview mirror, we see a trail of broken hearts or shattered dreams behind us. We see missed opportunities and neglected people, along with a destroyed reputation that we never thought we would possess. We can get back on track, but the damage is difficult to repair.

Reuter Information Service reports that a rash of deadly freight train accidents that occurred across the United States in the mid-1990s

could have been prevented if government reg-
ulators had responded faster to warnings from
safety experts. The *Los Angeles Times*, quoting
federal and union officials, said that braking problems contributed to at least ten
runaway freight train crashes over a
twenty-seven-month period of time during
the mid-1990s. The *Times* story went on to
say that officials with the National
Transportation Safety Board urged the Federal
Railroad Administration several times to issue an order
requiring that all mountain passage trains be equipped with electronic
braking control systems, but the agency failed to heed the NTSB's
advice.[8]

Every Christian has a built-in braking system that can stop these runaway thoughts.

Sounds simple: Install the necessary braking systems and prevent
runaway trains. Well, apparently not so simple. Simply *having* the braking system is not enough to ensure safe mountain passage. A train oper-
ator must *activate* the system before it can do its intended job.
According to this Reuter's report, a freight train traveling through
California's dangerous Cajon Pass broke free and jumped the tracks,
killing two crewmen, when its electronic braking system was never
activated.[9]

Every Christian has a built-in braking system that can stop these
runaway thoughts. "His divine power has given us everything we need
for life and godliness through our knowledge of him who called us by
his own glory and goodness" (2 Peter 1:3).

> We have been given the mind of Christ so we can think like him.
> We have been given the Word of God so we can know what
>   to do.
> We have been given prayer so we can realize the power over
>   temptation.
> We have been given the Holy Spirit so we can experience
>   freedom.
> We have been given faith so we can face whatever Satan
>   sends our way.

We have been given spiritual armor so we can experience true
victory.

We have been given the Name of Jesus so we can win, not
just endure.

The problem is not with the brakes—the Christian's tools for overcoming. The problem is with the activation—using those tools on a
daily basis. Perhaps we need a bumper sticker that says, "I brake for
runaway thoughts."

Thought Workout

Leaving the Gravitron exercise system, David stepped on the
StairMaster stairclimber to round out his high-energy workout. How
dare his wife comment that she thought his love handles were adorable!
Love handles—baloney! Those were only ripples in his well-defined,
albeit middle-aged, abs. He wondered if he was still attractive to
younger members of the opposite sex the way he was in his prime.
Nonsense! Of course he was. Anyway, going to bed early tonight was
not a good idea. There was no way he could possibly sleep. He had too
much on his mind. You know, he felt like exercising—exercising "just
because," certainly not because he was losing his physique.

As he was topping his third mile of "stairs," this used-to-have-it-all-
together-but-now-he-just-didn't-know leader looked up from the flight-
to-fantasy television show he was watching to notice the stillness of his
city and the emptiness inside of himself. What was it that made him so
restless tonight? What was he feeling? Was he depressed or something?
He had been unable to concentrate all day. He felt tense and on edge.
He didn't feel like talking to anyone. Nor did he feel like praying. He
just wanted to do something physical to numb the aching . . . and
the inner restlessness he was feeling.

From his penthouse rooftop, David had an unparalleled view of the
city. It was a beautiful night. The moon was full, and the stars brilliantly
lit up the night sky. The smell of spring was in the cool evening air.
Everything was perfect, except. . .

"You'd better drink some water, sir," his trainer suggested.

"Huh?"

"You probably should drink some water or Gatorade as you cool down."

"Sure. I'll take some water."

Stepping down from his exercise-machinery perch, David grabbed a towel and began wiping away the perspiration. As he cooled down, he leaned on the railing and looked down at the dwellings below.

"Whoa! And just who is *this*?" David thought as he noticed a beautiful, young woman who was bathing herself without curtains drawn. Captivated by her every movement, David could not take his eyes off this stunning creature, who seemed to be performing her bath rituals by flickering candlelight to rouse his attention. As she stepped out of the garden tub and began drying her attractive body, David began to fantasize about being with her: "Oh, I could make you happy. If I could just…"

"Sir, here is your water."

"Uh, thanks. Hey, do you know who she is?" David asked his trainer, as he pointed to the woman in the window below.

"Oh, my! I now see why you seemed distracted. Sure, I know her. I have seen her a number of times at the gym. Her name is Bathsheba. She's married to Uriah Hittite, who works in your company. Lucky man, her husband. She's something else, isn't she?"

"I'd like to meet her."

"Wouldn't every guy?"

"No. I am serious. I want to meet her and get to know her."

"But, sir. She's married, and her husband…"

"Find her number now and call her. She seems to be alone. Tell her that I have admired her and would like to meet her. See if she would like to come over …"

Stalking the Wild Taboo

A recent study by the National Institute of Justice found that stalking was far more prevalent than anyone imagined: 8 percent of American women and 2 percent of American men will be stalked in their lifetimes.[10] These findings equate to an estimated 1,006,970 women and 370,990 men who are stalked annually in the United States. A National Violence Against Women survey identified 90 percent of the stalking victims as being stalked by just one person during their life.[11]

Michael was an intimate partner stalker who just couldn't let go of his ex-wife. After their divorce, Michael became obsessed with Caroline. Still drawn to this man with whom she could not live, Caroline had time and again agreed "to be with him and talk with him one more time—always hoping that this time he would be different." A Christian, Caroline thought that Michael's "stopping his drug usage, going to rehab, and telling her that he was a changed man meant that there was new hope—that he might finally have learned all his lessons. Michael would be nice for a few days or weeks—even attend church with me—but each time it backfired." It seemed to fuel his compulsive belief that "if he could not have [her], then no one else could either."

In talking with her about the stalking that had been going on for years, Caroline recounted to Marilyn the many times that Michael would call her in the wee hours of the night to harass her: "He would threaten to harm anyone else I chose to date." She said that she would often see him sitting in his parked car and watching her house. Calling the police proved futile. He'd just come back later—after she would leave her house to go elsewhere. Then he would go to her front door and leave his "calling card"—a broom turned upside-down, leaned against the door with his crumpled cigarette wrapper on it—"or a note with all the exact times he had come by and found me not at home written down so that I would know he had been there."

When Caroline began seeing another man, Michael threatened to kill him. In actuality, he never came near the new boyfriend. Instead, he knifed all the tires of this new guy's car and hers on several occasions—sometimes at her home and sometimes at her business. "The police did nothing but file a report, because they said that without a witness to the crime they could not make an arrest." And on and on the stalking went . . .

My heart broke for this woman when I heard her story. In her thinking, "There seemed to be no way for me to get away from Michael's progressively illogical behavior. Caring for him and wishing to help him—yet knowing it was impossible to be in a 'normal relationship' with him—made me unable to move on, because Michael was unwilling to allow me to. Having to prove it was impossible to myself—and having him do so over and over—became a vicious cycle. There seemed no way for me to get on with my life without fear." Because of Caroline's feelings for this man and thinking that she might be able to help him change, she enabled Michael to continue to stalk her and control her life in many ways.

> For the first time in our history the weird and the stupid and the coarse are becoming our cultural norm, even our cultural ideal.
>
> —CARL BERSTEIN

Many of us are stalkers. We stalk because we harbor a desire for that which we do not have. Stalking invents promises in our minds that offer hope that that about which we are thinking and fantasizing could actually happen. We stalk the taboo areas of life. Taboo, referred to in some cultures as the gatekeeper of the mind, refers to certain people, things, or acts that are too sacred or inviolate to be mentioned or approached. We have been culturally conditioned over the past decades to think that we have the freedom to openly discuss— and even entertain—what has formerly been too taboo.

Monica Lewinsky has become a household name. As the news of former President Clinton's affair with this young intern broke, the sordid details were aired over the nightly news and talk shows. Things that were once taboo became fodder for public discussion and humor. When independent counsel Kenneth Starr offered his explicit report to the world, most newspapers and networks found the titillating accounting of events newsworthy. Tragically, it was not just the sensitivity of adults affected by such frank discussions. Our country's youth—as well as young children—heard the formerly taboo openly discussed as acceptable behavior by our nation's honored leader. As a nation, we were culturally conditioned one step further backwards to anything-goes. The gate has been opened a little further. And our thinking about the taboo has been further desensitized.

Thought Miracle-Gro®

A green thumb I don't have. I look at other people's yards and think, "Shoot! Why can't mine look this way?" Maybe it has something to do with my utter contempt for weeding, pruning, planting, trimming, mowing, edging, and fertilizing. Other than that, I love to garden! Understand: I am not a completely inept yardsman. I do love those Miracle-Gro® commercials with the stirring testimonials of miraculous lawn and plant growth. And I do aspire to achieve that kind of mani-cure-my-lawn-until-everyone-else-in-the-neighborhood-is-green-with-envy, show-off greatness.

Miracle-Gro® was born in 1950 when two men—Horace Hagedorn, an advertising executive, and his partner, Otto Stern, a nurs-eryman—invested $2,000 to introduce a new product to make house and garden plants stronger, healthier, and more beautiful. They initially began a mail-order garden products business. Otto, frustrated by com-plaints from customers that by the time they received their plants they were not healthy, began to ship a small packet of water-soluble fertil-izer with each plant. Customers loved it! Soon they were back for more of the miracle plant food. In 1951, Horace ran a full-page ad in a New York City newspaper telling readers about Miracle-Gro®. Three days after the ad appeared the mail brought $22,000 in cash orders, and the company was on its way to success.[12]

Consumers today can choose from a number of Miracle-Gro® products—from plant food to roses, from tomatoes to lawn food. There is also a Miracle-Grow for our thought lives. This product, how-ever, is not one marketed by the company from whom its ripped-off name is derived. Satan is the product developer. Just like the market-ing of the original Miracle-Gro® plant food packages, this thought Miracle-Grow is shipped along with wrong thoughts to consumers by the Supplier of all wrong thinking.

Just follow these devilishly easy suggestions, and a little of this Miracle-Grow will help wrong thoughts grow and reproduce with supernatural success:

- *Go* to places where you are easily tempted to give in to sin.
- *Allow* a wrong thought to enter and take up residence in your mind.
- *Fail* to immediately confess specific sin.
- *Expose* yourself to visual and/or audible stimuli that encour-age wrong acts.

- *Fantasize* about giving in to wrong thoughts.
- *Neglect* reading God's Word or praying daily.
- *Ignore* issues in your life that need to be confronted and resolved.
- *Refuse* to let go of grudges.
- *Dwell* on "what if's" or "if only's."
- *Believe* the wrong thoughts will get better over time without help.
- *Avoid* accountability.

I hate to admit it, but I *do* have a green thumb. The problem is that it is not with growing a beautiful lawn and garden, but in cultivating wrong thinking. Sometimes I think Satan dumps gallon-size packets of his Miracle-Grow in my water! Even though my relationship with the Lord grows more intimate and real every day, negative thought growth remains a constant challenge for me as I try to faithfully follow Christ. At times it seems like an overgrowth of destructive thoughts is trying to take over my mind and choke out the beautiful fruit of the Spirit growing inside of me. I know that I am not alone. We all face this challenge.

With this chapter, we have progressed to the second step of our sin flow-chart, which is *desire*, our want-to that calls out for us to give into the temptation. Temptation becomes stronger *"when by [one's] own evil desire"* (James 1:14), we are fascinated with the prospects of the pleasures of sin. Unless we stop that progression, we will begin to flirt with the desire. This is dangerous because what we experience is not a bad feeling at all. Rather, it is an exciting, usually quite appealing kind of feeling. We start to dance with that desire. And desire is that inner source that connects with temptation (which is the outer manifestation of our sinful thinking).

Step 1.
TEMPTATION
"But each one is tempted ..."

Step 2.
DESIRE
"When by one's own evil desire ..."

If the process is not stopped, the next step is found. . .

3

Behind Closed Door #1: Lust

FRANKLY, I WAS READY to leave the church I was pastoring. I had sacrificed everything I had in me to see growth take place in that small church. But to a few deacons who had run the church for years, enough would never be enough. This young pastor, early in his ministry, was out of patience. I simply had had it—and I was ready to exit quickly.

That's when the call came from a church in another state who said the magical words, "We are interested in your becoming our pastor." Soon thereafter Angie and I visited the church. I loved what I saw! According to those with whom we talked it was a perfect situation. Oh, it sounded so good, and so I told God that I would do anything to go there.

Within a short few weeks we moved and I became their pastor. Can you say "miserable"? Yes, I got what I so desperately desired, and it became the most miserable time of our lives. The church was wracked with problems of every kind. Don't get me wrong. Somehow in all of this, the church grew—but at a tremendously high personal cost. No doubt, it was the hardest time in our marriage and our ministry. I had gotten what I lusted for, but what I desired was not God's best for me. It took years to get over it.

Billions of dollars are spent each year to create lustful desires in consumers. Advertising targets us to encourage, convince, and seduce us into buying a product or service whether we really need it or not. Catchy jingles and snappy slogans plant covetous thoughts that we cannot get out of our minds until we go out and buy the product.

Let's try an experiment. See if you can fill in the following blanks from what some researchers have called the top ten slogans of the twentieth century.[1]

The Twentieth Century's Top 10 Ad Slogans

1. "Diamonds are _____ "	DeBeers
2. "Just _____ it!"	Nike
3. "The pause that _____ "	Coca-Cola
4. "Tastes great, less _____ "	Miller Lite
5. "We try _____ "	Avis
6. "Good to the last _____ "	Maxwell House
7. "Breakfast of _____ "	Wheaties
8. "Does she . . . or _____ she?"	Clairol
9. "When it rains, it _____ "	Morton Salt
10. "Where's the _____ ?"	Wendy's

If you answered: 1. forever; 2. do; 3. refreshes; 4. filling; 5. harder; 6. drop; 7. champions; 8. doesn't; 9. pours; and 10. beef, the advertising industry has been successful in getting you to flirt with the idea of buying that product!

The advertising agency of *World, Flesh, and the Devil* is constantly looking for ways to get you to flirt with the thought of doing something that is outside the boundary of God's will. This unscrupulous agency will do whatever it takes to grab your attention and get you to buy into what they are trying to sell. Their proven

Just as the advertising industry has many and varied approaches to get our attention, Satan employs a number of methods to create lust, a-wanting-it-even-if-it-doesn't-please-God mindset.

marketing strategy is to take the tried-and-true sales pitches that have worked for ages and put a new twist on them—so that they look hot, new, and inviting. Satan, the founder and CEO of this aggressive agency, has always been cutting-edge in his advertising campaigns to entice us, the customers. While his techniques are often over-the-top in pushing the envelope to do what has never been done before to make us think we gotta have what he's selling, his corporate purpose—getting us to sin—has never changed.

The Circus Has Come to Town!

The brass band and drums exuberantly call crowds of all ages to line the street to see brightly colored wagons caging exotic animals followed by the spectacle of clowns, flame-eaters, and acrobatics. The parade announces the circus has come to town: *"Ladies and gentlemen, come one, come all to see ferocious lions, terrifying tigers, gargantuan elephants, and dancing bears. Get your ticket and be dazzled by daring young men and women on the flying trapeze. And if it's the unusual, the startling, the bizarre you crave, see freaks of nature—including the bearded lady and mermaids of the deep blue sea."* Curious onlookers see just enough to make them desire more, to make them want to rush and get their tickets to go to the big top for the show of a lifetime.

Phineas Taylor ("P.T.") Barnum was called an all-American huckster for his showmanship that would mesmerize crowds as they gullibly fell for his bizarre setups. He was known for saying, "There's a sucker born every minute." He proved his point when he once promoted a "man-eating chicken" that turned out to be nothing more than a man chewing on a drumstick. Even in pulling such stunts, the people loved his likeable personality and flocked to see his circus in city after city. "Every crowd had a silver lining," quipped Barnum. And that silver lining was in Barnum's pockets. His Grand and Traveling Circus, Menagerie, Caravan and Circus grossed him $400,000 in its first year.[2] In the next decade Barnum would form a partnership with James Anthony McGinness (a.k.a. James A. Bailey) to produce Barnum & Bailey's "Greatest Show on Earth."[3]

I must admit that circus-going had become a little passé for my family, that is, until we went to the spellbinding twenty-first-century version of the circus, Cirque du Soleil. It was breathtaking and electrifying, fascinating and engaging, intriguing and appealing! This so-hard-to-describe show is dessert for the mind—absolutely scrumptious and appealing to so many tastes. From the moment the lights dimmed and the performance began, it was hard for us to know where reality ended and illusion began.

Like dreams, Cirque productions are surreal and unpredictable—a strange blending of Houdini, art, and athleticism.[4] Dozens of things go on simultaneously, keeping the mind engaged from start to finish. This unique production is all visual—not one word is spoken during the entire performance—yet there is not a boring moment in this fantastic two-hour presentation with its exquisite costumes, state-of-the-art lighting, stimulating music, dazzling choreography, and captivating set. Men, women, children, and youth sail high above the audience on long scarves, perform daring feats on bicycles, spring acrobatically from trampoline to trampoline, defy gravity by climbing steep walls, spin and toss tops while running all over the stage, and contort their bodies while doing things that disregard human limitations. This mental playground leaves the audience wanting more and more.

Satan's best performances of mind infiltration are also staged on mental playgrounds—our own cirque du so-imagine. Like the circus-come-to-town parade, Satan marches his enticements down the avenues of our thought-lives and teases us just enough to make us want to rush and purchase a ticket to the sin-circus. All too easily duped by his glitzy showmanship, we become suckers for Satan's sideshows where he promises us not a man-eating chicken, but a sin-will-make-you-happy setup.

As with Cirque du Soleil, we enter another world—this time the spirit world, the world where the mind is the staging area. This demonic ringmaster parades his enticements from city to city—often finding a silver lining in the minds of unsuspecting audiences all along the way. Satan's thought circus, like Cirque du Soleil, includes . . .

alluring perceptions,
fascinating people,
spellbinding possibilities,
enticing promises,
intriguing proposals,
engaging persuasions,
captivating pictures,
mesmerizing perspectives,
appealing plans.

Escaped! Caged Wild Thoughts on the Loose!

"Who let the dogs out? Woof! Woof! Woof! Woof!" Escaping wide attention of American audiences until the release of their Grammy-winning CD, *Who Let the Dogs Out*, the Baha Men have been stars for years in their native Bahamas. Combining the rhythmically rich indigenous music called Junkanoo with elements of contemporary pop, R&B, hip-hop, and reggae, this band's sound is energetic and fun! When I hear the title single from this CD, I can hardly sit still. First, I begin chanting with these guys in a street-savvy, "I-think-I-am-'down'" rapster voice. Then, for inexplicable reasons I bite my bottom lip and move my head in only what I know how to describe as a chicken-pecking motion as I begin doing something that probably looks like a painful version of upper-body-shadow-boxing-while-holding-on-to-the-steering-wheel. To those who may drive past my car at the time I plead, "I can't help it. Hey, what can I say? I've got the rhythm in me—and it just has to escape sometimes!"

It's not just dogs—or one "cool dude" pastor—who are on the loose, but occasionally it's those circus animals we admire during a performance at the big top. While doing research for this book, we ran across a recent story of six—not just one—escaped lions from a circus in a Brazilian town. The lions broke out of their circus cages before sunrise one August day and prowled around for almost six hours through San Simao, a town of 12,000 inhabitants located 150 miles northwest of Sao Paulo. A local police officer reported that one of the lions had been causing havoc in the middle of the street and another had attacked a horse. Soon there was panic throughout the town.[5] Can you imagine driving to work and encountering a lion on the loose in your lane? Do you blow your horn at it or do you give it a piece of your mind by hollering, "Either speed up or get out of the way!"

Apparently this was not the only problem that Brazil had experienced with circus animals within a span of a few months. An online news service also reported a tragic incident where a six-year-old boy was eaten by five lions in front of a circus audience after one of the big cats dragged him from his father's grip and into their cage. The report indicated that the lion struck when the man took his two children to inspect the animal enclosures during an intermission at the Vostok Circus in Recife, Brazil. The lion lurched toward the boy, pulled him through the bars, clamped its jaws on his head, and shook him violently as the other lions attacked. It took police officers more than four hours to recover the boy's torn body from the cage.[6]

Our thought life, unless properly controlled or "caged," can be like an escaped wild animal. Once it's out of its cage, irreparable damage can be done. Threatened by our runaway or escaped thoughts are our. . .

- character
- conscience
- commitment

And these runaway thoughts are then replaced by thoughts that are. . .

- condemning
- contemptible
- confining

That's why Paul reminded his readers: "We take captive every thought to make it obedient to Christ" (2 Corinthians 10:5). Furthermore, we must also be extremely cautious even when our thought life is under control that we don't allow anything into our minds that is outside the boundaries of God's will. Like the lion who lurched at the small boy and pulled him into its cage, our thought tendency is to seize those off-limit thoughts that also get too close to temptation.

Angela came for counseling as her eighteen-year marriage was coming to a tragic end. As she discussed her marital problems, it quickly became evident that there had been a history of disagreement and tension between her and her husband over his gambling addiction. Stan always had grandiose thoughts of striking it rich quick. He just knew the next wager, the next lottery ticket, the next bet would pay off big. Although they were constantly facing one household financial crisis after another, Stan would continue to spend at least fifty dollars a week on lottery tickets and scrape up whatever other money he could for other gambling ventures. Angela discovered to her shock that on his day off Stan was going to the dog races in a nearby city—and taking their children.

His gambling forced them into filing for bankruptcy, causing them to lose their home and forcing them to move in with her parents. While they were living there, Stan found another way to satisfy his addictive urges. He engaged in an affair with a woman from work. That affair proved to be the end of their marriage. Because of his out-of-control thoughts, he was now losing his wife, children, job, and reputation. His insatiable lust for more also caused the break-up of the home of the woman with whom he was having an affair. Satan had tempted Stan with alluring bait, and he bit down on the painful hook.

Taking the Bait

Imagine the world's largest river in the midst of the world's largest rainforest, hydrographic basin, and genetic bank. Then visualize this magnificent river teeming with some of the biggest and hardiest fighting fish in the world. Next, picture yourself aboard a seaplane flying to your jungle-based fishing camp on a tributary that flows into this grand river. Soon you, your fishing companion, and guide are aboard a craft boat headed into a protected ecological reserve to begin a fishing adventure of a lifetime. Sound alluring—like a too-good-to-be-true dream?

For years I have heard guys talking about game fishing in the Amazon. I have been fascinated by their stories of fishing adventures on the Amazon River, whose volume is ten times that of the Mississippi

River. I have drooled when I heard their descriptions of the incredible beauty of this river teeming with many exotic species of fish.[7] I was particularly interested in what many of these guys consider to be the fishing of all fishing . . . sport fishing in the Amazon for the peacock bass.

Apparently the peacock bass is one of the most beautiful and strong freshwater fish in the world. Anglers can expect to fish peacock bass that weigh from five to twenty-five pounds, with the unofficial known world record being around thirty pounds. The peacock bass routinely breaks forty- to sixty-pound test lines, straightens heavy-duty hooks, breaks rods, and strips reels. Their electrifying strikes as well as acrobatic jumps and dives amaze even the most veteran angler and spoil him forever.[8]

When interviewed for this book, peacock bass fishing expert and author Larry Larsen, who has led or taken forty-six fishing trips[9] into the Amazon and who has written three books on this subject, enthusiastically declared that the peacock bass "is the world's greatest game fish, because it is attracted to cover, strikes top water lures regularly, jumps when hooked, never gives up in battle, and is powerful enough to test anglers' skills and tackle."

A friend Don shared with Marilyn about a recent fishing trip to the Amazon where he had great luck catching the peacock bass using artificial bait that was much larger than that which is normally used for freshwater bass fishing. While the peacock bass would go after these seven-inch plugs with propellers on the back, they were also attracted to the smaller (one- to three-pound) fish that Don and his fishing pals would be in the process of reeling in.

New Testament author James, obviously familiar with fishing in the Galilean lakes, effectively uses the analogy of fishing when he says that each one is tempted "when he is drawn away, enticed and *baited* by his own evil desire" (James, 1:14 AMPLIFIED). Other translations use the word "lured."

- ". . . as he is beguiled and *lured* . . ." (Moffat)
- ". . . when he is *lured* and enticed . . ." (RSV)

A fishing lure is an attractive, often colorful bait that floats past the fish to gets its attention. Once distracted by the lure, it's usually just a matter of time before the fish bites into it—and then it's hooked. Satan has beautiful lures designed to distract us from God's purpose. Taking this analogy a little further, our thought life is like the fish and Satan's orchestrated temptations are the bait. Once we go for it, we are caught in bondage—hook, line, and sinker. Like the peacock bass, we may choose to fight and struggle, jump and dive, and never give up in the battle. Or, we can see the bait as being so desirable that we do not put up much of a fight—and Satan hooks another big one! He is the master gamesman—and he'll use whatever methods to hook us and lure us away from a pure thought life. This seasoned Angler is always after one more trophy fish to mount and hang on his den walls.

> After a time, you may find that "having"' is not so pleasing a thing, after all, as "wanting." It is not logical, but it is often true.
>
> —SPOCK, "AMOCK TIME," STARDATE 3372.7

James, in his play-by-play commentary on sin (James 1:13–14), conveys to his readers that the more attractive the bait, the more enticing it will become. The advertising industry knows that the right bait means interest—and ultimately the *Cha-ching!* of the cash register. Satan, the Master Marketer, knows that the most appealing bait is that which creates lust.

Lust Sells

Lust is commonly used to sell fragrances, automobiles, fashion items, and luxury goods—items with well-known labels (Gucci, Luis Vitton, Prada, Salvatore Ferragamo, Kenneth Cole). The most common strategies in advertising seem to center around lust and sex.[10] In a website for the University of Texas at Austin, the author of *Advertising Department Theories of Persuasive Communication and Consumer Decision Making*, Nathan Hamilton, theorizes how advertising works:

> Ads are compelling, creative, sharp, eclectic, stunning, flashy, boring, stupid, esoteric, but how they work is something to really think about. . . . How is it that an ad can make

someone do something, illicit a response, cause action, create need, evoke one's emotion? Does it have magical powers over one's psyche? Does someone have control over our persona like a witch doctor sticking pins into a doll? Are we all subjects of voodoo? Are we in control, or simply pawns in a chess game? Are there strings attached to our bodies? Is someone predicting our moves? Could it be that we are all hard-wired with special buttons that when pushed will induce a response? Could it be that marketers and advertisers know how to push these buttons on us? *How does advertising work?*

> It is my theory that most of all advertising follows the themes of the seven deadly sins.
>
> —NATHAN HAMILTON

The clothes we wear, the food we eat, the cars we drive, the scents we put on our bodies, the dwellings we live in, the brands we associate with, the service we feel obligated to provide—is advertising a product of us or are we products of advertising?

It is my belief that one must go past the models, the charts, and the graphs to understand how advertising works. We must look at the basic human desires that drive human behavior. We all boast, envy, hate, loathe, feed, want and lust to a degree— it is human nature to do so. Therefore, it is my understanding that most of all advertising mirrors that of these basic human weaknesses and desires. . . [11]

It is my theory that most of all advertising follows the themes of the seven deadly sins. This strategy, if you will, is more times than not a win/win situation as most people can identify with any one of the seven deadly sins. It is the ads that works through the sins that send the strongest emotionally charged messages.[12]

From blue jeans to burgers, from cars to cologne, from vacuum cleaners to chewing gum, from work-out equipment to shoes . . . it works!

Whether it's a billboard for Hooters or a trendy fitness center, the sex-to-grab-your-attention does the job—even for innocent passersby.

I have to admit it: I am not your typical male. I actually like to shop. Please don't broadcast this, or I'll really have to take the heat from my guy buddies. You see, I enjoy shopping for clothes, for books, for gifts. It's a great way for me to turn off the pressures and relax—especially if I am at a mall where I am not recognized by fellow shoppers. There are, however, a few beyond-my-comfort-zone areas of the mall—like the women's lingerie section or, worse yet, Victoria's Secret.

I don't get it. There doesn't appear to be much that this Victoria gal is secretive about. Okay, how shall I delicately say this? Those overtly seductive window treatments give me occasion to blush, especially when I'm passing by them with my teenage children or a buddy. Quite frankly, because of my discomfort when walking by that store, I've trained myself to keep my eyes peeled straight ahead—which, I must admit, is sometimes kind of difficult if I am trying to carry on a conversation with someone walking beside me. I have to be careful not to improperly engage my mind while I am talking to a pal as I go past this store, or I'm afraid that might slip and say something like, "John, how's your wife Victoria, er uh. . . Carolyn? Tell me, what's her secret? I mean, um, how does she do all she does?"

This is no new marketing strategy. Satan perfected it long before today's advertising firms discovered it. He has his own billboards, his own ads, his own commercials that target our thought lives. For example:

- Satan pitched to Eve the idea of gotta-have that exciting fruit—even though it was forbidden for a woman who walks with the Lord . . . and she bought it.
- Satan pitched to David the idea of gotta-have that desirable woman—even though she was totally off-limits for a vow-keeping man of God . . . and he bought it.
- Satan pitched to Solomon the idea of gotta-have more power and pleasure than anyone else—even though it was destructive for a wise leader . . . and he bought it.
- Satan pitched to the rich young ruler the idea of gotta-have money and possessions—even though it came with a selling-your-soul price tag . . . and he bought it.

There is one bright note: Satan pitched to Jesus the idea of gotta-have the world at his feet even though it would cost Jesus the abandonment of his purpose for coming to this earth . . . and Jesus did *not* buy it! Satan's sales strategies did not work on the one consumer he most needed to persuade to buy. And, praise God, Satan's marketing plan failed!

Frustrated Lust Life

I find in the Old Testament a story of a young man overcome by his lust life (2 Samuel 13). In this what-if-this-happened-today story, just imagine what could happen if lust, once created, led to such utter frustration that it pushed the individual struggling with it to "go for it"— even though it meant destroying his family in the process.

Jonadab arrived right on time to pick up his buddy for their standing Thursday round of golf. As he bounded into the house, he breezed past the servants as he asked where Amnon was. They gave him that here's-where-he's-been-hiding-out-lately look as they pointed upstairs to the master bedroom.

Not stopping to knock on Amnon's bedroom door, Jonadab burst in, and, foregoing any niceties, demanded, "Hey, man, aren't you ready yet?"

As he looked at his friend who was still in bed—and who apparently had slept all night in the previous day's clothes—Jonadab asked, "What gives?"

Empty liquor bottles and beer cans were strewn around the dark, draped-drawn room that reeked of a malodorous stench. Looking like someone who had been on a major drinking binge, Amnon struggled to reply, "Huh? What? Who . . . Jon, is that you. Oh—! What time is it?"

Knowing that his friend had been struggling with some kind of personal issues that really had him bummed out lately, Jonadab compassionately responded, "Amnon, man, you've got everything—riches, power, prestigious family—yet day after day I find you in this pathetic condition. I don't get it. What's going on? I don't know you anymore. Why are you so depressed? Why are you blowing off all your friends? Come on, tell me. This has gone on long enough."

Amazingly enough, Amnon rolled over and sat up halfway. As he pushed the hair out of his eyes, he squinted as he tried to focus on his friend who was now standing next to him. Holding his head as if every noise where amplified by many decibels, Amnon struggled to explain: "It's her. I am so desperately in love with Tamar, and yet she treats me like I don't even exist (2 Samuel 13:1–4). Everything is always about Absalom or my dad or her in-crowd friends. I try and show her how much I care, and she just blows me off."

Amnon paused and scrunched up his face as if he were about to get sick. As Jon stepped toward him to help him, Amnon seemed to recover and continued explaining, "It happened again last night. We had this family dinner, and after we had finished our meal, I followed Tamar outside into the garden. The evening air was brisk, so I took that opportunity to put my arm around her as I noticed she was shivering. I thought that finally I could show her how much I cared, and guess who walked up?"

"Absalom?"

"Bingo! Immediately she pushed me away, grabbed his arm, and walked away with him—leaving me standing there . . . alone. Oh, I hate her. But, Jon, I want her so badly that it's driving me crazy. I can't eat. I can't sleep. I can only think about her. And she doesn't even give a thought to me."

"So, did you talk to her later back at the house?"

"Are you kidding? No way! She went off with Absalom and his 'cool' pals. Of course, no one invited me to come along. So, I said my good-bye to the folks, and headed home—with a stop at the bar. I just sat there alone, wishing I could be with her. I guess I got pretty wasted sitting there—just wanting to feel numb and get her out of my mind. I drank a lot . . . until I passed out.

"Man, you're killing yourself over this woman. Are you sure she's worth it?"

"You know, I'm not sure any woman is worth this. But now I have something to prove to her. She cannot treat me like this. I just want to show her who's the real man. No woman is going to treat me like this and get by with it. Jon, you've got to help me. How can I get her alone to show her? You got any ideas?"

Jonadad thought for a minute, and then he suggested, "Get her up here . . . on *your* turf. You need her alone—away from all her friends and your family."

"Oh, sure . . . as if she would come if I invited her," Amnon quipped.

"You can get her up here. Just pretend you are sick. Then when your dad comes to check on you, tell him that the only thing you feel like eating is something of that delicious cake Tamar fixes. Ask him to have her come over and bake some right up here in your apartment . . . 'cause you want to enjoy the aroma as it bakes. And you would feel so much better if she took care of you" (2 Samuel 13:5–7).

Amnon did just that. He made sure the household staff stayed away when Tamar arrived. The two of them were finally alone. Tamar graciously prepared the cakes as Amnon had requested. As she approached him to feed him as he lay in bed, Amnon overpowered her. Despite her pleas to him to let her go, he continued to hold her down and then raped her. When he had finished violating her, he screamed with hatred in his voice, "Get up! Go away! Now you see that you can't treat me that way and get away with it. Get out!" When she hesitated, he called for the staff to throw her—violated and disgraced—out of the house (2 Samuel 13:8–18). In his mind, he had won.

Abortion in the Case of Rape

Every person—regardless of race, age, social or economic status, or lifestyle—is a potential victim of rape or sexual assault. Reported victims range in age from several months to one hundred years. No one is immune. While the most vulnerable target is a solitary woman— especially at night or if she is impaired by drugs, alcohol, or medical situations—men are victims of rape, too.[13] It is reported that 60 percent of all rape victims know their assailments.[14] Rape most often occurs in the home of the victim or assailant.

Sexual assault is not a crime of sex or even of passion. It is a crime of violence. Rapists view their victims as objects on whom they can vent their hostility, aggression, frustrations, and insecurities. Sexual gratification is not the major motivating factor. These assailants want to humiliate and degrade their victims, while trying to gain power and control over them.[15]

The Enemy is guilty of attempted rape. This repeat offender attempts to rape our thought life, violate our mind purity, and even deflower the mental virginity of the young and innocent. Why? He wants to corrupt our thought life—and when he does, he controls our lives.

I must confess, there are times when Satan has attempted to mentally and spiritually rape me—especially when I have been vulnerable to his attacks just before getting up before a group to communicate God's Word. Often, well-meaning—and some not so well-meaning— people will say something to me like, "Pastor, there is a serious problem. It's really bad, but don't think about that right now. We'll talk next week." Or, as I begin speaking, I notice someone who is obviously unhappy with me and is letting me know through his body language that he is upset. Or, I am distracted by an immodestly dressed female right in my sight path. At those times, I feel as though I have been victimized by a rapist at large as I struggle to regain my focus on God.

Once a sinful thought violates our thinking, we are faced with a choice: to allow the conception of sin or to abort the thought. Once impregnated with the seed of sinful thinking, the Christian must be pro-abortion[16] in the case of the raping of the mind by Satan if that person is to live in freedom.

The Word of God plays out the consequences of carrying sin to full-term: *"Lust gets pregnant, and has a baby: sin!"* (James 1:15 THE MESSAGE). Like sperm attaching itself to an egg resulting in conception, a wrong thought that is allowed to attach itself to our lives will result in the conception of sin—and eventually it will give birth to the offspring of the Evil One. And when that happens, the proud father of lies, Satan, no doubt says, "Congratulations! It's a sin!" as he hands out cigars to all his buddies.

When my wife, Angie, was expecting our second child, we all wanted a girl—including our then five-year-old son, Will. In fact, one day as we were driving somewhere, he announced to us, "It is a girl and her name will be Emily." Of course, I didn't want him to be disappointed so I began to pray in pink, believe God for pink, and even thought of going to work for Mary Kay Cosmetics to get the—well, you know— pink Cadillac.

The day finally came when Angie said to me, "It's time!" In the labor and delivery room I promise that I almost wore pink, but I opted instead for the "designer" green scrubs that the hospital issues to nervous soon-to-be fathers. In a matter of minutes I heard the doctor say, "Congratulations, it's a girl!"

"You're kidding!"

"No, Mr. Dennis, it's definitely a girl."

I was tickled pink! As I walked down the long hall, proudly carrying my little baby girl to the nursery, I heard the sound of giggles. I thought the nurses were just laughing at this silly dad. Later, to my embarrassment, I discovered that the whole back of green scrubs I was wearing was out!

> Like sperm attaching itself to an egg resulting in conception, a wrong thought that is allowed to attach itself to our lives will result in the conception of sin—and eventually it will give birth to the offspring of the Evil One.

In spite of that blushing-pink episode, Em's birth was such a happy time. But when lust gives birth to sin, the only one laughing is Satan. That's why it is imperative that we guard our minds from impure thoughts or we will get . . .

Zonked!

"Will you choose what's behind door number one, door number two, or door number three?" asked the ol' wheeler and dealer himself, Monty Hall, show after show to ridiculously costumed contestants on the game show *Let's Make a Deal*. This immensely popular television series—which first aired in 1963—enticed lawyers, doctors, plumbers, and even Beverly Hills housewives to dress as everything from kumquats to comic strip characters to buy, sell, or trade any and everything from aarddvarks to zithers.

Just before taping, thirty-five or so contestants—dressed in bizarre costumes designed to get Monty's attention—were selected from the studio audience to become the day's possible traders. The traders brought unusual odds and ends that they had retrieved from their homes, attics, or garages to trade in hopes of getting a chance at the big deal. Of those people seated on the trading floor, about eight people were chosen by Monty Hall to participate in three or four deals, plus the Big Deal, which involved major cash and/or merchandise.

Viewers of this show were familiar with this scenario: A trader decided to "take the curtain," and Monty offered to buy it back again for $1,000 . . . $2,000 . . . $3,000. Who knew the best choice! Packages were disguised so that traders were never sure of the contents. For example, a garbage can might contain a mink coat or just garbage. The decision-making was pretty suspenseful. Would the right choice be made? Would the trader have hostess Carol Merrill point out the features of a new, deluxe refrigerator with an icemaker, or would the always-animated announcer Jay Stewart be dressed as an old granny in a giant rocking chair?

Near the end of the show, Monty asked the most successful traders if they wanted to keep what they had or trade it for a chance at the "Big Deal of the Day." The first two traders who decided to risk their prizes for a chance at the grand prize were given a choice between Door #1, Door #2, or Door #3. While there were are no "zonks" (gag prizes) in the big deal, it was possible to trade down. Even when the big deal had been made, Monty continued to make "quick deals" until the end of the show: *"I'll give you $50 for a hard-boiled egg."* [17]

While *Let's Make a Deal* ended in 1977, the show continues to run in a new format on a supernatural network, in all time slots. Satan has replaced Monty Hall as the wheeler and dealer par excellence, who is more than happy to cut a deal with anyone. There is a difference with this game: Satan disguises himself, rather than the traders. "And no wonder, for Satan himself masquerades as an angel of light" (2 Corinthians 11:14).

What does Satan offer in his trades? He offers . . .

- a short-term thrill for a long-term happiness.
- a lust fulfilled for the joy of purity.
- a desired quick-fix for the pleasure that accompanies lifetime obedience.
- a fleeting excitement of compromise for the resultant peace of godly convictions.

- a split-second feel-good of popularity for the honor of leaving a legacy of faith.
- a get-you-ahead benefit of a lie for the impact of integrity and character.

As Satan tries to make his deal, remember, there is something behind the door that can destroy you. With more pizzazz than Monty Hall, Satan will pitch the alluring possibilities behind that door. While it may be tempting to go ahead and trade, don't even let your mind entertain the thought—for the more you think about it, the more appealing it will become. The crowd may even spur you on: "Go ahead, go for it! Trade!" However, once you walk through the door of lust, you will soon realize that you have been zonked (that is, ripped off) by the world's biggest con man.

> He that but looketh on a plate of ham and eggs to lust after it hath already committed breakfast with it in his heart.
>
> —C. S. LEWIS

That what's-behind-door-number-one can easily become a skeleton in your closet.

You have just read about the third step in the progression of a sinful thought—lust: "He is carried away and enticed" by his own lust (James 1:14). A temptation crosses our path. We are curious and have a desire to try it. Then that desire turns evil and becomes lust—which is a craving for something sinful. It's the "I want-it-gotta-have-it" stage in our sin flow-chart.

Step 1.
TEMPTATION
"But each one is tempted . . ."

Step 2.
DESIRE
"When by one's own evil desire . . ."

Step 3.
LUST
"Dragged away and enticed . . ."

Unless the sin progression is stopped, you will start . . .

4

Peeking Behind the Skeleton Door . . . Sin

I FEEL SO BLESSED to have many young couples and families in the congregation I pastor. Because of these demographics, our church is constantly blessed to have babies being born. One of my incredible privileges as pastor is to present these newborns to our congregation for what we call "baby dedication." We covenant with the parents to pray for that child and to help them raise him or her in a way that fosters the child's coming to a saving knowledge of Jesus Christ.

Whenever I make contact for the first time with the parents after the birth of their child, I always sense the great joy they have in sharing their child's name with me. Now this tiny individual has an identity of his or her very own (even though we know our heavenly Father gave this small one an identity long before he or she was born). This tiny person is no longer the baby they were "expecting"; rather, he or she is the "real" child they now hold. And the name declares that new identity.

Parents often struggle right up to the moment of the birth of a child with what they should name their baby. Should they give the child a family name or name the baby after a friend? Should they choose something unusual and distinctive? Smart parents weigh their name options against what the child will have to face in grade school when other kids apply their creativity to the name. Then again, some parents don't seem to think through these things.

When my son Will was born, I remember discussing names with the labor and delivery nurse. I asked her what unusual names she had seen parents give their babies. She immediately responded, "There were twin girls born here not long ago, and the mother named them Lemongelo and Orangelo." When the nurse inquired of the new mom where she had found those unique names, the mother said, "*Good Housekeeping Magazine.* I saw an ad for lemon Jello and orange Jello. . . ."

Virginia, Marilyn's mom, who worked for years as the assistant county treasurer, shares her most-unusual-name-encountered story of a woman who came into the treasure's office to pay her taxes. Virginia asked her what her name was, and the young lady said something that sounded like *Pheh-mah-lee.* Not familiar with that name, Virginia asked the woman how she spelled it—and the woman spelled, "F-E-M-A-L-E."

Trying as hard as she could not to get tickled, Virginia felt compelled to comment on that being such an unusual name. "Did your mother name you after a relative or someone close?" Virginia inquired.

"Well, actually, no. The hospital where I was born named me. Shortly after I was born, they brought me into my mother's room. As the nurse handed me to my mother, my mom noticed that the hospital had put a bracelet on my wrist with *Female* written next to where it called for the name. When my mother, who did not read well, sounded out the apparent name given me by the hospital staff, she thought that it was such an unusual and beautiful name that she decided to go along with their choice of name for me!"

When parents are not so fortunate as to have the hospital come up with a name for their newborn, they can always refer to the many one-of-these-is-a-definite-sure-fit-for-your-precious-baby name lists that are published in books, in magazines, and on websites. The following list was compiled from the most frequently used given names for births in the first eight months of 2000. The data comes from a 1-percent sample of Social Security card applications for births from January through August 2000.[1]

Top 100 Baby Names

Rank	Male	Female
1	Michael	Hannah
2	Jacob	Emily
3	Matthew	Madison
4	Joseph	Elizabeth
5	Christopher	Alexis
6	Nicholas	Sarah
7	Andrew	Taylor
8	William	Lauren
9	Joshua	Jessica
10	Daniel	Ashley

Unlike excited parents planning the birth of their child, many of us do not stop to consider what is developing in our thought lives. Too often we do not stop and specifically name—then confess to God—the lustful thoughts we carry around in us. Unfortunately, we often wait until we are in the delivery room giving birth to fully developed sin, and then are faced with what to do with this newborn creation.

Carrying Sin to Full Term

A man was helping deliver one of his cows, when he noticed his wide-eyed four-year-old son standing at the fence, soaking in the whole event. The man thought, "Oh, great. Now I am going to have to explain the birds and the bees to my four-year-old." Then he thought about it for a moment and decided not to jump the gun. He'd just let the child observe the birth and then ask any questions he might have.

After the calf had been delivered, the man walked over to his son and asked, "Do you have any questions, son?"

"Just one!" gasped the still wide-eyed child. "How fast was that calf going when he hit that cow?"[2]

Many of us are like that young child when it comes to the birthing of sin in our lives. After the sin has been born, we stand there and say, "How did that happen?" Like gestation in humans, so sin develops by stages in our life. To borrow analogies from the stages of pregnancy, I think there are some similarities between growing, developing sin and fetal development.

Conception

Having dealt with this in the previous chapter, let me amplify by giving three of the signs of sin-pregnancy:

- missed period(s) of intimacy with God because fellowship with him has been interrupted
- morning sickness where one cannot stomach feeding on the riches of God because of guilt
- feeling exhausted from trying to fight a losing battle with temptation

Are you aware of the sin-pregnancy tests? Most are do-it-yourself tests that can be performed in the privacy of your own home. To detect a growing sin problem in your life, you need only to try *E.P.T.*— *Examining Private Thoughts*—which, when properly administered, yields 100 percent accuracy in its results. You perform this self-test by coming before God and asking him for his guidance as you search his Word while imploring the Holy Spirit to examine your heart. In the last section of this book we will further examine this test as a God-provided way to overcome sinful thoughts that lead to sinful actions.

First Trimester

In human development, a normal baby is born around nine months after conception. In the development of sin in our life, the pregnancy length can greatly vary. In the first trimester of sin gestation, the parent-to-be is going through the acceptance phase of sin in his or her life. The body can reject—or miscarry—this sin or adjust to accommodate it. The sin fetus, while small at this

> Then, after desire has conceived, it gives birth to sin; and sin, when it is full-grown, gives birth to death.
>
> —JAMES 1:15

point, implants itself inside the parent and begins to develop. It assumes form and defining features as it lives and breathes inside its parent. The biblical author James informs us that it should be no surprise that unless sin is dealt with prior to its conception, it will give birth.

Second Trimester

In the second trimester, the parent is experiencing a sort of sin-pregnancy honeymoon. He or she feels pretty good again as the adjustment has been made to handle growing sin inside. There's less of a strain on the person giving birth to sin. Euphoric feelings—sometimes identified as a "glow about this person"—often accompany this phase of sin development. During this trimester of sin development it becomes harder and harder for the parent to hide their sin-pregnancy. They begin "showing," and it becomes obvious that something is different about the person who has given in to sinful thoughts. Her attitude changes, his countenance changes, her words change, his "things of God" habits change.

> He who is pregnant with evil and conceives trouble gives birth to disillusionment.
> —Psalm 7:14

Third Trimester

The growing sin more and more resembles the parent during this last trimester. As sin continues to grow and position itself for delivery, the parent begins to become more and more uncomfortable—oftentimes experiencing difficulty in sleeping. The parent is being stretched to accommodate this growing sin life inside of her. By the end of this trimester, a state of total sin maturity allows the sin to live and breathe on its own.

In the Bible we read of David's ongoing struggle with the consequences of allowing temptation to turn into sin and his saying, *"There was a time when I wouldn't admit what a sinner I was. But my dishonesty made me miserable and filled my days with frustration"* (Psalm 32:3 LB). All the partying in the world couldn't remove David's misery and remorse.

Labor and Delivery

Satan's obstetricians and midwives are always "on call" to deliver a full-term sin so that the world can see the proud parent with his or her newborn. While the parent may experience pain in laboring over its delivery, the sin-infant now forces its way into the world. Fully dilated and effaced, the parent begins to push uncontrollably—and the sin newborn is delivered! While still dependent on its parent for care and nursing, the bouncing baby sin has already developed an independent attitude. And Satan is right there with cigars, balloons, and stork signs to announce the birth. However, rather than this being a joyful moment for the new sin parent, it is often a time of remorse, pain, guilt, and disgrace. And no matter what the parent chooses to call or name this newborn, it is still sin.

> They conceive trouble and give birth to evil; their womb fashions deceit.
>
> —Job 15:35

I remember a time during the earlier years of our marriage when Angie innocently answered the phone at our house after I had asked her not to as it was my only day off. She had forgotten that, mistakenly picked up the phone when it rang, and called out, "Jay, it's for you!" Sure enough, it was another one of those "Pastor-you-have-to-leave-your-house-and-come-deal-with-this-right-now" situations. When I got off the phone, I lost my temper and said some things to my wife that were extremely hurtful. True to course, sin had followed the flow chart precisely:

1. I was tempted to get angry.
2. I wanted to lash out.
3. That want-to became a feeling of I-have-to.
4. Then sin was given birth as I was unreasonably ugly to my wife.

After I had vented my frustration, I could not believe what I had just said to her. My heart was devastated as I watched the most important person in my life start to weep at my thoughtlessness. I can't describe the sadness I felt as I allowed sin to give birth that day, and I was left holding something I had created that caused such pain.

A Death Announcement Is Born

Imagine for a moment that we could turn back the clock and listen in on an interview with Jesus' beloved disciple John that would help us better understand how sin brings about death—and how easy it is to give in to sin, even for those who are "close" to Jesus Christ.

"Excuse me! Judas! Over here! May I have a moment of your time? Good. Hello. I am Starr Scoop with *The Daily Inquisitor*. Sources inside the Sanhedrin have identified you as the one of the key figures in the plot to expose Jesus as the fraud many claimed him to be. Can we have your side of the story?"

With crowds pushing him on either side, he stops for a moment and addresses this reporter's accusation, "First of all, I am not who you think I am. My name is John. I *am* a follower of *The Way* and a disciple of Jesus, but I am not Judas Iscariot. Besides, have you not heard? Judas is dead."

"No! What? Don't you mean to say instead, '*Jesus* is dead'?"

"It is true that Jesus is dead, but so is Judas. He committed suicide yesterday. It's horrible, unbelievable. We are shocked and grieved by all that has transpired over the past few days."

"This *is* news! I guess we in the media have been so focused on Jesus' crucifixion that we missed this important story. Please, can you give me another few moments of your time to answer some questions that might clarify what really has happened to your leader and followers—especially this Judas?"

"I'm sorry, but you have no idea what you are asking of me at this point. I am so exhausted and . . . "

"But, please. Readers want to know the real truth about . . ."

"Truth? That's a new one! You want the real truth! Sure, I'll give it to you—but only a few questions. I simply can't handle much more today. Plus, I must go soon to meet the others."

"Fine. Would you like to step over there under the portico? Maybe we can have a little more privacy."

John follows the reporter, and quickly the two resume the interview. "John, what happened with Judas? Had there been an ongoing dispute or problem between him and Jesus? Why did he do what he did?"

"No, nothing major between them. Judas seemed to be a trusted and loyal follower. While he did not always agree with Jesus' views on things, he stuck with Jesus ... even though, at times, he did, in fact, grumble about some of these differences (John 6:60–71). Of course, Jesus never talked about him to the rest of us. That wasn't how he operated."

"Then why did Judas sell out Jesus to the high priests?"

"That's the question we've all been asking ourselves. He did struggle with the problem of greed, and yet—because of his good business sense—Jesus put him in charge of our group finances. Over the course of time, it became evident that he was stealing from our modest funds (John 12:6; 13:29)."

"Judas was a thief?"

"The truth is that Judas never seemed to be released from the stronghold of greed in his life. None of us realized how big a problem this was in his life. Something happened this week—in Bethany at a friend's house—that seemed to push Judas over the edge."

"What was that?"

"When we were guests in Lazarus's house, Mary—a dear friend of ours and follower of Jesus—opened an alabaster jar of the very expensive perfume nard. In an amazing act of devotion, she poured it all over Jesus' feet and began wiping his feet with her hair. At this Judas became quite indignant, shouting, 'Are you crazy, woman? Why are you wasting this perfume? We could sell it and ... uh ... give the money to the needy. That's a year's worth of wages!' Judas wasn't concerned about the poor, only himself!" (John 12:1–6).

"So, what did Jesus say to him?"

"Jesus nailed him—in a loving, but to-the-point way. He told Judas to back off ... that Mary was using the perfume for the purpose it was intended: his burial preparation. And then he said that while we will always have the poor among us, we wouldn't always have him

(John 12:7–8). Sadly, it wasn't till yesterday that we really understood what he meant."

"Was it after that incident in Bethany that Judas sold out Jesus to the high priests?"

"Yes. From what we have been able to piece together, Judas lost it. I guess his sin problem had grown to the point that Satan was able to take complete charge of him—causing him to do the unthinkable. He went to the high priests and negotiated to betray Christ in return for a substantial sum of money" (Luke 22:1–6).

"And then what did he do?"

"Two nights ago, we all gathered to celebrate the Passover and what turned out to be our last meal together. At that meal, Jesus made the accusation that one of us would betray him. We were all shocked that he would say—much less think—such a thing. Simon Peter asked him who would do such a thing. And Jesus responded, 'It is the one to whom I will give this piece of bread when I have dipped it in the dish.' And then he did so, gave it to Judas, and said, 'What you are about to do, do quickly.' We were totally clueless about what was going down. We assumed he was sending Judas out for some more food since Judas kept our money (Matthew 26:19–25; John 13:21–30). Instead, Judas went after the authorities who would later come and arrest Jesus in the Garden of Gethsemane."

> Sin will take you further than you want to go, keep you longer than you want to stay, and sink you deeper than you thought you would go.
>
> —UNKNOWN

"When did Judas kill himself?"

"Yesterday. When Judas saw that Jesus was condemned to death, he apparently was so overcome with guilt that he went back to the chief priests and tried to undo what he had done. When that proved futile, he went away and hanged himself (Matthew 27:1–5). Oh, look at the time. I'm sorry, but I have to go now. Please excuse me."

"Thank you, John. Thank you very much for this."

Unbelievable, isn't it? That sin could grow inside of someone so close to Jesus. We, too, must guard our lustful desires lest they grow to the point that sin—perhaps unthinkable sin—is given life within us. Such out-of-control sin-growth could lead to deadly consequences. It has been said that sin will take you further than you want to go, keep you longer than you want to stay, and sink you deeper than you thought you would go.[3] Could it happen to you?

Dumpster Diving

New sport? Apparently for some. What's the enticement? Others' still-usable-or-consumable-but-discarded stuff (i.e., trash). It's not just disposed-of home garbagio that dumpster divers prize. Some sift through the refuse of offices or technical installations to extract confidential data—especially security-compromising information. Others target grocery stores and restaurants, looking for edible items. Still others raid the dumpsters behind producers or sellers of high-tech equipment, hoping to snatch up still-valuable equipment that can be nursed back to health by some hacker's hand.[4]

The Art and Science of Dumpster Diving (yes, there's a book by that title!) provides the following helpful—I am sure, to some—"how-to" suggestions:

- Be careful around dumpsters. Lids can slam shut amazingly quickly from the wind.
- A good long stick with a sharp end is really nice to poke at bags and reach way into the corners.
- Avoid meat, eggs, and dairy food. Everyone knows this, but as a reminder—the stuff get really nasty quick.[5]

I was surprised to discover that rules of etiquette govern dumpster diving:

- Be aware of what you are taking. You can run afoul of people if you take sensitive materials (e.g., office refuse with bank numbers).
- Be conscious of how much you are taking and how much you use. It's simple ethics: Taking more than you can use

and throwing it away takes it away from other potential users, some of who may be far more dependent on dumpster treasures than you are.
* Leave the dumpster looking better than you found it.[6]

Dumpster diving isn't just limited to trash bins. Satan has been promoting this game from the beginning in the Garden. He seeks to entice us to dumpster dive in our thought life. He wants us to dive into the dumpsters of . . .

trash television
garbage magazines
filthy Internet sites
dirty jokes
rubbish relationships
spoiled thoughts
worthless ideas
junky language
foul attitudes
polluted morals
corrupted values

Can't you hear Satan saying, "Just dive in!"? While Satan promises that it will be free and fun, God has already posted his *No Trespassing* signs on these trash bins. God has done it for our protection, yet Satan encourages it for our destruction. Then when we go for the dive, the very one who promised us freedom and fun becomes the one who points his diabolic finger in our faces and condemns us. No wonder he is called "the accuser of our brothers" (Revelation 12:10).

Sometimes I get preoccupied and fail to take out the trash at our house. I can walk right past to-the-point-of-overflowing trashcans and not even notice the need to empty these receptacles—that is, until Angie lovingly draws my attention to what needs to be done. I am embarrassed to admit that too many times I have been caught up with ministry details and failed to notice the accumulating garbage in my thought life. The mounting garbage may go unnoticed until a loving and gracious Holy Spirit prompts me to remove the trash accumulating in my thought life. Likewise, he warns me about climbing in the sin dumpster and pulling out past attitudes that were negative, present anger that is bent on destruction, and future needs about which I am worried. It seems the hardest garbage for me to toss is the stuff I find when I look back at past sin with a regretful eye.

Nightmare on Looking Back Street

I'm an Alfred Hitchcock fan. Still when I hear the "Good e-v-e-ning" at the beginning of his films, it sends chills down my spine. And when I see hundreds of *Birds* in the sky, I begin to cringe. And, of course, after seeing *Psycho*, I was never quite as comfortable about singing in the shower!

My daughter must have inherited the fright-fest gene from me. When she had a sleepover with her girlfriends to celebrate her thirteenth birthday, they decided to rent the supernatural thriller *What Lies Beneath*. In the wee hours of the morning I was awakened by screaming, hollering, giggling, and crying coming from the other end of the house. The girls had been frightened by the movie's effective scare tactics as they watched this frightening tale of a college professor's wife's (Michelle Pfeiffer) picture-perfect life being completely disrupted by the ghostly apparition of a young woman in her bathtub. It soon becomes apparent that this woman's husband (Harrison Ford) has betrayed her, and that his past has returned to haunt him— literally. After watching the movie, none of the girls wanted to take a bath for days!

This genre of movies is so popular . . . from Freddy—the man with the claw, the nightmare of Springwood—to Jason—the man in the mask, the terror to teens at Camp Crystal Lake. The American public apparently loves to be scared out of its wits by movies such as John Carpenter's "Was that the bogeyman?" in the 1978 horror classic *Halloween*, to the 2001 gruesome "I should tell you . . . I've given some serious thought . . . to eating your wife" horror flick *Hannibal*.

I Still Know What You Did Last Summer (1998) actress Jennifer Love Hewitt explains why this film engages audiences: "What makes this one scarier is that this one is allowed to be sort of wild and violent and psychotic because it all takes place in Julie's head, which is no longer filled with any sort of reality." Hewitt adds, "In a horror film, anything is possible. I don't think horror films ever end."[7]

Horror films take place in our heads, too. The tape is popped in and *Power, Rewind,* and *Play* are punched to play the memory—not Memorex—tape. The recorder in our minds repeats this process day after day as Satan pushes the buttons. Our thought-life horror films—memories of our past when we have given in to temptation— become old, but they are still terrifying reruns in our minds. Featured in this fright flick are skeletons from our past that threaten our future, alarm our fears, terrorize our feelings, and intimidate our faith.

> *Digging Up Skeletons II* is the movie Satan rushes to get whenever he wants to indict us.

The skeletons' dialogue is somewhat predictable, but frightens us nonetheless:

"What makes you think you will get by with this?"

"Why do you believe that you can ever get beyond this?"

"When are you going to concede that you will never be free?"

"How are you going to explain it when it gets out?"

"Where could you ever go to get away from this?"

These thought skeletons seem to have a thousand lives. We kill them, and Satan brings them back to life again. We bury them, and Satan digs them up again. We put them in a closet, and Satan releases them again. Always available for rental, *Digging Up Skeletons II* is the movie Satan rushes to get whenever he wants to indict us.

Skelaphobia

Marilyn's husband, Jon, phoned her to say he was stopping by the gardening center to pick up some pine straw on the way home from work. Task completed, he headed home. As he was cruising along the highway at sixty-plus miles per hour, he noticed, out of the corner of his eye, something that seemed to be moving on the dash. As he glanced to his right to see what it was, the object came into clear view. An at least five- to six-foot snake—half on the dash and half hanging down to the floorboard—was slithering his direction.

Not taking the time to determine if this was a "bad" snake, Jon instinctively reacted by slamming on the brakes as he pulled off the road. You may have guessed: The snake fell off the dash and onto the seat next to him! Panicked, Jon jumped out of the now-stopped car. He was successful in escaping the snake, but in doing so he failed to put the car in "park."

> According to most studies, people's number one fear is public speaking. Number two is death. So to the average person, if you have to go to a funeral, you're better off in the casket than doing the eulogy.
>
> —JERRY SEINFELD

Now with the car rolling toward a ditch, Jon had to open the car door, sit on the seat next to the snake, and apply the brakes as he put the car in "park." Mustering all of his courage, he did what he had to do—and then quickly got back out of the car! As he stood there trying to figure out how the snake got in his car, he deduced he had brought it into his car when he put the pine straw in the trunk.

Still not knowing what kind of snake it was—because the snake had gone into hiding when Jon got back into the car—Jon phoned a wildlife official to see if he had any idea how to coax the snake out of the car. The guy instructed Jon to get back in the car one more time, turn the heater on full blast, and crack the windows just enough that the cool-air-seeking snake could crawl out. He did—and it worked! Within a few minutes the snake—which turned out to be non-poisonous—crawled out. However, before Jon got back into the car, he opened the trunk and thoroughly examined its contents to make sure there were no other hitchhikers!

This episode would have "done in" most Americans if recent Gallup survey results are correct. According to these pollsters 51 percent of adults said that they most feared snakes.[8] Would Jon's experience have given you a heart attack? What do you most fear?

Fred Culbertson has compiled and posted online *The Phobia List*,[9] an extensive "A to Z" catalogue of phobias. He admits that he knows little about curing phobias, but he is fascinated by their names—and, oh, what names there are for our phobias! Do you suffer from any of these?

Phobias from A to Z

Arachibutyrophobia: fear of peanut butter sticking to the roof of the mouth
Bogeyphobia: fear of the bogeyman
Cacophobia: fear of ugliness
Dentophobia: fear of dentists
Ecclesiophobia: fear of church
Frigophobia: fear of cold, cold things
Genuphobia: fear of knees
Hippopotomonstrosequippedaliophobia: fear of long words
Ideophobia: fear of ideas
Jayophobia*: fear of people named *Jay* or of the name *Jay*
Kopophobia: fear of fatigue
Logizomechanophobia: fear of computers
Macrophobia: fear of long waits
Obesophobia: fear of gaining weight
Pteronophobia: fear of being tickled by feathers
Quackaphobia*: fear of fakes
Rhytiphobia: fear of getting wrinkles
Sociophobia: fear of people in general
Tropophobia: fear of making changes
Uranophobia: fear of heaven
Venustraphobia: fear of beautiful women
Wiccaphobia: fear of witches and witchcraft
Xanthophobia: fear of the color yellow
Yuckaphobia*: fear of yucky substances or tasks
Zoophobia: fear of animals

---

*These phobias are not real names of phobias, but my attempt at humor where there were no phobias either given or appropriate for our purposes in Culbertson's list.

I searched Culbertson's list but did not find an all-to-common pho-bia: *skelephobia*—the fear of being found out. Many live with the fear that what they have done in their past will come back to haunt them—which, in fact, it often does.

Larry Flynt, publisher of *Hustler* magazine, capitalized on skele-phobia. As one of former President Bill Clinton's chief defenders when Mr. Clinton faced impeachment for the Monica Lewinsky debacle, Flynt spent four million dollars of his own money to produce *The Flynt Report: Hustler's Hard Evidence of Adultery, Lies, and Fraud.* He referred to it as an unmasking of the Republican Party hypocrites in Washington. Flint dug back into the closet to find skeletons on prominent Republican leaders who had been critical of Clinton.

If Flynt were searching for skeletons to expose from your sin closet, what would he uncover? Would there be the skeleton of an affair, divorce, or moral failure? Would there be the skeleton of a past drink-ing, gambling, or drug problem? Would there be the skeleton of a past crime, debt, or scandal? Would there be the skeleton of a long-held grudge, jealousy, or resentment? What skeletons haunt you and hold you captive?

At Attention!

Cathy's skeletons surfaced after years of keeping them locked away in her closet. She was married to a military officer and loved life as the offi-cer's wife—especially the formal dances and events. She was an attrac-tive and outgoing woman and made friends easily with "other men."

When her husband retired, Cathy was in her fifties and became dissatisfied with nonmilitary life, her empty nest, and no longer feel-ing important. While her job was not all that satisfying, she did like the attention she received from the men at her workplace. She began hav-ing fantasies about these men who were willing to give her the atten-tion she craved. More and more she began flirting with these men, which ultimately led to a string of affairs. For a long time Cathy suc-cessfully hid her affairs from her husband and family, but eventually these sin skeletons came out in the daylight. One night her husband confronted her after he had discovered her past affairs.

Devastated by her unfaithfulness, he gave her an ultimatum: Move with him to another city and put an end to these extramarital relationships or be divorced. She did move with him, but their life together was never the same. Both of them were miserable, and Cathy found escape only in her ongoing fantasy world.

Like Cathy, each of us deals with skeletons of one kind or another in our closet. Some are from innocent mistakes we have made, while others are there because we acted on a sinful thought. Many of us live with the fear of being found out. Yet we won't take the necessary steps to deal with those secret sins that are hidden away in a closet labeled "Past."

> Sin is not a pretty baby to be held and cuddled, but an ugly skeleton that can haunt us for the rest of our lives.

Did you hear about what they encountered while tearing down that large, old building in Chicago to make room for that new skyscraper? Because of its proximity to other buildings, the old building could not be imploded. So it had to be dismantled floor by floor. While working on the forty-ninth floor, two construction workers found a skeleton in a small closet behind the elevator shaft. They immediately called the police.

When the police arrived, they directed them to the closet, showed the officers a fully clothed skeleton standing upright, and said, "This could be Jimmy Hoffa or somebody really important."

Two days went by, and the construction workers couldn't stand the suspense any longer. They had to know whom they had found. So they called the police and said, "We are the two guys who found the skeleton in the closet. And we want to know if it was Jimmy Hoffa or somebody important."

The police said, "It's not Jimmy Hoffa, but it was somebody kind of important."

"Well, who was it?"

"The 1956 National Hide-and-Seek Champion!"[10]

Playing hide-and-seek takes on a new meaning as we try to hide our sins, but they come after us, seeking us. Sin, like the birth of a baby, cannot be hidden forever. Our sin is the only thing that has the simultaneous effect of birth and death. Once it's birthed, a funeral notice is posted. Satan congratulates, but God pronounces something dead. Sin is not a pretty baby to be held and cuddled, but an ugly skeleton that can haunt us for the rest of our lives.

It's inevitable. It's simply going to happen if we don't S.T.O.P. the sin process. Temptation leads to a desire to go for it. And that desire, when left unchecked, leads to lust—an evil craving. We shouldn't be surprised that lust gives way to sin. "It gives birth to sin . . ." (James 1:15).

Martin Luther said, "Sin is essentially a departure from God." That defining moment—when you choose to follow Satan's leading instead of God's directions—occurs prior to the sin, when we can either say *yes* or *no* to our sinful thoughts. You may be struggling right now with lust for someone or something. The sin process will continue and sin will be born into your life, unless you S.T.O.P. it now.

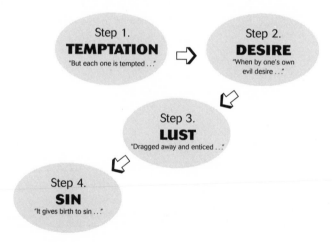

The next step in the devastating progression of sin is . . .

Part Two

Examining Sin's Consequences

You may be sure that your sin will find you out.

NUMBERS 32:23

Death of Pure Thoughts

DON HENLEY, FORMER SINGER and drummer for *The Eagles*, went solo with his album *The End of the Innocence*. The title song tells how "happily ever after" fails us. The song depicts how the fairy tales of simpler days are poisoned by lies. This commentary on life concludes with the words, *"Offer up your best defense but this is the end of the innocence."*[1] How sad if that song were to be dedicated to us. For with each of us, there comes the time—and it's different for each person—where innocence is lost. It could be through one or more of these. . .

- the first look at a porn magazine or website
- the first introduction to sex
- the first time hearing one's parents arguing, fighting, or threatening to leave the marriage/family
- the first time to use cigarettes, alcohol, or drugs
- the first realization that one's parent is doing something very wrong
- the first time a "dirty" word is heard or used
- the first time of cheating on a test
- the first awareness that there has been a shooting at one's school
- the first time saying something that is offensive—like a negative nickname or slur—to another individual

- the first time a child realizes that a parent doesn't love him or her
- the first time of seeing America under terrorists' attack

The loss of innocence begins in the thought life. In this chapter we will consider the process of how innocence first goes to war with sinful thoughts and how, if not stopped, will ultimately lead to the death of pure thoughts. Being aware of how it happens can help us to avoid the pure-thought funeral.

The Killing Fields

Lakhina Chin, a young Cambodian lady in her early twenties, bravely stepped to the podium at our church and shared the following riveting story of the loss of her pure thoughts and the tragic way she acquired accusing thoughts that nearly cost her life.

Being a survivor from the "Killing Fields," I have had to face death in all its dreadfulness as I witnessed the relentless brutal massacre of my people by the millions. Yet, despite the wide range of evils my eyes have been exposed to, nothing haunted my soul more than witnessing abortion.

I was fifteen years old and attending a youth rally at a Catholic high school when I first saw a film on abortion. I had thought I had seen all the faces of evil, through the experiences in Cambodia, but shockingly, while viewing the film, I quickly learned otherwise. Never in a million years could I have ever imagined a more senseless death than the killing of innocent babies. Gripped by a deep sense of sorrow, I burst into tears as I watched the metal prongs crush their little tiny skulls and cut them up into tiny pieces. I then watched as these now-lifeless fetuses were sucked out, bagged up, and stacked up on hundreds of other mutilated victims, waiting to be dumped like worthless disposable garbage.

Viewing this horror was too grotesque for me to tolerate. Feeling sick to my stomach, I ran out of the classroom. The youth pastor found me on the bathroom floor, curled up in a fetal position, holding my stomach, and screaming, "Why, Lord? How could you let this happen? They're innocent! They're just babies! They haven't done anything to anybody! How could you let this happen?" With tears gushing uncontrollably, I kept on crying out, "But they're so helpless!"

I would have never imagined it even remotely possible that ten years later I would become like those women who had stopped a beating heart. I, too, ended up doing the unthinkable—denying the precious gift of life to an innocent child. And—as I have thought about it so many times since— the only explanation I can come up with was that I was scared—scared of the rejection of being left to go through motherhood alone, scared of being a disgrace to my family, scared of raising an illegitimate child alone, scared of failing as a mother. I was so scared! There is no other explanation.

I remember waking up from the operation and finding myself surrounded by a roomful of other young, hurting women who, too, had believed a lie. The nurses had told us before the surgery, "Don't worry. You won't remember anything." As I lay there—frightened and hurting, and with a sick awareness of the reality of what I had just done—I realized that what the nurse had said was a lie from the pit of hell. I had made a deal with the devil over an innocent soul. Trembling with remorse, I cried out, "What have I done, God? What have I done?" All I wanted to do at that point was die in place of my baby. I knew that I had destroyed God's beautiful, little creation. It was the darkest day of my life! I could almost see the frowning face of God as he turned his back towards me—or, at least, that was another lie Satan wanted me to believe.

Because of my lack of knowledge on what the Word of God says about the cleansing blood of Jesus, I hardened my heart to numb the pain. I pursued every avenue that I could to help ease the pain of living with the reality of what I had done. I was drinking alcohol for breakfast, lunch, and dinner. It seemed to relieve some of the hurt for a short period of time, but I needed something else to enhance my mood. So I would smoke marijuana. Soon I needed something that could take me higher, so I began taking Ecstasy. I wanted to go as high as the sky so the pain could not reach me; however, once the drugs wore off, I was down again—as low and miserable as ever.

One day, after living months of this destructive lifestyle, I had decided I did not want to live any longer. I prayed and pleaded for God to let me die: "Just let me die, please...." I had seen so much evil in my life that I was convinced that a good God did not exist. Asking God to let me die became my desire and my plea for many weeks.

That has been over two years ago. As you can see, God did not let me die. Instead, he gave me life! Even better than that, God spoke to my heart and said, "Come to me, and choose life—the abundant kind of life that I have always desired to give you." God wasn't talking about the just-barely-getting-along type of life. He was talking about a complete and victorious life filled with his joy and peace.

In desperation, I accepted his invitation for that new life. Immediately, as the Spirit of the living God came to live in me, I felt all of my pain, hurt, and confusion lifted off my weary soul. His love has set me free and his mercy has restored my restless soul! His grace has healed my broken heart, and I have received complete forgiveness for all of my sins. I have become a new creature in Christ Jesus!"

Lakhina's loss of innocence began at an early age—in the killing fields of Cambodia. Her pure thoughts died many deaths as she grew into adolescence and adulthood. She experienced repetitious cycles of innocence-loss as she sought escape from the mental scars of pain and searched for happiness in all the wrong places. Lakhina wanted to escape from the pain she felt, but it led her to a spiritual and moral killing field.

When we give into our sinful thoughts, we kill—for the duration of our disobedience until the time of our genuine repentance—purity, godliness, peace of mind, and unfettered communion with God. Our thought life is a battleground, a war that is daily waged against us. The constant skirmishes being fought between our ears could easily be called . . .

World War Thought

Together with the rest of the world, I was glued to the television set as I watched in stunned disbelief as the passenger airlines were flown into the World Trade Center towers. It caused me to think about

When we give into our sinful thoughts, we kill—for the duration of our disobedience until the time of our genuine repentance—purity, godliness, peace of mind, and unfettered communion with God.

warfare in a different light and to recall my feelings as I—with the world—watched Bernard Shaw and Peter Arnett broadcast live from their room in Baghdad's Al-Rashid Hotel on CNN on January 16, 1991. Five and a half months after Iraqi forces had invaded Kuwait—and seventeen hours after the deadline for their withdrawal, which was set by the opposing coalition of nations—Baghdad bunkered down beneath the strongest concentration of air defenses in the world. This included seventy-six surface-to-air missile (SAM) launchers and nearly three thousand anti-aircraft artillery (AAA) guns. And the world waited in fearful anticipation with Baghdad. "We haven't heard any planes yet," reported Shaw. Neither he nor the Iraqi radar operators detected any approaching B–52 bombers in the moonless sky.

Six hundred and fifty miles south of Baghdad, at Khamis Mushayt in Saudi Arabia, U.S. Air Force pilots of the Thirty-Seventh Tactical Fighter Wing were also glued to the CNN newscast. Two hours earlier some of their squadron had departed their air base on the first air strike of the war. One of their targets, located on the west bank of the Tigris River, was the 370-foot Al-Kark Communications Tower, by which CNN was broadcasting to the world. If all had gone according to plans in the past two hours, the network would go off the air . . . *now!*

Shortly before 3:00 A.M. local time, January 17, 1991, eight black F–117 Nighthawk jets (a.k.a., stealth fighters) arrived above Baghdad. Captain Marcel Kerdavid, who was assigned to bomb the Al-Kark tower, locked his laser beam on the tower and, using a fingertip control on his throttle stick, locked his aim point onto the laser glint. Ten seconds before release, Kerdavid hit the "pickle" button that enabled his weapons system. The Nighthawk's bomb bay snapped open and lowered its one-ton GBU–27A/B guided bomb into the slipstream. Freed of the necessity of dodging anti-aircraft fire, Kerdavid delivered his bomb above his target.

In their room in the Al-Rashid Hotel, the CNN reporters' microphones picked up the rising sound of an air raid warning. "Now the sirens are sounding for the first time," reported Arnett. "The Iraqis have informed us . . ." At that instant, Kerdavid's GBU–27 took out the Al-Kark tower, snapping it in two. And CNN promptly went black. A surviving audio-only land link allowed Arnett to verbally describe the spray of aimless return fire above Baghdad skies.

In the first twenty-four hours of the Gulf War, the forty-two Nighthawk or stealth fighters at King Khalid—only 2.5 percent of the total allied aircraft deployed—accounted for 31 percent of the targets attacked. Because the stealth fighter offers virtual immunity to radar because of its "invisible" design and its ability to deliver weapons with unprecedented accuracy, these black jets were consistently assigned the most dangerous, high-priority targets throughout the Gulf War.[2]

Every reader of this book is also fighting in a war. Even if you aren't a Gulf War veteran with memories of Baghdad, you should realize that a war is now being fought wherever—and also because—you have chosen to read this book. It may be peacetime where you and I are living, but there's always a battle raging for the mind. In my own mind there are days I simply want to call for a cease-fire. *Please, Lord, give me two or three days where no sinful thoughts attack my thought life!*

But on this side of heaven, there is no armistice. The attacks come like rapid-fire weapons targeting our thoughts. Stealth-like pure-thought fighters are deployed by Satan to remain undetected as he zooms in to fire away at our thought lives. Unless our anti-sinful-thought, surface-to-Prince-of-the-Power-of-the-Air weapons are up—that is, the Holy Spirit's control, renewing the mind daily through Scripture, and our instant and total obedience to the will of God—

sinful thoughts can invade our unguarded thought-lives. We should live in readiness for these mind attacks because in an instant—at the speed of thought—we can lose control, and our thoughts will take us to places we never intended to go.

> We should live in readiness for these mind attacks because in an instant—at the speed of thought—we can lose control, and our thoughts will take us to places we never intended to go.

Through our thought life we can escape into places where we lose any kind of biblical convictions, personal morality, and passionate commitment to Christ. We fool ourselves into thinking we can lay aside our values for a sin-filled moment, and no one ever has to know. But in reality, it is one step removed from losing those things that are most dear to us.

Lose Something?

Little Rock (AP)—Things went from bad to worse for the University of Arkansas men's basketball team. They lost their last game of the season, then they got lost on the way home. Returning the Razorbacks to Arkansas on a late Thursday night flight from New York, the pilot of the private charter plane mistakenly landed at the wrong airport. The Boeing 727 touched down at a small airport in Springdale, some 12 miles north of where it was supposed to land. "Everybody in the plane knew we were at the wrong airport except the pilot," Rick Schaeffer, director of Arkansas's sports information department, said Friday. Eventually, the 137 weary passengers—basketball players, cheerleaders, boosters, the school band and alumni—carried their luggage across the runway, regrouped on buses, and headed back to the Fayetville airport, where the plane was supposed to land and where they had parked their vehicles. The Razorbacks were home after losing 74–64 to Connecticut in the consolation game of the National Invitational Tournament.[3]

Like those basketball players, you know that losing something can be frustrating. Have you ever lost a credit card, set of keys, airplane ticket, or even a pet? Upsetting, isn't it? Losing valuables can be so frustrating and cause you to have that sick-to-your-stomach feeling when you realize what may have just happened. Some reports have estimated that lost merchandise costs us millions of dollars each year.[4] "Lost and found" services in department stores, amusement parks, airports, restaurants, hotels, and even churches seem to confirm that we are a serious bunch of losers!

> Good news, pastor: You've baptized seven people today in the river! Bad news, pastor: You lost two of them in the swift current![5]

Not long ago, my writing partner and I met up in another city to do some book interviews. It was a particularly meaningful day where we had seen God orchestrate the impossible—including a visit with Billy Graham at a time when his health was not allowing him to do this sort of thing very often. We were on Cloud 9—pumped about what God had done that day—as we rushed to the airport to fly back to our respective cities.

As it ended up, Marilyn and I were both booked on the same connecting commuter flight to Atlanta. Because our time with Mr. Graham had concluded close to our flight time, we just made it to the gate as they were boarding passengers. After the less-than-an-hour flight arrived in Atlanta, we deplaned and stopped at a newsstand immediately to the left of the gate so that we could grab newspapers before we caught our other flights. As Marilyn went to retrieve her wallet to pay for a paper, she said, "Jay, I don't have my wallet." Surprisingly calm, she looked through the purse she was carrying, and it obviously was not there.

Confident that it had slipped out of the drawstring purse when she had it on the floor beneath her seat, she asked some airline personnel to go back on the plane and check the area where she had been sitting to see if they could locate it for her. The airline representative soon came back and said that he didn't see it. Using her cell phone, Marilyn quickly and systematically made the calls one makes when this sort of thing happens. After coming up on one dead-end after another, she filed the appropriate reports for a missing item and flew back to Orlando— and refused to let this loss ruin what had been an incredible God-day.

The wallet never was recovered. And as we collaborated on some writing projects via e-mail over the next week, she commented on what a pain it was to handle all the matters associated with losing a wallet. Lost were some things she could not replace—and also some things, like her driver's license, which were replaceable but a pain to do so.

I could easily empathize with Marilyn. Even though I hate to lose things, I still do. Some of my "losing-itis" is acute and some is chronic. I sporadically lose money in my suit pockets (that ends up at my honest dry cleaners) or those "Hey, pastor, here's some vital info—call me later—I'll be waiting" notes that I receive when I am trying to talk to forty people at once. As I think about it, there was even that elusive paycheck that somehow disappeared and inexplicably ended up in our outside trash can. Some people—like my wife or assistant—would say I have a bad case of chronic lose-it syndrome when it comes to my keys, sunglasses, CDs, tapes, phone numbers, and to-do lists.

Marilyn and I decided to come up with separate his and her would-really-hate-to-lose lists. See if you would agree with any of our half-facetious, top-ten selections.

	Top Ten Things He'd Really Hate to Lose	Top Ten Things She'd Really Hate to Lose
#10	*Electricity:* He can't watch TV in the dark.	*Restroom-bonding:* It's a female privilege.
#9	*The TV remote:* It's the surest way to defeat a man.	*Her girlish figure:* Was it Baskin Robbins or having a baby?
#8	*His temper:* He'd hate to say, "Pardon me, may I borrow your temper? I seem to have lost mine."	*Carpool:* Love those days she doesn't have to drive!
#7	*His keys:* They are never where he left them. It must be his wife's fault.	*Charge cards:* Enough said.
#6	*Directions:* Of course he'd rather drive all day than stop and ask!	*Parked car:* Okay, who moved the parking lot?

#5	*His athletic physique:* He doesn't want chest and drawer disease where his chest drops down to his drawers.	*Her smooth complexion:* Where did these crow's feet come from?
#4	*His hair:* Where's that number for Hair Club for Men?	*Telephones:* Never enough said.
#3	*His wallet:* Forget the money. His Blockbuster Card was in there!	*Her favorite "soap":* Better than Calgon to take her away.
#2	*His job:* He'd rather be caught dead than wearing a pink slip.	*Chocolate:* Sometimes it's the only thing that helps.
#1	*His marbles:* He'd hate to use someone else's!	*The last word:* Always!

While it's easy to shirk off some losses, others are far more difficult for us to handle. Beyond losses that are just temporary setbacks, other losses may be some of the most difficult challenges we will ever face—if not life-changing. Satan wants us to think that there is no way we can possibly survive the . . .

- *Loss of family* . . . Not only is the loss of a loved one by death something that impacts the way we think about things, but so, too, the death of a marriage. The pain of hearing and living with the judge's words "divorce granted" can devastate our lives—and the way we perceive ourselves, others, and life events.

- *Loss of finances* . . . The words *down-sizing, flat-broke, lay-off, bankrupt, more-month-than-money, Nasdaq nose-dive, maxed-out credit card* impact not only our financial security but also our sense of well-being, worth, and purpose. The death of finances, for many, signals a loss of self-esteem.

- *Loss of future* . . . The death of a promising or hope-filled future can be brought about as the fateful result of bad choices and wrong decisions. When we give in to sinful thoughts, other things die as well. God's plan for maximum happiness and fulfillment is replaced with the painful and disappointing consequences of sin.

- *Loss of faith* . . . The death of faith is the saddest of all. It takes the once-upon-a-time virgin belief in God's Word, God's goodness, and God's exciting plan for your life and exchanges it for thoughts of "God doesn't care," "God can't do anything about it," "God isn't involved in my everyday routine," or "God is not worth serving if he is going to allow such evil and tragic things to happen." Faith limited to what-we-can-figure-out-and-work-out-on-our-own is faith that is far from live, true-to-the-promises-of-God faith.

Recently I had a disturbing visit with a college student who was struggling with her faith. Kara was distraught about all the doubt she was having about God's being real and having a specific plan for her life. She, like many her age, sought something other than her parents' answers for the important, faith-shaping questions:

- "Does this God-stuff work?"
- "God may be there, but is he really involved in my day-to-day life?"
- "God seems to be working for others, but why has he never told me specifically what to do with my life?"
- "How can I accept with blind faith what my reason tells me isn't so?"

Sadly, Kara and other fellow students had been challenged by more than one professor at this established-as-a-Christian university to question everything about their faith in God. In the name of academic freedom, professors had taken her out on a theologically dangerous limb, but had never brought her back to a biblically based foundation. The final blow came when a friend—who was a graduating senior—said to her, "I wish I was leaving here with the same faith I had when I came." Kara, discouraged and disillusioned, withdrew from that school and came home. While she was still in the search mode, wanting answers, she was too mentally exhausted and disillusioned to search for truth by herself.

Where did this loss of faith begin? It all started with a runaway thought that everything she believed should be now filtered through her unaided human reason, devoid of genuine faith. For the moment, it felt to her that she had been defeated in Round 1 of her adult thought-life wrestling match.

Thought Wrestle-Mania

Have you heard of the apocryphal story of a United States Olympic wrestling match against Russia? In the first match, the Russian wrestler beat the American decisively. In the second match, the Russian prevailed over the American opponent. The American coach—devastated and embarrassed—could bear no more. In the final match the coach told his wrestler, "Just go out there and do the best you can and get it over with."

The coach could not bear to watch, so he put his hands over his eyes. He could not see the action, but only heard the crowd as it went crazy, cheering and applauding. By the time the coach removed his hands from his eyes, the match was over and the American had won!

The coach ran over to his wrestler and asked, "What happened out there?"

"Well, Coach, it's like this. While I was in the match I saw this big toe and I just bit it as hard as I could. And you know, Coach, it's amazing what a man can do when he bites his own toe!"[6]

> Round 1 is where we either allow a sinful thought to enter and stay, or we pin it to the mat and declare the fight to be over by a T.K.O.—a *Thought Knock Out!*

When the apostle Paul spoke of this spiritual warfare, he borrowed a term from the world of wrestling: "For our struggle is not against flesh and blood" (Ephesians 6:12). The word "struggle" means to wrestle, a hand-to-hand, *mano a mano* fight. R. Kent Hughes describes this idea of struggle as "swaying back and forth while locked in mortal battle . . . sweat against sweat, breath against breath."[7]

Where does Round 1 begin in this ongoing wrestling match with the devil? It begins in the thought life. That's where the real battle is either won or lost. Most matches go for several rounds, but when it comes to the thought life, the first round determines the outcome. Round 1 is where we either allow a sinful thought to enter and stay, or we pin it to the mat and declare the fight to be over by a T.K.O.—a *Thought Knock Out!*

Claiming to be the most electrifying man in sports entertainment today, Dwayne Johnson, better known by millions as "The Rock," transcends boundaries of age, culture, and sex in his appeal to audiences. The Rock has become a World Wrestling Federation superstar. His talent, good looks, athletic ability, and arrogant attitude hold an attraction for countless wrestling fans. The undisputed champion of "The Nation of Domination" comes out with his signature battle cry, "If you smell what The Rock is cooking." At "No Way Out" The Rock added to his legacy by becoming the first-ever six-time WWF champion.[8]

The thought battle isn't fought in a fan-packed arena. Instead, it is fought in the unseen stadium of the spirit world. The winner of this match is not guaranteed by using smart techniques, slick moves, fancy footwork, or death-holds. The Rock, Mankind, Steve Austin, or any of the other WWF or WCW wrestlers are not the champions in this arena of the mind. Most often these matches are not well publicized. Yet, at any time or any place, they can instantly become the main event in our lives.

Our toughest wrestling matches are most commonly fought at places where it is much easier to give in to sin—places where the atmosphere entices us to let down our guard. While these unrelenting matches can occur at any time, they can almost be guaranteed to occur during those times when we are emotionally and physically tired. We must be aware that our pure thought life, if not protected and defended against Satan's sinful-thought onslaught, will go down for the ten count and die.

Pick Out Your Casket

Many times I have been with families who were dealing with the shock and reality of death. One of the most difficult times they face is when they have to make the funeral and burial arrangements. The last thing anyone wants to do at a time of the loss of a loved one is to be thrown into the midst of dozens of decisions about who is going to lead in the funeral service, who will sing, who will be the pallbearers, what kind of casket to buy, whether a grave vault should be purchased, and what kind of grave marker they want.

Under such emotional stress, most of us are not at our best for making decisions that can be so costly, especially given the high expense of funerals. And often, when faced with this dreaded task, we do not know where to turn to get the objective advice we need to make informed and wise decisions.

Nowadays there are a number of funeral websites to assist in securing information about consumer law regarding funeral arrangements as well as how to select and purchase caskets, vaults, urns, monuments, and flowers at costs they claim as being only slightly above wholesale prices. Did you know that since 1994, federal law states that a funeral home must accept a casket secured elsewhere and cannot charge a handling fee or manipulate their prices in any way to penalize you? They must treat you as if you purchased the casket from them.[9]

On an online consumer law site, the Federal Trade Commission explains that the coffin is frequently the single most expensive funeral item you may have to buy if you are planning a traditional funeral. Most caskets sold in the United States today are made from either steel or hardwood. A casket is not required for a direct cremation or an immediate burial. With the latter, the body is generally buried without viewing or embalming and is usually placed in an alternate type of container made of unfinished wood, pressboard, cardboard, or canvas.[10]

Funeral and burial practices vary almost as much as individuals themselves differ from one person to the next. This may be a good thing. I know that funerals are not supposed to be funny, but as a pastor I have been involved in some funeral services where I have been— pardon the pun—tickled to death.

One funeral in particular completely took me by surprise. Contacted by a funeral director to see if I could do the funeral of a man who was not associated with a church, I agreed, since I felt it would be a great outreach opportunity. As I arrived at the funeral home I immediately noticed that something was different. Only a few cars were parked in the lot. Instead, there were Harleys everywhere.

Once inside I found out that the man who died was a biker. Never have I seen so many tattoos in one single setting. I made it through the funeral, and at the end of the service I stood at the head of the casket as the people filed by. What transpired over the next few minutes is beyond description. Instead of solemn organ music, Queen's cult hit *Bohemian Rhapsody* blared out of the sound system. Stunned, I stood there trying to compose myself and look "pastorly" while the blaring words "*Oh, mama mia, mama mia, mama mia, let me go. Beelzebub has a devil put aside for me, for me, for me*"[11] shook the funeral home as the mourners rocked and rolled past the deceased.

Not only have I participated in some unusual-to-say-the-least funerals, I have heard stories of some that were quite bizarre. While serving as pastor in the Dallas area, one of our church members who worked for a huge cemetery told of one funeral procession that arrived late to the internment because the hearse driver had gotten hungry and took the entire processional on a detour through a Church's Fried Chicken drive-through. The hearse was not the only vehicle in the procession to stop so that a "to go" order might be placed, but literally the whole funeral party got their buckets of chicken and stood graveside licking their fingers!

He also told an extraordinary story of a man who was buried with a case of whiskey, a sizeable sum of cash, and a large amount of gold. My friend asked the family of the deceased why in the world this man was being buried with these three unusual things. Their response shocked him. They explained, "The whiskey is so he will enjoy the trip. The cash is for any emergencies on the way to where he is going. And the gold is so he can live a rich life when he gets there."

After hearing that I jokingly told my friend, "Tell you what ... I think we should dig up the grave when no one is looking, leave the whiskey, take the cash and gold, and simply write the man a check!" (Before you think I am some kind of thief, please know that I was just kidding!)

On the serious side, many of us are buried in coffins of our own choosing with far greater riches that will never wisely be used. When

> Stunned, I stood there trying to look "pastorly" while the words "*Oh, mama mia, mama mia, mama mia, let me go. Beelzebub has a devil put aside for me, for me, for me*" shook the funeral home.

we allow our mind to run away from pure thoughts and continue running away from God's way of thinking and living, we are picking out a made-to-order casket for ourselves. We have killed—at least for a time or at worst for an eternity—what God intended for us to be and to do. Unlike our having to purchase a casket for a loved one who has literally passed away, Satan has provided a style and model to accommodate us. Allowing sinful thoughts to continue hands him another nail for the coffin of pure thoughts. Some of the nails that we hand to Satan to use in sealing our coffins are:

- the nail of continuing to do something even when our internal alarm is sounding the warning, "Danger!": *"But when he, the Spirit of truth, comes, he will guide you into all truth"* (John 16:13).
- the nail of allowing ourselves to go to places where we know it will be easier to think sinful thoughts and give in to sin: *"Avoid every kind of evil"* (1 Thessalonians 5:22).
- the nail of not listening to godly counsel: *"For lack of guidance a nation falls, but many advisers make victory sure"* (Proverbs 11:14).
- the nail of failing to be involved in those things that strengthen us spiritually: *"We will in all things grow up into him who is the Head, that is, Christ"* (Ephesians 4:15).
- the nail of running with the wrong crowd: *"Do not be misled: Bad company corrupts good character"* (1 Corinthians 15:33).
- the nail of feeling we will be the exception to the rule of where sinful thoughts usually lead: *"Pride goes before destruction, a haughty spirit before a fall"* (Proverbs 16:18).
- the nail of compromising in the "little things": *"So whether you eat or drink or whatever you do, do it all for the glory of God"* (1 Corinthians 10:31).
- the nail of feeding our sinful thoughts with pornographic— or suggestive—pictures or print: *"I made a covenant with my eyes not to look lustfully at a girl"* (Job 31:1).

Scan the list you just read and ask yourself, "Have any of these 'nails' ever been held in my hands? Am I flirting with any currently?

Have I failed to heed these Scriptures?" As we walk through Satan's cemetery and view the inscriptions on the tombstones, one headstone seems to stand out. It is one of which Satan is particularly proud—as it leads to so many other deaths. Its inscription reads: *Pure Thoughts*.

In the process of moving to another town to assume a new pastorate, we had difficulty finding a house to buy. A realtor in the church offered to help us. We were delighted when he told us that he had found a house that we could lease with the option to buy.

A year later when we found another house—one we wanted to buy—we also found ourselves with a potential lawsuit on our hands. The owner of the house we were leasing assumed that we were going to buy his house—which was not at all our understanding, nor did it meet our needs. Our real-estate friend had not fully disclosed to us just what kind of deal he had made on our behalf.

I remember on the day of the move, the owner of the house followed me as I took loads of furniture to the house we had just purchased. He got out of his truck and let me have it: "What kind of preacher are you anyway? You reneged on your end of the deal. I'm going to sue you."

> As we walk through Satan's cemetery, one headstone seems to stand out: *Pure Thoughts*.

I was tired from the move and exasperated by all that had transpired, and I lashed back at that guy with a forked-tongued vengeance. That was inexcusable. My witness with this prominent man in town died right there in my new front yard. I have grieved about this for years. I know now that I should not have assumed anything or trusted someone else to speak on my behalf. I should have gone to that man and tried to work it out.

I am embarrassed to admit that I allowed the progression of sin to continue and my testimony to be buried. James's words appropriately depict my not stopping the sin process: "It brings forth death" (James 1:15).

Whenever any of us fail to deal with our sinful thoughts—those that lead to sinful actions—our witness receives the death penalty.

Be aware that in this forward progress of sin, it initially feels good and there is . . .

The Exhilaration of Deceptive Thoughts

FROM THE TIME WE ARE LITTLE, we sneak and do those things we have just been told not to do. It's as if a little voice goes off in our minds that starts saying, "Do it anyway!" Such has been my life experience. When I was two years old, my mom no sooner had told me not to stick the fork into the electrical outlet that I felt compelled to do it anyway. So, I waited until I was certain that she was not looking and then *carpe "de opportunity"!* Boy, was I shocked at what happened next! I would like to tell you that I learned my lesson at age two and never did an I-know-I-shouldn't-but-I-did-it-anyway thing again. However, if I did, I would be breaking one of God's *Top Ten*. I can proudly say that I no longer stick forks into electrical sockets, but I do cheat on diets, break the speed limit (of course, I'm just speeding for "religious reasons"—like I'm late for church and I'm the pastor), and struggle with "www.don'tgothere.com" in my thought life.

"Don't touch that."
"Don't go there."
"Don't eat that."
"Don't wear that."
"Don't say that."
"Don't do that."

What is it about those words? Why are they so inviting—even though we know we may face some dire consequence for choosing to do what we've been told not to do. Is it the thrill of doing something we shouldn't do? Is it that momentary high—however short-lived—we get from being sneaky? Every day we are faced with a decision: whether to give in to our wrong thoughts or choose to do the right thing.

The Whether Report

As I'm getting ready to head out the door and face the no-more-memory-left-on-my-Palm-Pilot day, I catch the latest on the Weather Channel. Dr. Steve Lyons informs me that "today we're under the influence of high pressure." He, of course, is talking about how that will affect the day's weather.

I, by contrast, hear a different kind of report—a *whether* report, that is, a whether-or-not-I'm-prepared-to-face-the-pressures-of-my-day report. I instantly begin to think about my being ready to face the high-pressure schedule for the day. I stop and look at Dr. Lyons and say, "Man, you can't begin to know what high pressure is about to descend on my corner of the world. Today I've somehow got to handle my men's prayer group, incoming e-mail to answer, fifteen calls to return, a two-hour staff meeting, five radio spots to tape, sixteen calls to return, three sermons to prepare, a 'live' interview, seventeen calls to return, a premarital counseling session, a funeral, eighteen calls to return, refereeing a staff conflict, convention duties, nineteen calls to return, finish my column for the bulletin, visit the hospital, twenty calls to return, and bond with my family before returning for prayer meeting tonight!"

> For everything in the world—the cravings of sinful man, the lust of his eyes and the boasting of what he has and does—comes not from the Father but from the world.
>
> —1 JOHN 2:16

Whatever is on our "to-do" list for today, daily we are all under the influence of high pressure to allow sinful thoughts to enter our minds, to linger there until they turn to lust, and then to give in to those thought cravings.

Our fascinated-with-the-pleasures-of-this-world minds constantly battle doing that which will feel good but can never be pleasing to God. Each of us has a choice—God's way or my way? We have a daily "Whether Report" concerning our actions . . .

- whether we are going to turn our thoughts in God's direction or allow them to run away with sinful thoughts
- whether we will turn our bodies over to God's control or allow them to control what we do
- whether to turn our emotions over to God's protection from our misdirected feelings or to let our feelings decide what we will do
- whether to commit our eyes, what we allow ourselves to see, over to God's supervision or allow them to wander into the lust-zone
- whether to commit our ears to hearing and obeying God's voice or allowing them to listen to Satan's "go ahead and live a little" whispers

The question we each need to ask is: "How's my whether?" When "my whether" is God-controlled, I experience peace; however, when "my whether" is sinful-thought-controlled, I experience anything but peace. A turbulent front moves in with a major downpour of impure thoughts. I also have to be aware of possible tornado activity of confusing thoughts with accompanying damaging winds of worried thoughts.

> My "whether" determines how I play out my thoughts—a dress rehearsal for the action to follow.

You may be thinking, "But, Jay, you're a pastor—a Christian leader— you should be beyond struggling with such things." Ha! I am tempted like every other person. Sure, some in the ministry would deny that pastors struggle with those kind of thoughts, but they are denying the truth. We are all human. And unless God is in control of our thought lives, we all are vulnerable to the devil's sinful suggestions. My "whether" determines how I play out my thoughts. My thoughts—like yours—are a dress rehearsal for the action to follow. That's why it is vital that you and I choose the right thoughts, because the wrong ones lead to wrong feelings and to wrong actions.

Hooked on a Feeling

Recently I was talking with a friend who is a pastor in another city about his ministry. He commented that so much of his time is spent in counseling church members—specifically in helping hurting people deal with their addictive behaviors. Something he said rang true: "It seems that everybody—men, women, children, Christians, non-Christians, everyone—these days is addicted to something." I, too, see it all the time in my ministry—men seeking counsel for their addiction to work or pornography, women seeking counsel for their addiction to food or relationships, and teens seeking counsel for their addiction to music or substances. Food, money, alcohol, power, drugs, sex, romance, relationships, music, work, shopping, gambling, cultism, hobbies, and even churchianity (an unhealthy religiosity) grip millions upon millions of individuals in our gotta-have-it-all society.

In his excellent book on understanding dependencies of the heart, *Addicted to Love*, Stephen Arteburn explains that some experts believe that addictions to romance, relationships, and sex are at the root of people's other addictions. People who crave romantic attachment or sex turn to other addictive behaviors in order to cope with pain and emptiness. Arteburn identifies intimacy as being the core issue for the romance, relationship, or sex addiction. In the absence of intimacy, addicts look for substitutes—other addictive behaviors—in an attempt to find relief. This he offers as the reason why addictions so often seem to occur in clusters.[1]

Debra was searching for the intimacy that she lacked in her marriage. She, too, would fill the void in her life with other addictive behaviors—shopping, overeating, fantasy. When those substitutes no longer met her need for being able to give herself without reservation to another and to receive back the affirmation and closeness she craved, she easily took the next step—an affair with someone at work.

When Debra was asked in an interview by my partner, Marilyn, why she risked her marriage, her family, her reputation, and her career for an affair—the thousand-dollar, "What did you get out of it that made it worth it at the time?" question—Debra stared into vacant space and seemed to be replaying the not-too-distant past in her mind. The painful, confessional look that had just been on her face was replaced for a moment by an all-too-knowing-of-the-pleasures-of-sin twinkle in her eye as she emitted a soft half-chuckle.

Are you serious? Okay. I'll tell you. It felt good . . . so good. Initially it was that sexy, I-am-desirable-again feeling that this handsome, successful man gave back to me. I felt like I had lost all desirability—and, with that loss, I had pretty much lost all interest in sex. From the first time Greg, the guy with whom I had the affair, looked me in the eyes—when we bumped into each other in the sandwich shop in our office building—I began coming alive again! Each time—after that first encounter— when we would run into each other, the flirtation became more blatant. We were both definitely interested in knowing each other better.

That went on for about a month or so. At first, we would "just happen" to run into each other at work—and those encounters would make me float throughout the rest of the day. We began to linger longer and longer with each other as we talked and sought to be alone with each other. We would plan coffee breaks or lunch times together. It was so exhilarating! I really did not feel guilty at that point—only aroused by thoughts of this man-of-my-dreams.

The playful flirtation was such a high. The electricity between us was powerful—every glance, every touch. Both of us wanted the same thing. Being with him made me feel so good—so complete. He was all I could think of—whether I was alone or at work, with my husband or with my children. I lived to see him, to talk to him, and to be with him again.

We had good marriages and happy family lives. Neither of us had ever considered—much less done—anything like this before. As to who suggested we meet for more than flirtation and talk . . . I guess he did—although I jumped right on it. I wanted to be alone with him as badly as he wanted to be with me. Together we made the decision to arrange out-of-town business trips at the same time in the same city—staying in the same hotel. Never before had I been so excited about anything. It was like a fairy tale . . . like the movies.

I was so exhilarated during the several-hour drive to our hotel. I didn't play any music—only fantasized about what could happen over the next couple of days. I could not wait to see him.

When I arrived at the hotel—after he did, as he had had business meetings all that day—I checked into my room and found that he had already left a phone message for me. He asked that I call his room as soon as I got there. And I didn't waste a moment in doing that!

Soon I was on my way to his room. My heart was beating so loudly that it drowned out any thoughts that what I might be doing was wrong. I quietly tapped on his door, and I will never forget the look in his eyes when he cracked open the door. He looked at me with such desire—like I was the only one in the whole world who mattered to him.

In those two days together—with our alone-times being sandwiched between business obligations—we experienced extraordinary bonding, an intimacy I had never known—and, yes, passionate sex. It was everything in a relationship that I had ever fantasized about.

When asked about her relationship to God during this time, Debra—who professed to being a Christian since childhood—responded:

Two things happened. First, I put my faith on hold. I guess I wanted this guy at the time more than I wanted God. I know that sounds awful, but my actions bore that out. Just before the affair—when we were flirting and meeting—and during the affair, I quit seeking God. I quit praying or reading my Bible. Worship times were only rote actions to fool others. I felt guilty. I knew what I was doing was wrong. I knew it was sin. I figured that I would only be with him for a while—and then I would quit it and get right with God again.

And, as things have worked out, that is what happened. After almost a year of having an affair with Greg, I came under tremendous conviction for my sin. The guilt of what we were doing—and what I was not doing in my relationship with God—became more than I could bear, and so I told Greg that it was over. That was the hardest thing I had ever done. I felt so alone.

During these months of trying to restore my relationship with God, my faith has changed. I no longer take God for granted. I need to know his love and acceptance of me as I never have known before. It has been extremely difficult for me to feel worthy of receiving God's forgiveness—and I have really battled with Satan over this guilt thing. I know I am growing in the Lord—as there is no pretense on my part, only honesty and deep neediness. I still struggle with thoughts about Greg and our times together, but I am determined not to give into that wrong desire again. I want God too badly. And I want to make things right again—even better than before—in my marriage.

What made it worth it? During the affair, I thought all the love, the intimacy, the excitement made it worth it. Now, in the aftermath, I would have to say that nothing made it worth it. I would give anything to undo what I have done . . . to escape this mental, emotional, and spiritual anguish. It was not worth it—that was only a lie I allowed myself to believe at the time so that I could manage the guilt.

Debra is like so many of us—choosing to believe the whopper-size lies of Satan.

The Whopper

F. E. Smith served as the British Attorney General from 1915 to 1919. On one occasion, this quick-witted lawyer cross-examined a young man claiming damages for an arm injury caused by a bus driver's supposed negligence. "Will you please show us how high you can lift your arm now?" asked Smith.

Grimacing with pain, the young man gingerly raised his arm only to a shoulder level.

"Thank you," said Smith. "And now, could you show us how high you could lift it before the accident?"

The young man eagerly shot his arm up above his head. He lost the case.[2]

"Sometimes you've gotta break the rules" or so Burger King suggested in their Whopper of an advertising campaign. They tried to encourage us to forget the fat grams, forget the cholesterol, forget the calories, forget the consequences, and enjoy a delicious burger. Breaking the rules—or at least the way Burger King promotes it—is sometimes necessary for us to get what we want.

> No sooner had God established the "thou shalt" and the "thou shalt not" rules than Satan began making people feel like those rules were restrictions to their enjoying happiness and freedom.

They didn't invent the concept. Satan's been using that line for a very long time. I am guilty of having a B.K. mentality when it comes to my driving—to which I alluded in an earlier chapter. My children have asked me, "Dad, why do all the idiots come out when you're driving?" What does that say? Angie recently told me that she could tell God was really working in my life; however, when it came to my driving, God had given me over to a reprobate mind. Of course, she said it in love—I think. The hardest place for me to be a Christian is in my car. I know the posted speed limit may be fifty-five, but, come on, there's just too much to do to drive that slowly. I suppose when it comes to that area of my life, I have earned the B.K. crown many times over for breaking the rules.

No sooner had God established the "thou shalt" and the "thou shalt not" rules than Satan began making people feel like those rules were restrictions to their enjoying happiness and freedom. But let's consider it from another perspective. When God says "Thou shalt," he is saying, "Help yourself! Enjoy it!" When he says "Thou shalt not," he is saying, "Not wise. Don't hurt yourself." Satan, however, whispers, "These are just dumb laws, dumb rules to keep you from having fun."

I was amused by the *Dumb Laws*[3] website, which lists state by state many of the antiquated or humorous laws that are still on the books. As I read through these laws, I was amused when I thought about the possibility of some of these laws' actually being enforced today. Let's consider a "dumb law" from twenty-four of our fifty United States:

Dumb Laws

Alabama	It is illegal for a driver to be blindfolded while operating a vehicle.
Arkansas	Dogs may not bark after 6 P.M. (Little Rock)
California	No vehicle without a driver may exceed sixty mph.
Colorado	Tags may be ripped off pillows and mattresses.
Delaware	It is illegal to wear pants that are "firm fitting" around the waist.
Florida	Men may not be seen publicly in any kind of strapless gown.
Georgia	It is illegal to use profanity in front of a dead body.
Hawaii	Coins are not allowed to be placed in one's ear.
Illinois	You may be arrested for vagrancy if you do not have at least one dollar bill on your person.
Indiana	Mustaches are illegal if the bearer has a tendency to habitually kiss other humans.
Kentucky	It is illegal to transport an ice cream cone in your pocket. (Lexington)
Louisiana	It is illegal to gargle in public places.
Michigan	All bathing suits must have been inspected by the head of police. (Rochester)
Mississippi	It is unlawful to shave in the center of Main Street. (Tylertown)
New York	The penalty for jumping off a building is death.
North Carolina	It is against the law to sing off key.
Oklahoma	Females are forbidden from doing their own hair without being licensed by the state.
Pennsylvania	You may not sing in the bathtub.
South Carolina	Horses may not be kept in bathtubs.

Tennessee	It is illegal to use a lasso to catch a fish.
Texas	You can be legally married by publicly introducing a person as your husband or wife three times.
Utah	Birds have the right of way on all highways.
Virginia	It is illegal to tickle women.
Wyoming	You may not take a picture of a rabbit during the month of June.

Contrary to Satan's lies, God's laws are anything but dumb. There's a good reason they are kept on the books—actually in his Book—for us to observe to this day:

God's laws bring freedom rather than bondage to the thought life.
God's laws bring happiness rather than sorrow to the thought life.
God's laws bring direction rather than confusion to the thought life.
God's laws bring satisfaction rather than lust to the thought life.
God's laws bring peace rather than turmoil to the thought life.

In spite of all the benefits of obeying God's laws, some people choose to buy Satan's whoppers in their search for happiness.

God's Laws and Satan's Whoppers

God says: "Stay pure."
Satan says: "Everybody's doing it."

God says: "Don't put anything harmful into your body."
Satan says: "You only live once."

God says: "Dwell on those things that will lead to integrity."
Satan says: "Think about what will bring you pleasure right now."

God says: "Be faithful to your spouse."
Satan says: "Everybody's fooling around."

God says: "Follow my Word as your moral compass."
Satan says: "That archaic book doesn't apply today."

God says: "Keep the rules for maximum freedom."
Satan says: "Gotta break the rules to enjoy maximum freedom."

When we "break all the God-rules," we soon discover that our choice to do so ends up breaking us morally, ethically, physically, and relationally. Let me explain what I mean by that statement. God says, "Flee from sexual immorality" (1 Corinthians 6:18), yet many who have broken that law have suffered the consequences of a sexually transmitted disease or an unplanned pregnancy.

God says, "You shall not steal" (Exodus 20:15), yet many are behind prison doors today because they took something that didn't belong to them.

The Bible says, "Therefore, honor God with your body" (1 Corinthians 6:20), yet many have chosen to abuse substances and are now suffering from addictions or substance-related diseases.

God says, "You shall not commit adultery" (Exodus 20:14), yet many today are living in loneliness, financial ruin, or guilt because they did it anyway. The very laws that could have made these individuals happy became the laws that—when broken—made them miserable.

In the first chapter of this book we considered the first time Eve bought a whopper of a lie, the "sometimes you've gotta break the rules" lie that Satan sold her. If she and Adam had kept the rules given them by a loving and gracious—not an unreasonable or selfish—God, they would have had every blessing and benefit they could have ever needed or enjoyed. But as soon as they bit into the "gotta-break-the-rules" fruit, they became charter and lifetime members of The Gotta-Keep-on-Breaking-the-Rules Club.

Why Adam and Eve joined it is beyond sound reasoning. There are no benefits for club members: no exclusivity—anyone and everyone can join; a loss—instead of gain—of God's choicest privileges; and exorbitant, constantly escalating dues. In spite of all these drawbacks, we all join this club through the initiation of wrong thought. At some point in all of our lives, Satan has masterfully snowed us all into believing this is The Gotta-Have Club membership.

Snowmen in the Desert

Thomas Edison did not like the fact that visitors to his office helped themselves to his expensive Havana cigars. To remedy this, his secretary suggested he have some cigars made from cabbage leaves and substitute them for the Havanas. Edison agreed and then forgot about it. He only remembered some time later when the Havana cigars started vanishing again.

When Edison asked his secretary why the bogus cigars had not arrived, she informed him that they had. In fact, she had given them to his manager who—they learned upon further investigation—not knowing the cigars were fakes, had packed them for Edison to carry on a trip. "And you know," Edison laughed, "I smoked every one of those cigars myself!"[4]

Sometimes we fool ourselves. Our minds play tricks on us. We think something is real when it is not. It's like the scene from the movies where a cowboy in Death Valley or a French Legionnaire in the Sahara Desert staggers and crawls toward what he believes to be a thirst-relieving pool of water. Then, as hey draws closer, the water disappears! Or it's like when we are driving down the highway and see those apparent pools of water lying across the pavement—which disappear before we can reach them. We often experience "mind mirages" when we encounter what appears to be very desirable and almost within our reach, only to be fooled by our fairy-tale perception of these deceptive mind tricks.

> We often experience "mind mirages" when we encounter what appears to be very desirable and almost within our reach, only to be fooled by our fairy-tale perception of these deceptive mind tricks.

The American Meteorological Society, in the *Glossary of Weather and Climate*, defines a *mirage* as "a phenomenon wherein an image of some distant object is made to appear displaced from its true position because of large vertical density variations near the surface; the image may appear distorted, inverted, or wavering." It's the pencil in the water that appears to be bent—but, when it's removed, it is as straight as can be. The effects of these distortions of the image create the optical illusion we see. Although the mind may misinterpret the mirage it receives from our eyes, the image is no figure of the imagination—it can be photographed. It's real—but it is not what it seems.[5]

When we were doing the research on deception—on "being snowed," or "having the wool pulled over our eyes"—Marilyn laughed and said, "I can relate. My trusting in the good I see in people sure has left me feeling disappointed or foolish more times than I like to admit. The wool's been pulled over my eyes so many times that when I blink I can knit a sweater." Are you there with her? Are you easily fooled? Have you been duped by people you trusted?

> The wool's been pulled over my eyes so many times that when I blink I can knit a sweater.

Not long ago, the Internet carried stories of students—and adults—being fooled by a hoax perpetrated on *EverQuest* game players. *EverQuest*—a popular design-your-own-character, pick-your-own-world, alternative reality game—has attracted huge numbers of players around the globe who enjoy escaping to an interactive, role-playing fantasy world. Because participants "e-chat" as they play with and against other players in this virtual kill-and-survive fantasy world, they form relationships with new friends. Day after day they meet online to continue the role-playing. Whether or not they allow their true persona to be known is up to them. It's only a game to many who play, and the pretending often doesn't stop even in their e-conversations—no matter how intimate—with others.

EverQuest player Jeff was stunned to hear the tragic news that a fellow player had committed suicide. He was devastated by the news because he had formed what he thought was a deep relationship with this suicide victim. It was not until Jeff decided to make contact with the family of the victim and to check out the "obits" in the victim's hometown newspaper that he discovered it was all a hoax. In a virtual reality world he had believed what he was experiencing was real.

What an awful feeling it is to realize that we have been duped or "taken for a ride." We all know that sick feeling when we ask ourselves, "How could I have allowed myself to fall for this?" We often become deceived because we have an eye problem—that is, a spiritual eye problem. Whenever we fail to daily renew our minds in God's Word, we set ourselves up to become blinded to the traps Satan sets for us. We become easy marks to be taken in by Satan's believable, sounds-so-right-that-it-must-be-true lies. Why? Scripture says, "The heart is deceitful above all things" (Jeremiah 17:9). Our human nature has a propensity toward evil, toward that which is wrong. And our desire-those-things-that-are-not-good-for-me feelings so often pull the wool over our eyes.

When Italy's mandatory use of seat belts went into effect on April 27, 1989, enterprising Claudio Ciaravolo saw an opportunity to make a killing. Dr. Ciaravolo, a psychiatrist in Naples, invented a "security shirt"—which was simply a white T-shirt with a diagonal black stripe designed to deceive the police into believing the motorist was buckled up.[6] Likewise, Satan often deceives us and sells us something that looks like it is designed for our good. Yet when we crash and burn, Satan just smiles as he rings up another bill of goods.

The Intimidator Wins

Racing fans were stunned and saddened by the death of NASCAR superstar Dale Earnhardt. Known around the world as "The Intimidator," Earnhardt moved stock-car racing into mainstream America. His hard-charging charisma brought new fans to the sport. Some fans and drivers, however, despised his reckless ways. He was not above using his bumper to knock a leader out of the way. He is quoted in the *Orlando Sentinel* as saying, "They [other drivers] ain't ever seen the kind of rough racing I've had to do in my life just to survive. They don't want to mess with this ol' boy. I want to give more than 100 percent every race, and if that's aggressive, then I reckon I am. It's not a sport for the faint of heart." Hence, he was dubbed "The Intimidator."[7]

All of us have known "real life" intimidators. Our first exposure to these bully-types was probably a childhood experience on the school-yard or playground. We are all familiar with their intimidator rhetoric:

"You're a little Sissy."
"Scaredy Ca-a-at! Scaredy Cat!"
"Hey, Stupid, I'm talkin' to you!"
"Come here, Dumby!"
"Ha! Ha! Fatso!"
"You're nuthin' but a beanpole!"
"Wanna make something of it?"
"Get out of my way, Cream Puff."

Many of these intimidator-types grow up perfecting the art of the put-down. Have you heard of these intended-to-be humorous put-downs?[8]

"He does the work of three men: Larry, Curley, and Moe."
—RON DENTINGER

"I never forget a face, but in your case I'll make an exception."
—GROUCHO MARX

"I want to reach your mind—where is it currently located?"
—ASHLEIGH BRILLIANT

"When you go to the mind reader, do you get half price?"
—DAVID LETTERMAN

Satan, the Supreme Intimidator, is anything but joking in his relentless pursuit of the lead in our racing thoughts. He will resort to many methods of put-downs, intimidation, or bullying in order to play mind games on us and lead us away from God. He will taunt us with:

- "Why are you afraid of a God you've never seen?"
- "All your friends are doing it. What are you—a wimp?"
- "You just don't fit in—do you?"
- "You are a loser with a capital 'L.'"
- "Enjoy your misery, Sucker!"
- "A real man would do it."
- "You're not much of a woman—are you?"
- "You're dumb to pass up a golden opportunity like this one."

If this Master Intimidator were on a life-NASCAR circuit, his race-track would not be the tracks at Daytona or Indianapolis, but in the minds of everyone—young and old alike. Each of us has a race to run, and Satan wants us to crash and burn in this race. His pit crew—the world and the flesh—are always looking for ways to improve Satan's chances of defeating God's best vehicles. The cheering crowds—that is, those who couldn't care less about the things of God—encourage us to "go full throttle and live a little." In the end, Satan waves the checkered flag each time we run with sinful thoughts. We, however, never get to stand in the winner's circle or take a victory lap. That's Satan's trophy.

You may be asking yourself, "Now what? How can I avoid the problems of a Debra? How can I avoid being duped by Satan's whoppers? How can I overcome his intimidation?" There is hope! Just ahead there is a method that I promise—when applied—will work. God has not left us to deal with sinful thoughts alone. I know at this point you may feel bruised spiritually and emotionally, but hang on. Be encouraged. No matter what you have done, God—in his wonderful grace—has provided the solution to your sin dilemma.

Satan, the master deceiver, attempts to make wrong things look right, good things look bad, and dangerous things look safe. If we aren't daily walking in the will of God and seeking the wisdom of God, we can easily fall into the trap of a "real-good, feel-good" moment and be deceived.

James warns us, "Do not be deceived . . ." (James 1:16). *Deceived* means "to go off course." How easily our thinking and our lives can get off base, off track, off course when we allow sinful thoughts to continue.

Step 5.
DEATH
[of Pure Thoughts]
"[It] gives birth to death . . ."

Step 6.
DECEPTION
"Do not be deceived . . ."

They must be stopped or you will be saying . . .

7

I Never Thought It Would Lead to This

M‌AYBE YOU HAVE SAID, "I never thought it would lead to this," as you have dealt with the consequences of your actions. We've all been there at some point. We didn't think—or at least we dismissed the "this might mean trouble" preamble to our declaration of independence from possible consequences for our behavior. I remember learning in science: "For every action there is an opposite and equal reaction." And I have found this true in lessons I have learned in life.

We often do little things—which appear to be insignificant at the moment—that, when we look back, were the first small step that led us so far away from God. Who would believe that . . .

- a simple wink could lead to an affair?
- a brief lustful look could lead to a wrecked marriage?
- a single click of the mouse could lead to a wrong relationship?
- a meager bet on a game could lead to a gambling addiction?
- a small giving in to fear could lead to being socially paralyzed?
- a no-big-deal take could lead to a shattered career?
- a short-lived high could lead to a destroyed life?
- a tiny lie could lead to a life of denial?
- a one-time, unwise swipe of a credit card could lead to financial bondage?

125

Sin's downward spiral in our life is rarely preceded with the thought, "This is going to ruin my life and hurt the ones I love, but I am going to do it anyway." Does the thought, "It's no big deal and I can stop whenever I want," sound familiar?

Does That Ring a Jingle Bell?

Do you remember the commercial jingle: "Winston tastes good like a cigarette should"? When I hear those words, I picture in my mind's eye the debonair Winston Man who, with his James Bond kind of savoir-faire, made smoking look like the cool, manly thing to do. As a young boy, I wanted to look and feel like a dude. So, being a Dragnet fan, I would pretend to be cool Joe Friday. When no one was looking, I would roll up a gum wrapper and pretend it was a cigarette.

While I never had the desire to smoke "real" cigarettes, I did smoke some grapevine once! Someone had told one of my friends that you could smoke grapevine. So, as young teenagers, we visited a stash-vine and loaded up our front pockets with some vine. Then we lit up. Oh! The light-up was short-lived. Not only did it quickly burn my tongue, it tasted absolutely awful. Right then and there my smoking career ended.

Alan Landers is the former Winston Man who did the majority of the print ads for the company in the late 1960s and early 1970s—during my impressionable years. He projected the man's man image. While touting this lethal and addictive product, he himself smoked up to four cartons of cigarettes a day. Now he is a different Marlboro Man, a two-time cancer survivor.

At age 57, Landers was diagnosed with lung cancer in 1987. He underwent painful surgery to remove a significant portion of lung. Five years later, this man who had been deceived by the industry he promoted received the devastating news that the cancer had returned—this time in his other lung. Surgery a second time was complicated by his vocal cords being accidentally cut. Now this actor could barely speak. This was not the end of Lander's health battle, for in 1996 he underwent heart bypass surgery. His body has been left permanently disfigured from the surgeries, plus he is extremely short-winded.

Alan Landers, who now donates his time fighting against tobacco use and cancer, has become a national spokesman for anti-tobacco campaigns—especially urging young people not to smoke. He regularly appeals to lawmakers in the U.S. to regulate tobacco products and to curb cigarette advertising.[1] I am sure that he never imagined he'd end up doing what he is doing, having faced what he has faced as a result of his buying into a lie about smoking.

Isn't that just like Satan to hide from us the consequences of giving in to sinful thoughts? With slick and attractive appeals, Satan seduces us into giving sinful actions a taste; however, we soon are left with the bitter "I never thought it would lead to this" burn of our decision-making. What may begin as an advertising jingle in our thought life can lead our lives off-course as we buy into Satan's false advertising.

Off-Course by an Inch

On December 20, 1995, an American Airlines Boeing 757 passenger jet crashed into a mountainside in Colombia, killing 159 passengers and crew members. On its northern approach to the Cali Airport, Flight 965 made initial radio contact with the Cali Approach Control while descending to a lower altitude. According to a National Transportation Safety Board report on this accident,[2] the control tower issued clearance to Cali VOR and radioed to the flight captain that he was to fly "straight-in" to Runway 19.

The crew had been expecting the usual procedure of using Runway 1, which would require flying past the airport and turning back. The crew became confused over the clearance. They were not familiar with the Rozo One arrival they had been given. Having less time than usual to make their approach, needing to make an expedited descent, being very busy, trying to communicate with tower officials who lacked fluency in English, and operating under the very archaic South American traffic controls, the crew used procedural shortcuts.

In the flight crew's efforts to expedite their approach, they apparently gave up on their raw data flying skills and relied too heavily on automation. In doing so, the wrong flight code—the letter "R" which the crew erroneously believed to denote "Rozo" navigation beacon at Cali—was entered into the onboard computer. Instead, flight-management-systems-generated navigational information uses a different naming convention from that published in navigational charts. Its database uses "R" to denote "Romeo," a beacon located 132 miles to the left and behind the plane at the Bogota airport.

The crew assumed their actions would cause the autopilot to fly the plane in the direction of the "Rozo" beacon; however, the onboard computer diverted the plane to the "Romeo" beacon. This confusion over two navigation beacons in the area with the same identifier and frequency led to the aircraft turning left—away from the arrival path—a departure not noticed by the crew for ninety seconds. When they noticed, they chose to fly parallel to their cleared path. However, they had not arrested their descent and were in mountainous terrain. Unable to precisely execute an escape maneuver and with speed brakes left out, the aircraft flew to impact. According to the Glasgow Accident Analysis Group, the aircraft should have never been so far off course, so low.[3]

This one-letter designation, seemingly such a little thing, led to this off-course tragedy. Likewise, one little wrong thought can misdirect our emotions and bodies—resulting in moral tragedy.

We've all probably heard or used the expression "off by an inch." Just think about what a difference an inch makes . . .

- Off by an inch in surveying property lines could create disputes between neighbors somewhere down the road.
- Off by an inch in figuring the depth of a pool could mean the difference between breathing and drowning for someone who cannot swim.
- Off by an inch in doing brain or heart surgery could mean the difference between life and death.
- Off by an inch in either choosing to "open" or "close" Internet sites could mean the difference between staying pure and giving in to lust.

We are commanded in Scripture: "Love the Lord your God with *all* your soul and with *all* your mind and with *all* your strength" (Mark 12:30). Off by an inch, a foot, a yard, a mile—any amount other than *all*—in offering perfect devotion and conforming 100 percent to God's moral law is sin. Sin, sometimes defined as "missing the mark," is not measured in increments, because all sin—whether big or small, grave or peccadillo—is rebellion against God. R. C. Sproul has called sin "cosmic treason against a perfectly pure Sovereign . . . an act of supreme ingratitude toward the One to whom we owe everything."[4]

Off by a moral inch can have serious—if not destructive—consequences in our lives, as with a young lady from my city who was not wise about . . .

The Little Things

Making national news were the accounts of a fifteen-year-old girl from the Lakeland, Florida, area who was lured to Greece by a thirty-five-year-old German man who had met her on the Internet a year prior. Convincing this middle school eighth-grader he, too, was fifteen years old, Franz Konstantin Baehring developed an online relationship with her. Enlisting the help of two Americans, Baehring was able to lure her to Athens, Greece.

This young victim started her journey on August 28, 2000, when she left her home to catch a flight from Orlando to Cleveland, Ohio. Then on September 16, she took a bus from Cleveland to New York City to board an international flight to Greece. On September 17, this teenager finally met Baehring—who turned out to be a man twice her age.[5] According to law enforcement reports, this middle-schooler had an emotional, as well as a physical relationship, with this older man. Sadly, this child did not even realize that she had been a victim.

On February 1, 2001—almost a year after she began her relationship with the man—this deceived runaway was found by Greek authorities inside or near an apartment used by Baehring in the northern Greek city of Thessaloniki. He was subsequently charged with child abduction and sexual assault.[6]

The girl's mother is making it her mission to educate teenagers and their parents about the dangers of the Internet and of people like this man who prey on unsuspecting victims. When she became aware of her daughter's correspondence with Baehring, she tried unsuccessfully to block her daughter's communication with him—but to no avail, since he just used several aliases. "She's smart, but she was lured," explains her mother. "Those kind of people are so manipulative. He had her so under his control. He had her against everyone ... and he never even stepped into the country."[7]

A little thing, a less-than-one-inch mouse-move on the computer screen—the approximate distance between "send" and "close"—made all the difference in the life of this teenager. Her thinking, her decisions, her actions, and her life got off-course by this inch. It is often the little things—the little compromise, the little missed time with God, the little lustful look, the little innocent flirting, the little step away from God's will, the little sinful thought, the little turn in the wrong direction—that get us off course in life and in our relationship with God. Over the course of time, the little things, as with inches, begin to add up and make a big difference.

> A pig ate his fill of acorns under an oak tree and then started to root around the tree. A crow remarked, "You should not do this. If you lay bare the roots, the tree will wither and die." "Let it die," said the pig. "Who cares as long as there are acorns."
>
> —Unknown[8]

The Song of Songs is the beautiful story of a relationship between Solomon and his wife. One of the foci of this book is Solomon's acknowledgment that that there are many things that, if allowed, can eat away at their marital relationship. He mentions one thing—even though it is a little thing—that if left undetected, can destroy their marriage: "Catch for us the foxes, the little foxes that ruin the vineyards, our vineyards that are in bloom" (Song of Songs 2:15). Pictured in this analogy are the little foxes that sneak into the vineyards and gnaw away at the vine roots. Life's "little foxes," when left unchecked, can do tremendous—and sometimes irreparable—damage. Their silent and gradual destruction can destroy what really matters in our lives and in our relationship with God.

I Could Never Have Imagined . . .

As I was concluding my message one Sunday morning, I noticed a young woman sitting toward the front of the church who was obviously upset. Her tears could not be hidden. When I gave the appeal for people to come to the altar to pray, I noticed that she got up and prayed with one of our pastors. Later, as I greeted our guests in a reception after the worship service, this woman came to speak to me. Julie was shaking and crying as she shared with me what God had done in her life that day as she worshiped. She had come face-to-face with the reality of her sin and misery.

Convinced of the genuineness of her repentance and her commitment to living a Christ-filled life, I asked Julie to share her gripping story with our congregation several weeks later. The people in our congregation were moved to tears as they heard her share with honesty the consequences of the choices she had made.

> I have spent the last ten years of my life living a lesbian lifestyle; denying God and trying to prove my parents, family, and friends wrong. When they said things about how I lived my life, I just tuned them out and ignored them. I felt guilty about the way I lived, but I kept going back to the thought, "If it feels so right, how can it be so wrong?" I questioned God on many occasions—why and how could he let something like this happen. I questioned what in the world was wrong with me—this goes against everything that I was ever taught. As time went on, I pushed those thoughts to the back of my mind and decided I was having too much fun to dwell on the fact that it was wrong.
>
> I went to the gay bars, I had a lot of worldly fun—drinking and partying with my homosexual friends. I made my partner number one in my life instead of Christ. I lived a very public lesbian life. There were not too many people who have known me in the last several years that did not know about my lifestyle.
>
> Even though I was a very happy person on the outside, the questioning thoughts started coming back to me. I began to

pray, "God, please let my lover get up the courage to leave me, because I think I will be strong enough to continue. Lord, however, I don't think that if I left her, she would be strong enough to go on." Three months ago she left me. Initially I was devastated. Even though I knew that what we had was not godly, I didn't think I was ready or would be able to move on. I lived with this woman for over eight years. There was great "emotional dependency" on each other.

> I didn't live a very private lesbian lifestyle, so I don't intend to live a very private Christian lifestyle.
>
> —JULIE

I knew at that point in my life, I had a decision to make. I could continue going down the destructive path of homosexuality, or I could start living for God. I got down on my hands and knees and asked God to forgive me for the way that I had lived my life and for how I had rebelled against him. He forgave me right then and there.

I have completely done a 180-degree turnaround. I didn't do this by myself; I was only able to do this via the grace of God. God never shut the door for me; I shut the door on him. When I opened the door, he was right there waiting on me. I have now replaced the ring on my left hand that signified my love for a woman with a necklace with a cross on it to act as a daily reminder for me that he is always with me. I didn't live a very private lesbian lifestyle, so I don't intend to live a very private Christian lifestyle. God is responsible for my turnaround.

In a follow-up interview, Marilyn asked Julie what were some of the tough, I-never-thought-it-would-lead-to-this consequences of her lesbian lifestyle. Julie thought for a moment and shared the pain of her initially having to pretend she was somebody she was not in order to hide the fact that she had chosen this lifestyle. She pretended with her family, the people at work, and at church. "I was faking it . . . teaching a fifth-grade Sunday school class at the time."

Gossip about Julie and her lesbian partner had begun to circulate in her church—even before she went public with her lifestyle. "My partner and I were going to church, but church members were starting rumors. Everywhere we turned we faced criticism." Julie was hurt and angry with the cruelty and lack of compassion of fellow church members, so she and her partner stopped going to church. She said, "It killed my personal relationship with God. I quit even saying blessings before my meals."

When Julie finally decided to "come out of the closet" and her family found out about her choices, she said, "I felt like the black sheep of my family. I felt like an outsider to some degree—realizing I had let them down tremendously." During this time, Julie was plagued with guilt. She became depressed. "I no longer cared about myself. My weight shot up from 140 pounds to 260 pounds during this time. My partner and I—with no public display of affection— would walk through the mall and people would stare and talk about us." Julie lost the glow out of her life.

The glorious good news is that Julie has been transformed in Jesus Christ. He has put "the glow" back into her life. She looks joyful— plus, she's had a major weight loss—and acts like a new woman. "I strive now to live my best. I have a tremendous burden for lost people. I now care." She rejoices in God's delivering her from this lesbianism. "God is now giving me so many opportunities to make a difference in other people's lives."

Failing to stop runaway sinful thoughts leads to consequences that are unexpected, unwanted, uncomfortable, undeniable, unfortunate, unfavorable, unhappy, unhealthy, uninvited. Blinded to the consequences, we fail to see the traps Satan sets for us through the thought life.

Watch Out for the Landmines

Undersea dredging to reclaim land for a Disney theme park in Hong Kong has unearthed dozens of old bombs and artillery shells. It's not all that unusual to find World War II bombs from time to time in Hong Kong, but the work on the new theme park uncovered larger than normal amounts of explosives—which kept disposal crews busier than usual during this land reclamation. The bombs did have the potential to cause what Alick McWhirter, an assistant bomb disposal officer, called "fairly extensive" damage. So every time dredging workers dug up a bomb, they would stop work, and explosive teams would be summoned. McWhirter commented on the future safety of the theme park area: "Once [a bomb] goes into the landfill, that's about it, unless you're tossing it about. It's really not an issue."[9]

My writing partner, Marilyn, kind of smirked as we discussed the bomb unearthings at the Hong Kong Disneyland and reported the following:

> I can relate to that! Jon, James [her son], and I went to Israel with a group from my seminary to work at the dig site at Bethsaida before it was open to tour groups. The upper site was just starting to show some resemblance to a New Testament fishing village, and the lower site was beginning to be identifiable as the Old Testament palace of the King of Geshur.
>
> When we arrived on the site, the supervising archaeologist warned us about a couple of safety concerns. He told us that if in our digging we hit metal, to stop and carefully look at what we were uncovering. It might not be a coin, fishhook, or a tool. It might well be an unexploded bomb or landmine. We should stop immediately and let him know if we unearthed one of these explosives. Duh. As if we would want to put that "find" in the big sifter so that we could check out the serial numbers on it to see if it was first-century issue!
>
> Then he warned us to heed the "Danger Mines!" signs and not step over the barbed wire surrounding the perimeter of the dig site to walk down the hill to the restroom facilities below. He informed us that not all of the unexploded landmines from the Six-Day War had been removed, and it would be too dangerous to take that route. So, we had to take a long road down the other side of the hill and around to . . . well . . . you know.
>
> About the time we got accustomed to the explosives thing, we were warned to stay away from the scorpions near the food tent and the viper housed in the tree above our backpacks—

and to ignore the sound of bombing in the Golan Heights. Other than that, the whole dig experience was a blast. Oops! Maybe that's a poor choice of words.

I heard of one mean-spirited man working for a dynamite company who went by the initials K. B. Everybody wanted to know what the initials stood for, but no one had the courage to ask him. Finally one day someone got his nerve up and asked. He harshly responded with, "It stands for Ka Boom!"

We are warned in Scripture about landmines that can go "Kaboom!" in our lives: "Be careful, then, how you live—not as unwise but as wise" (Ephesians 5:15). This biblical passage and many others encourage us to make wise choices in the way that we go. We must be careful and watch our steps to avoid life's landmines. With the Holy Spirit directing our every move, we can sidestep . . .

> moral landmines
> emotional landmines
> physical landmines
> relational landmines
> mental landmines
> financial landmines
> ethical landmines
> sensual landmines

Often there are no posted warning signs around these landmines. Many are so well hidden that unless God directs our paths, they can blow up in our faces and be fatal to our character. Then we get . . .

Stuck in the Penalty Box

I really like hockey. My son and I saw our first game together—watching the play-by-play ice aerobics of the Dallas Stars—when he was eleven years old. It felt like a real "guy thing" for a father and son to do together. There's just something about this fast-paced sport to get a guy pumped up. It is anything but boring to watch the two opposing teams of skaters use their long, curved sticks to try to almost maliciously drive that hard rubber disk into each other's goals—and get into each others' faces as the points are scored.

Hockey—played in about thirty countries, principally in North America, Europe, and the countries of the former USSR—had its genesis in Canada, where the game is the most popular. Great players like Wayne Gretzky, Bobby Orr, Mario Lemieux, Maurice Richard, Doug Harvey, Bobby Hull, Gordie Howe, and Valeri Kharlamov are synonymous with the sport.[10]

I kind of hate to admit it, but I do enjoy the rough-and-tough, action-filled competition. Yes, even the fights among the players—which are the rule and not the exception. At that first game, my son was fascinated by the penalty box. I tried to explain to him that during a game penalties are given when players commit a significant foul against an opponent or official. Penalized players are required to leave the ice and spend time in the penalty box—that small, confined area that looks like a cage.

The penalty box is the price for breaking the rules. Lloyd Freeberg, an off-ice official with the National Hockey League who is assigned to "supervise" the penalty box, has written a book called *In the Bin: Reckless and Rude Stories from the Penalty Boxes of the NHL*, based on his experiences. By his accounts he is in charge of "men half [his] age, twice [his] size, evil in spirit, and carrying long sticks," who believe they should not be in that box. Many are in need of medical care and some, he says, seem to be in need of psychiatric care. They have a language of their own—and it doesn't include "nice." Emotions in the box are volatile as Freeberg counts the seconds until those being penalized can return to the ice. Interestingly enough the penalty box has a nickname: the "Sin Bin."[11]

> When we give in to sinful thoughts and break God's laws, we end up in the "Sin Bin."

When we give in to sinful thoughts and break God's laws, we end up in the "Sin Bin." We cause ourselves to be penalized when we choose to dwell on and then act on an impure thought. The apostle Paul was concerned that this would happen to him, so he disciplined himself in order not to step out the bounds of God's will: "Therefore I do not run like a man running aimlessly; I do not fight like a man beating the air. No, I beat my body and make it my slave so that after I have preached to others, I myself will not be disqualified for the prize" (1 Corinthians 9:26–27). He did not want to be in the penalty box and miss God's best.

Most of us don't set out purposefully to end up in the sin bin. We are usually shocked at how far we have gotten away from God when we find ourselves in sin's penalty box for . . .

a ruined testimony because of moral compromise

a destroyed marriage because of unfaithfulness

a lost job because of downloading sexual images on the computer while at work

a wrecked home because of alcoholism

a harmed body because of wrong choices

a defeated spiritual life because of ignoring God's Word

a damaged emotional life because of not dealing with unforgiveness

In the game of ice hockey, the penalized player eventually gets out of the penalty box. In life, however, we can spend the rest of our lives in the sin bin unless we quit breaking the rules and fouling out because of giving in to sinful thoughts.

The End Is Mir!

The kamikaze homecoming of Russian space station Mir on March 23, 2001, was one of the most extraordinary celestial events in recent history. Launched on February 19, 1986, this trouble-prone old junker paved the way for long duration space trips, space assemblage of large space stations, and international space cooperation.[12] After fifteen years in orbit, the Mir received Russian Mission Control commands to begin its deorbit the day prior to its suicidal descent to Earth.[13]

Taco Bell floated a forty-foot-by-forty-foot target for the fiery Mir debris in the South Pacific off the coast of Australia. If a big chunk of the Mir splashed down on that 1,600 square-foot bulls-eye, Taco Bell promised to give everyone in the United States a free taco. (Actually, Taco Bell had purchased an insurance policy to cover the cost of this extravagant promo in the event that Mir hit their target. So, it would have been the insurance company picking up the lunch tab for a couple hundred million tacos.)[14]

Alas, the Mir did not ring the food franchise's bell, but instead its 1,500 fragments—about forty tons of debris with some as large as a compact car—rained down on a remote part of the South Pacific between New Zealand and Chile. About 80 percent of the 135-ton space station burned up upon reentry into the earth's atmosphere.[15] The Mir, the biggest object ever brought back down to earth, made a big media splash as the world anxiously prepared to duck—just in case.

Russian space engineers probably never thought it would eventually come to this—their once high-tech, third-generation space station becoming the proverbial "tail" for the world's largest pin-the-tail-on-the-floating-Mexican-burro game. As I think about the crashing and burning of Mir, I am reminded of an Associated Press article I read today of a twenty-four-year-old man, Ajay Jindal, who arrived last spring from India to tap into the Silicon Valley gold rush as a computer programmer. In this capacity, he earned $80,000 a year—ten times what he earned in India. However, because of the recent job-cutting frenzy of so many technology-related businesses, Jindal became another victim of the high-tech market crash. He has not worked as a Java programmer since January.[16]

Many would have never predicted the collapse of the Internet bubble—which some call one of the largest financial fiascoes in U.S. history. It came after a three-year period, starting in January of 1997, when stock market investors bought up almost anything associated with the Internet. Dot-com stocks that once soared, however, crashed. "Stocks that skyrocketed north in a fashion never seen before will plummet south in a fashion never seen before either," said Steve Bengston, a managing director at Pricewaterhouse Coopers in San Jose, California. When the market became glutted with new, money-losing Web companies in 1999, the bright picture dramatically changed.[17]

With dot-com burnouts blazing across the Internet like a meteor shower, many dot-com companies are struggling to survive. There have been huge cuts in the dot-com job market—including a high turnover of CEOs, who were offered up as the sacrificial lambs to appease impatient investors.[18] Unfortunately crashing and burning are not limited to space stations and dot-coms. It happens to a lot of people, including Christians.

Why is it that many who start out strong in the Christian faith, somewhere along the way crash or burn morally? No one sets out with that in mind. Yet, it happens all too often. What happened to the pastor who felt such a strong call from God into the ministry, but is now pursuing a nonministry career and seldom opens his Bible or attends church? What happened to the young groom or bride who entered marriage with a "'til death do us part" commitment, but who ended up hearing the words "divorce granted"? What happened to the teenager who made a commitment to sexual purity until marriage, but in a moment of passion gave in and gave his or her treasure away? What happened to the Christian business person who started out building the business on biblical principles, but because of competition caved in to the pressure to be unethical?

Why is it so many ministries, marriages, commitments, and great beginnings end with a crash-and-burn ending? Paul's warning to the church at Rome is as fitting for us today in the twenty-first century as it was to the first-century Christians: "So be careful. If you are thinking, 'Oh, I would never behave like that'—let this be a warning to you. For you too may fall into sin" (1 Corinthians 10:12 TLB).

I believe it often happens ever so gradually—beginning with an unguarded thought life. In Paul's letter to the church at Colosse the apostle warns: "See to it that no one takes you captive through hollow and deceptive philosophy, which depends on human tradition and the basic principles of this world rather than Christ" (Colossians 2:8). We are bombarded with messages that can be summed up as . . .

You deserve a break today, so have it your way.

You only go around once, so go for the gusto!

As we allow the *Just do it* mindset to shape our thought lives, we will ultimately crash into a moral wall and burn out our lights that once shined brightly for God.

> As we allow the *Just do it* mindset to shape our thought lives, we will ultimately crash into a moral wall and burn out our lights that once shined brightly for God.

When the advancement of sin is allowed to go uninterrupted, consequences will no doubt follow. It's not a matter of if, but when. J. Kenneth Kimberlin has said, "We are free to sin, but not to control sin's consequences."[19] Unfortunately, when the consequences of sin come, many refuse to take responsibility for their actions, or perhaps they blame God. Although God's forgiveness is immediate when we ask for it in true repentance, the aftermath of sin is not instantly removed. However, when we cooperate with God, his grace helps us to deal with those consequences.

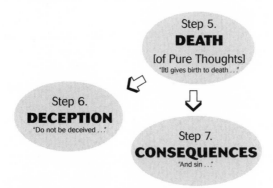

Step 5.
DEATH
[of Pure Thoughts]
"[It] gives birth to death . . ."

Step 6.
DECEPTION
"Do not be deceived . . ."

Step 7.
CONSEQUENCES
"And sin . . ."

However, if you let sin continue, it will make you a . . .

8

Slave to Your Thoughts

VISITING CORRIE TEN BOOM'S home in Haarlem, Holland, evoked all kinds of emotions from me. As I entered her father Caspar's watch shop and made my way up the cramped stairway, I felt a sense of awe—as if I were entering a sacred place. And then as I entered the family home on the top floor—the place made famous in Corrie's book *The Hiding Place*—I felt distressed being reminded of one of the darkest periods of history, the Holocaust.

On May 10, 1940, German forces invaded Holland. Soon after this invasion the ten Boom family began their underground work, helping Jews escape from the Germans. Someone with the Dutch underground suggested that the ten Booms construct a secret room in their home to hide the Dutch Jews during the Gestapo raids.[1] As I observed when visiting, their home was the perfect place for a secret room—as there were so many unsuspecting nooks and crannies throughout the old house. A tight space—about 30 inches wide and just tall enough for six people to stand side-by-side—was constructed behind a false wall in Corrie's room.

I was overwhelmed—to the point of fighting back tears—as I stepped into that tiny safe haven. It was a portal to another time—a cruel time when desperate individuals became prisoners, slaves by choice, choosing freedom over the German prisons (actually death camps) in this hiding place. While touring this quaint home, I found myself transfixed at times—staring out the windows, imagining Nazi troops storming the store-lined street below. What fear must have come over the Jewish people—and the friends of the Jews—as they hoped against hope that these atrocities would come to an end.

My visit to that hiding place has forever touched my heart and provoked my sensitivity to those who have suffered—and those who today suffer—for their faith. One man, Hitler, was essentially responsible for all of this torment. But there is another evil incarnate—far more sinister than Hitler or even Osama bin Laden—who is responsible for an ongoing destruction campaign, bringing misery, oppression, grief, and sorrow throughout the world. This insidious leader is known by a number of names, but the most familiar are *devil* or *Satan*. Tyrannical despot Satan does not want to annihilate us, but rather to make us his obedient subjects, his at-his-beck-and-call slaves.

Freedom: Going, Going, Gone!

On March 11, 1744, Samuel Baker, founder of Sotheby's, held the first-ever sale under his own name. The library of Rt. Hon. Sir John Stanley—described as "containing several hundred scarce and valuable books in all branches of polite literature"—sold for a few hundred pounds. Two centuries later, on December 6, 1983, Sotheby's sold a single book, *The Gospels of Henry the Lion*, for over eight million pounds.[2]

Since those early days, not only have prices grown considerably, but so, too, have the scope and size of Sotheby's itself. In the last century, the original London company has expanded from book auctions to cover all areas of the fine and decorative arts. Sotheby's is now not just one of the oldest fine art auctioneers in the world, but also the largest, with more than one hundred offices around the world. In 1998 auction sales produced a turnover of just under two billion dollars.[3]

The Wall Street Journal cited auctioneering as one of the top ten highest paying professions in the United States. In a survey of 321 members of the Certified Auctioneers Institute, the average age for an auctioneer is 42.8 years. Forty-seven percent of auctioneers made $35,000–

$100,000 a year, with 13 percent making between $100,000 and $200,000, and 4 percent making over $200,000 annually. Most auctioneers have some college education or a college degree. There are, in fact, colleges of auctioneering, where students are trained in bid calling, voice control, breathing, public speaking, auction history, auction laws, appraisals, marketing, advertising, salesmanship, and types of auctions.[4]

In the year 2000 over thirty million people attended auctions. Auctions are the fastest growing segment of the real estate industry. What is most commonly auctioned?[5] Real estate (46%), household/estates (20%), antiques (16%), equipment (15%), and livestock (2.5%).

Auctions can be a lot of fun—listening to the auctioneer talk at the speed of light in what sounds like a foreign language, watching people raise their hands or cards to indicate they are making a bid, and hearing the auctioneer's vivid description of the item to be auctioned. From paintings to pottery, from Jackie O's BMW to Madonna's wardrobe, from farm equipment to cattle, auctions are a great way of selling valuables—unless that something valuable is our freedom. God has given us the power to experience freedom in our lives. Unfortunately, because of our choosing to do the wrong thing anyway, we too often put that freedom on the auction block. But there is a conflict of interests here. Satan is not only the auctioneer, but he is always willing to be the highest bidder.

> Satan is not only the auctioneer, but he is always willing to be the highest bidder.

I have watched so many individuals—including undiscerning church members—place their happiness, their future, their peace, their reputations on the auction block. They traded their freedom for slavery, their peace for a quick thrill, their reputations for a moment of popularity, their future for fleeting glitters-like-gold enticements, and their happiness for a quick buck. The price paid? The seller was carried away from the auction block in chains of bondage instead of walking away in freedom.

The master auctioneer leads people away from the auction house with a variety of different chains. Let me suggest some links to the chains that Satan uses to lead us away from the auction block. There are the links of . . .

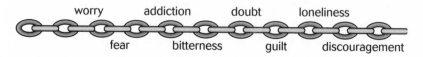

worry   addiction   doubt   loneliness

fear   bitterness   guilt   discouragement

Each of these links fortifies Satan's chains of bondage, which he uses to hold us captive. Paul's warning to the church at Galatia is also for us: "It is for freedom that Christ has set us free. Stand firm, then, and do not let yourselves be burdened again by a yoke of slavery" (Galatians 5:1). This issue of bondage is certainly not limited to those who are not Christians. We, too, struggle with these same sinful thought-choices that can lead us to putting our freedom on the auction block and cause us to swap our freedom for bondage.

Swap Shop

Gretchen bravely stood before our congregation and shared the heart-wrenching story of her older brother Dustin's slavery to drugs—a tragic illustration of the power of a runaway thought life. Gretchen and Dustin grew up in a Christian family who always attended church. Both became Christians at a young age. However, life events changed, and Dustin swapped his freedom in Christ for Satan's tyrannical chains.

At age twenty Dustin served as a Marine in Desert Storm. His work in Graves Registration—registering and handling the bodies the enemies killed in action—took a huge toll on this young soldier. He returned home a changed person. The emotional turmoil he was experiencing caused him to seek psychiatric help to ease the pain. Also, he drastically changed his lifestyle and behavior. He began hanging out with a different crowd—not the church kids he used to befriend. Drug use and an immoral lifestyle characterized the new Dustin. His young wife divorced him. He lost his home. His life was a mess. He was angry and bitter. To escape the pain and to join in with his friends, he began using—and soon became addicted to—crack.

Late on June 2, 1995, while Gretchen was on a date with her boyfriend—who is now her husband—she attempted to call her parents, but got no answer. She knew her parents were alone with her brother in their home. And Gretchen became concerned about what might be going on in that home since her brother frequently became angry. Fearing something might happen and not wanting to face the situation alone, she called a number of people, including the sheriff's department. She asked the deputies to go with her and some of her family to check things out.

Her worst fears were realized when the deputies knocked on the front door. Dustin was holding her parents at gunpoint. When the officers approached the house, Dustin panicked and shot both parents. While he was attempting to escape, he encountered two other people who lived behind their family's house, Dustin shot and killed them as well.

Gretchen's brother took three innocent lives that evening, including their father. Their mother was also critically injured and hospitalized for weeks. The family then had to endure what Gretchen calls "the worst nightmare of all": her brother's court trial. Dustin was found guilty of three counts of murder and one count of attempted murder. He was sentenced to life in prison with no parole when the judge decided to intervene and overrule a fourteen-to-one jury decision calling for the death penalty.

Prior to her sharing this testimony with our church, Gretchen told Dustin what she would be doing. She asked him, "What would you say to someone facing an addiction?" He responded, "Don't ever believe you have to fit in with the crowd. When you start doing bad things just to fit in, it starts to take control of your life." Dustin is now living with the painful consequences of becoming a slave to his thoughts. While Dustin has recommitted his life to Christ and knows spiritual freedom from his sins, he still must live the rest of his life captive—in physical bondage.

As Gretchen concluded her moving testimony of what God has done in helping her family recover from this tragedy, she encouraged our congregation to deal with the enslaving problem of addiction: "Today, if you are addicted to something, you can be set free, but you must make a decision right now. You must turn to the Lord and turn to the people you love to reach out for help. You are destroying not only your life, but the lives of people you love. If you are tempted to do something that may become addictive, don't do it! Let me also say a word to those with whom I most identify: Family members of those who have faced an addiction, you must forgive. You must let it go, release it, or it will destroy you as well."

For Gretchen's brother it was an addiction to something, for others it may be . . .

lust toward someone
depression about something
bitterness toward someone
worry about something
anger toward someone
fear about something
jealousy toward someone

Just as Dustin exchanged his freedom for an imprisoned life, we too exchange our freedom for a prison of our own choosing. It's like a "swap shop" where we go in and swap something we have of value—money or another possession—for something someone else wants to dump off on us. In the spiritual realm, we enter Satan's "swap shop" through our thought lives and trade what we have of value for the junk he wants to swap with us. Gretchen's brother's experience all too clearly attests to this. For Dustin it began when Satan whispered, "You want your new friends to accept you—don't you?" Because of swapping his Christian lifestyle for a momentary high, for the rest of his life this young man is to be in prison, a prison of choice.

Prison of Choice

There are some places that I just shouldn't go. Bookstores are problematic because I always find so many great books that I want to read and that, no doubt, will help me with ongoing research. Men's clothing stores pose another kind of dilemma: I really do need stylish work clothes, and it just stands to reason that I would be losing money if I didn't take advantage of sale signs. If I ever relax long enough to go to a Harley Davidson shop, I'm in serious trouble. Let me confess that I'm more than a little envious of Chuck Swindoll and his Harley bike.

I have explained my thinking on this to my wife with the reasoning, "He's a preacher. He needs an escape—and his wife even rides with him. I respect him, and, therefore, I think it would be wise for me to follow his lead in this. So, dear, I believe it is the 'will of God' for me to purchase a Harley—along with all the cool Harley accessories." It took my loving Angie only seconds to respond, "That's great, Jay. But there's a problem with your flawed reasoning. You are *not* Chuck Swindoll; I am *not* his wife. And *if* you need an escape, you can escape to the backyard and mow the grass! Plus—and most importantly—it is *not* the 'will of God' for you to get a Harley. It's the nonsovereign will of Jay." (Please don't tell on me, but I still sneak into the shops and dream every now and then.)

And then there's Fuddruckers. That's a whole other temptation. It's a fatal choice for me. Once there, I forget all the rules. Gone is my self-control. Lost is my good judgment. Departed is my common sense. As soon as I walk through the doors and go past the meateteria, I lose it. I crave the whole Fudd-experience: hearing my name called over the loudspeaker, being handed the large plastic tray with my burger and French fries on it, and heading for the crème de la crème of all condiment bars. I get oh-so pumped as I respond to the Herculean challenge of piling on the lettuce, tomatoes, salsa, ketchup, onions, pickles, their "world famous" mustard—and don't forget the cheese sauce! It soon becomes evident—after only a bite or two—that it's going to take more than a couple of trips to the soda fountain to wash my sin away!

This I-know-I-shouldn't-eat-this challenge has been a stumbling block for others besides me. Have you heard the story of a fourteenth-century duke, Raynald III, who lived and "duked" in what is now Belgium? Raynald, who was grossly overweight, was often called by his Latin nickname *Crassus*, meaning "fat." Thomas Costain's history, *The Three Edwards*, recounts a violent disagreement between Raynald and his younger brother, Edward. This led to a successful revolt against Raynald during which he was captured, but not killed, by Edward.

Instead, Edward built a room around Raynald in the Nieuwark castle that became his prison. There, however, was a way out and to freedom for Raynald! He could regain his title and property as soon as he was able to leave the room.

Here's the catch: The room had near-normal size windows and doors, but Raynald was too fat to escape through them. To regain his freedom, he had only to lose weight. Knowing his brother's love for food, Edward sent a variety of delicious foods to Raynald every day in order to keep him captive. Instead of dieting to get out of prison, Raynald ate and grew even fatter. When accused of cruelty, Edward responded, "My brother is not a prisoner. He may leave when he so wills." Raynald stayed in that prison of choice for ten years. He was not released until Edward died in battle. His health, however, was so ruined that he died within a year.[6]

After I "Fudd" it, I always feel like fat Raynald, a prisoner of my own appetite—a prisoner of choice. When I make an unhealthy or unwise choice, I almost always come to regret it. *Choice* is a powerful word. It conveys determination, decision, judgment, opinion, discrimination, selection, commitment, discretion, volition, conclusion, discernment, and will.

Dr. Patricia Maclay,[7] an Orlando internist and rheumatologist, devotes her practice to the care and study of people with fibromyalgia and chronic fatigue syndrome. Through her patient education program, *Choosing Wellness*, Dr. Maclay examines the health choices of wellness and prevention. Her unique program explores the various ways the human body responds to stress and why illness may develop as a result of experiencing stress. A critical part of her approach is a look at how and why spirituality may be the most important factor in achieving health. In an interview for this book, Dr. Maclay explained, "God gave us the gift of free will—the presence of at least two options. We can choose to be well or, when we don't, default into illness. People who have spirituality have the edge."

God really spoke to my heart when Marilyn and I talked with Dr. Maclay. My world is 24/7 stress. And it has impacted my health. The good news is that spirituality gives you and me an edge in dealing with stress when we choose to put God in control of our lives. Experiencing the pain and stress that life brings can actually be the catalyst to help us see God at work. The issue is how we respond.

We have life-altering choices to make. And I admit it: I sometimes struggle with choices—choices that impact my life, my health, my family, and my ministry. I particularly struggle when I am tempted to make life-changing decisions at the wrong time or when I am confused.

My long-time friend Jay Strack introduced me to something he calls the H.A.L.T. principle. Simply put, don't ever make a decision when you are Hungry, Angry, Lonely, or Tired.[8] That principle reverberates with everything in me because that's exactly when I am most tempted—and most at risk—to make poor choices. I'm learning to hold off on making decisions during those vulnerable times when my stomach is growling, when my face is red, when I feel alone, or when I'm physically and emotionally worn out. Experience has taught me that when I have not "halted" at those times and gone ahead and made less than wise choices, I end up finding myself in a prison of my own making.

Kermit in the Pot

Columnist Ellen Goodman wrote a powerful editorial on the topic of countering the culture, in which she said:

> At some point between Lamaze and PTA, it becomes clear that one of your main jobs as a parent is to counter the culture. What the media deliver to children by the masses, you are expected to rebut one at a time. . . . Mothers and fathers are expected to screen virtually every aspect of their children's

lives. To check the ratings on movies, to read the labels on CDs, to find out if there's MTV in the house next door. All the while keeping in touch with school and in their free time, earning a living. . . . It isn't that they can't say no. It's that there's so much more to say no to. Without wallowing in false nostalgia, there has been a fundamental shift. Americans once expected parents to raise their children in accordance with the dominant cultural messages. Today they are expected to raise their children in opposition.[9]

Often referred to as the frog-in-the-kettle syndrome, cultural conditioning threatens the moral fiber of our nation and our world. As the water heats up—through the raising of the what's-acceptable-to-think-and-say-and-do practices cultural temperature—the frog in the pot (a.k.a., unsuspecting, average Joe Kermit) doesn't notice the threat of being boiled alive until it's too late.

> A common complaint I heard from parents was their sense of being overwhelmed by the culture. Parents see themselves in a struggle for the hearts and minds of their own children.
>
> —BARBARA DAFOE WHITEHEAD, INSTITUTE FOR AMERICAN VALUES

Dr. William J. Bennett, drug czar under former President George Bush and U.S. Secretary of Education under former President Ronald Reagan, published his first *Index of Leading Cultural Indicators*—a compilation of facts and figures about the state of American society—in 1993. He continues to update and release the *Index*, which affords its readers an overview of where we, as a nation, are culturally. Some highlights from the most recent *Index*[10] show some disturbing trends that did not reverse during the 1990s but only escalated. In the 1990s:

- The percentage of families headed by a single parent increased by 13 percent.
- The marriage rate decreased by 9 percent.
- Cohabiting couples increased by 48 percent.

- Out-of-wedlock births increased by 18 percent.
- Teen use of alcohol decreased in the 1990s, but according to the National Institute of Drug Abuse, one in three twelfth graders, one in four tenth graders, and one in seven eighth graders had downed at least five drinks in a row.
- Candidates for drug treatment are nineteen times more likely to have been introduced to illicit drugs by a family member than a professional drug dealer, and five times more likely to have been introduced to drugs by a parent than a dealer.
- Suicide is the third-leading cause of death among persons between the ages of ten and twenty. Motor-vehicle accidents and homicide are the two leaders.
- In 2000, 57 percent of children ages eight to sixteen reported having a television set in their bedroom.
- Between 1993–1999 the percentage of households with computers more than doubled.
- About one in four regular Internet users—or about twenty-one million Americans—visit a pornographic website at least once a month.

In an interview with United Press International, Bennett interpreted the latest *Index* findings and added this commentary, "We're embarking on a social experiment the likes of which history has never seen before—of raising more and more children outside of a two-parent family. . . . The family is the fundamental unit of society, and cultural, demographic, economic and political factors have weakened the bonds that used to hold us together."[11] This breakdown of the family unit will change the culture in which we live.

> We have now become the kind of society that in the nineteenth century almost every Christian denomination felt compelled to missionize.
>
> —DAVID MURRAY,
> ANTHROPOLOGIST

What is "culture"? In *Winning the New Civil War*, Robert Dugan Jr. defines *culture* as being "the ways of thinking, living, and behaving that define a people and underlie its achievements. It is a nation's collective mindset, its sense of right and wrong, the way it perceives reality, and its definition of self."[12] Our nation's mindset has clearly shifted from a foundation of moral absolutes to the quicksand of relativism. And when a nation's thinking changes, so does its heart.

Out of Egypt, But Not Egypt-ed Out

What does it take to capture a nation's heart? You would think being God's beloved children—his chosen people—would command unequalled loyalty, devotion, and love. You might also think being rescued from captivity by a Savior who delivered them to the Promised Land would elicit unparalleled gratitude— reflected in a "Lord, we owe you everything, and may our lives forever reflect that" attitude. Again and again, the Jewish nation was called to remember—to remember their miraculous delivery from the bondage of Egyptian slavery, to remember how God sustained them with manna from on high, and to remember how God led them to a land "flowing with milk and honey." If they carefully considered all God had done for them, it should have been enough to cause them to serve him passionately all of their days. However, according to the biblical record this did not happen.

> We have learned to live with unholiness and have come to look upon it as the natural and expected thing.
>
> —A. W. TOZER

God's people may have been delivered out of Egypt, but the problem was Egypt was not out of God's people. This is evidenced in that God's chosen ones—shortly after they were formed into the Jewish nation—reverted back to the cultural mindset of their former homeland, Egypt. Moses had departed from them to meet with God on Mount Sinai. When he had been delayed in returning to the Jews, these disgruntled people got together and told Moses' brother, Aaron, that they wanted a new god[13]—one fashioned from their precious gold possessions—to lead them out of the desert.

Much like the temptation Adam and Eve faced in the first Eden, Aaron and God's chosen people—who were on the threshold of a new Eden—had the option to either obey God or take God-matters into their own hands. They chose the culturally convenient solution and fashioned the infamous golden calf. But if you remember the story, Moses returns with the tablets of law, loses his cool, and ultimately serves them up a pot of calf stew (Exodus 32). This incident marked one of the first times that Israel corporately sinned as a nation.

When our nation starts putting its stamp of approval—either through enthusiastically espousing or remaining apathetically silent—on activities to which God is opposed, it makes it much easier for each of us to concede and follow the path everyone else seems to be going down, a path that leads away from God. In his book *The Boiling Point*, pollster George Barna paints a troubling picture of the paradigm shift that has taken place in America. "More and more Americans are embracing the idea that there is no truth, or at best, that it is defined by each individual, from moment to moment."

Barna offers these twenty-first-century mores as proof:[14]

- Divorce, homosexuality, and abortion are no longer moral issues to be decided on the basis of God's law but are now decided on the basis of personal preference.
- Pornography is generally protected as "free speech," but prayer at public schools and the posting of the Ten Commandments in courthouses is outlawed.
- Widespread and public use of foul language is accepted as a right of personal expression.
- Lying and cheating are described as inappropriate behaviors; however, most people believe that the problem is not the act of lying or cheating but in being caught.

The spirit of what is now accepted corporately as a nation puts increased pressure on us to think like the majority thinks.

Attempted Jail Break

Alcatraz, the penitentiary often referred to as "The Rock," was called the inescapable prison. From the mid-1930s until the mid-1960s, Alcatraz was America's premier maximum-security prison, the final stop for the nation's most incorrigible inmates. Surrounded by the San Francisco Bay, this former federal prison presented no-win odds of conquering the freezing water temperatures, sharks, and the long distance to land against swift currents for those who might attempt to escape. Over the twenty-nine years (1934–1963) the prison operated, thirty-six men (including two who tried to escape twice) were involved in fourteen escape attempts.

Twenty-three of the inmates were caught, six were shot and killed during their escape, and two drowned. Officially, no one ever succeeded in escaping from Alcatraz, although to this day there are five prisoners listed as "missing and presumed drowned." Three of these five prisoners were made famous by Clint Eastwood in the movie *Escape from Alcatraz*.

On June 11, 1962, Frank Morris and brothers John and Clarence Anglin vanished from their cells and were never seen again. An intricate plot was devised that involved using homemade drills to enlarge vent holes, false wall segments, and even realistic dummy heads (complete with human hair) placed in the beds to fool the prison guards. The three inmates escaped through the vent holes, climbed the utility pipes, and gained access to the roof through an air vent. They then climbed down a drainpipe and made their way to the water. Using raincoats issued by the prison, they made life-vests and a pontoon-like raft to assist in their swim.

Did they make it? Morris and the Anglin brothers are officially listed as missing and presumed drowned. One body wearing prison-type clothing was found up the coast several weeks later; however, the body was beyond recognition.[15] Alcatraz is still known as the prison of no escape.

Every day there are those of us who unsuccessfully attempt jail breaks and find ourselves back in the slammer after our futile efforts have been foiled. Trying feverishly to escape the bondage caused by wrong choices, we plan and attempt to break out of our prisons of choice, using whatever tools necessary to . . .

> dig out of our debt
>> break out of our bitterness
>>> spring out of our sin
>>>> get out of our guilt
>>>>> bust out of our burdens
>>>>>> bolt out of our binds
>>>>>>> escape out of our existence.

Like trying to mastermind an escape from Alcatraz, it is seemingly impossible to break out. It's not that many of us don't try. It's just that we find ourselves in situations that appear to be more than we can handle. Feeling defeated because of past failures to escape our bondage, we simply concede to an imprisoned life.

Of course, Satan and his many associates will gladly assist us in our attempted jail break. The escape route most often will be through quick fixes, short-term solutions, pat answers, or suggestive ideas—none of which includes God:

- If overweight, try the route of binging and purging.
- If in debt, try the route of get-rich-quick schemes, gambling, or stealing.
- If addicted, try the route of denying there's a problem.
- If lonely, try the route of calling a "900" number for an exciting time.
- If sexually needy, try the route of an adult book store, Internet porn site, or "for mature audiences only" pay-per-view movie.
- And if all hope is gone, try the route of suicide as the quickest way out.

> The escape route most often will be through quick fixes, short-term solutions, pat answers, or suggestive ideas—none of which includes God.

Satan's "helping us" with our great escape only leads us to a greater trap. He bombards our thought lives with ways of supposedly meeting our needs, but all the while bypassing the God-solution.

James speaks of "sin, when it is full-grown" (James 1:15). Sin is birthed, grows up, and provides the chains that enslave us. The progression of sin inescapably leads to bondage. It has been said, "A single sin, whatever its name, may enslave you for life. A single wrong turn of a railroad switch may cause a great disaster. A single leak in a ship may cause it to sink beneath the waves. It does not require many sins to ensnare us."[16] Many are living in bondage because they acted on a sinful thought, and then once that thought gave birth to a sinful action, they neglected or refused to deal with it.

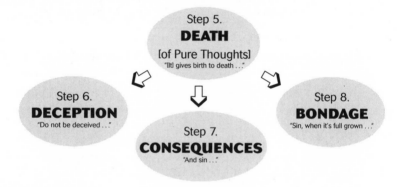

But, if you want to become free, even if you are in chains created by your own choices, there is hope that you can S.T.O.P. it.

Part Three

Stopping Sin's Control

Stop doing wrong, learn to do right.

ISAIAH 1:16–17

Stopping Sin's Control

S.T.O.P. It!

Over the first eight chapters we have focused on how our thought life can get off track. Perhaps you, like me, have felt a sense of heaviness at times in coming face-to-face with these thought-life issues. Maybe the Holy Spirit has been prompting you to deal with getting your thought life back on track and under his control. Does the following sound like anything you've thought?

> I'm full of myself—after all, I've spent a long time in sin's prison. What I don't understand about myself is that I decide one way, but then I act another, doing things I absolutely despise.
>
> I decide to do good, but I don't *really* do it; I decide not to do bad, but then I do it anyway. My decisions, such as they are, don't result in actions. Something has gone wrong deep within me and gets the better of me every time.

It happens so regularly that it's predictable. The moment I decide to do good, sin is there to trip me up. I truly delight in God's commands, but it's pretty obvious that not all of me joins in that delight. Parts of me covertly rebel, and just when I least expect it, they take charge.

I've tried everything and nothing helps. I'm at the end of my rope. Is there no one who can do anything for me?

—Romans 7:14– 15, 19–24 THE MESSAGE

Yes, it is tough! But not impossible. The Romans passage goes on to offer the solution to our common dilemma: "The answer, thank God, is that Jesus Christ can and does. He acted to set things right in this life of contradictions where I want to serve God with all my heart and mind, but am pulled by the influence of sin to do something totally different" (v. 25 THE MESSAGE).

There *is* a solution for this seemingly no-win thought battle that fiercely rages inside each of us! It is found in the finished work of Jesus Christ, who, as a real human being, found a way to win the thought war in his life. He did it! And while none of us can expect Christ-like perfection in this life, we can look to his example of not giving in or giving up. We see from his very own WWI—that is, "Wilderness War One—or Won" (Matthew 4)—that he faced the always-present thought battle head on and dealt with the temptation onslaught.

The past eight chapters have examined some of the reasons for this ever-raging thought war. The case studies presented could become our story unless we learn to get our thought life under God's control. They are presented not only for our encouragement—as we are not alone or without hope in this struggle—but also for our warning—as it could happen to any one of us. The next four chapters will offer some real, life-altering solutions with a sound biblical basis. In these chapters, you will be introduced to the S.T.O.P. method of dealing with sinful thoughts.

While a student in the Doctor of Ministry program at Fuller Theological Seminary in Pasadena, California, I took a psychology seminar entitled *Stress in the Life of the Minister.* My professor, Dr. Archibald Hart, shared with us a technique for interrupting a sinful thought. His suggestion, "Whenever a sinful thought comes into your mind, say out loud, 'Stop the thought!'" I have used that simple technique over and over to stop sinful or wrong thinking.

Marilyn and I took his idea of saying *Stop!* to a sinful thought and developed it into an easy-to-remember acrostic to introduce four principles of stopping sin where it starts—in the mind. We will discuss our S.T.O.P. method in the final four chapters. By employing this method, you can successfully "stop the thought." What is the acrostic?

1. **S**inful thoughts confessed
   1 John 1:9
2. **T**hink on these things
   Philippians 4:8
3. **O**rder every thought
   2 Corinthians 10:5
4. **P**ursue Christ-mindedness
   Colossians 3:2

9

S. Sinful Thoughts Confessed

IT HAS ALWAYS BEEN HARD for me—especially since becoming a pastor—to confess my sins to anyone other than God. It's not that I don't sin—far from it. Just ask my family. I guess it has to do with my commitment to maintaining a credible witness. I fear that if the people I pastor knew me as God knows me—particularly my sinful or wrong thinking—that they may not believe how much I truly love the Lord and desire to faithfully obey him. This is such a contradiction to the realness and transparency that I appreciate in others—and that I try to project!

In one of our first writing sessions, Marilyn looked me in the eyes and asked, "What is the worst thing you have ever done?" I hemmed and hawed as I beat around the bush—not willing to bear my soul to someone whose respect I wanted to maintain—and gave an anything-but-to-the-point answer. And it's not that I have some deep, dark, heinous past that I am trying to keep hidden. I am just embarrassed that I have let God down too often in un-Christlike thought and conduct. And I am afraid that if I let others see my weakness, they will change their opinion of me—or, worst of all, change their opinion of my Lord.

162

Yes, I know my thinking on this is messed up. But I am getting there. All the things I have shared with readers in this book were big risks for me. I am trying to open up more so that others can see the struggles in my life—and better appreciate the victories the Lord has given to me as an ordinary-Joe believer.

There *is* a place and time every day that I do bear it all. It's when I am before God—in the early morning hours before the sun even rises—when he and I are alone. Then and there I "come clean"—confessing my weaknesses, my wrong thoughts, and the sins I have committed in spite of knowing better. In my ear-lier Christian life, I did not always do this. But now, I cannot survive without it. I just cannot live with the thought that there is something between my Lord and me—keeping me from enjoying the intimacy with him that I have come to crave. Also, I have come to realize expe-rientially that dealing with my sin is necessary not only for me to be right with him, but also for me to act rightly with other people.

> For God will bring every deed into judgment, including every hidden thing, whether it is good or evil.
>
> —ECCLESIASTES 12:14

There's one other reason I feel compelled to confess my sinful thoughts and actions daily to God. I would hate to think that one day when I stand before the Lord to give an account of my life, he would point out to me that there were unconfessed sins that could have been forgiven, and a deeper fellowship with him might have been enjoyed while I was on this earth.

You're Being Recorded

On February 9, 2001, the USS Greenville—armed with Tomahawk cruise missiles—was on a routine operation nine miles south of Diamond Head, off Honolulu, Hawaii. But cruising in the same area was the Ehime Maru, a 180-foot training vessel from a Japanese fish-ery high school. As the Japanese vessel continued to engage in its two-and-a-half-month training mission, the United States submarine performed an emergency main ballast tank blow, which caused the ship to rocket to the surface at a steep angle. As it surfaced, tragedy ensued. The 7,000-ton submarine emerged from of the water with a huge force, hitting and sinking the Ehime Maru.

According to Hisao Oonishi, captain of the crippled ship: "I felt two great shocks all of a sudden. I looked back and saw the submarine surface." His fishing vessel sank quickly. Although twenty-six people were rescued from its life rafts, nine people were never recovered, certain to be dead. The crew of the USS Greenville claimed that they had looked through the periscope to check the ocean surface for any vessels prior to surfacing. The periscope checks were visible on a video screen inside the submarine, but the video recorder that would have recorded the images from the periscope is reported to have been switched off at the time.[1]

God's video recorder is never switched to the "off" position. He knows everything we do. There is nothing we ever do about which God would say, "Whoa! How did that one get past me?" Or, "I wish I had known this earlier." Or, "When did you do that?" Has it ever occurred to you that nothing ever "just occurs" to God? He knows it all from before the beginning and beyond the end.

When I teach a group of people about the nature of final judgment and arrive at the verses about there being no more hidden secrets at the time of judgment—no hidden thoughts, no hidden deeds, no hidden sins—the reality of God's knowing everything hits home in a big way. Inevitably I get those "uh-oh, that's not good, not good at all" looks. You know the verses of which I am speaking, don't you?

> Nothing is covered up that will not be revealed, or hidden that will not be known. Therefore whatever you have said in the dark shall be heard in the light, and what you have whispered in private rooms shall be proclaimed upon the housetops.
> —Luke 12:2–3 RSV

> For all of us must appear before the judgment seat of Christ, that each may receive recompense for what has been done in the body, whether good or evil.
> —2 Corinthians 5:10 NRSV

How do you picture final judgment? Do you see yourself standing before Christ and other people, hearing the heavenly bailiff call your name? And as you come before the Judge of all humanity, do you see yourself watching your life played back on some sort of huge IMAX screen in plain view of everyone? Do you imagine feeling shame or horror as your family and friends view such a video of your life? While I am not suggesting this is how the judgment scene will look, I am being honest about the gut reaction of individuals when they first consider their private lives and thoughts being publicly exposed.

Personally, I would be major embarrassed for all my thoughts and actions to be known. I can just hear someone in my congregation saying, "Brother Jay, you said *that* when the other driver cut you off?" Or my children saying, "Dad, I can't believe you thought that!" Or one of my parents saying, "Jay, what in the world were you thinking when you did that?" Or one of the men in my mentoring group saying, "Pastor, I'm shocked!"

> Sometimes it silently sizzles, other times it surfaces with the force of a USS Greenville, with a Wham!—surfacing, colliding with the lies we have led others to believe about us, and sinking us.

Let me get off the hot seat for a moment and ask you what would you not want anyone else to know about the private you. Well, you don't have to wait for what transpires at final judgment for your secret sins to be found out. Sin that is unconfessed—not dealt with before God—has an ugly way of surfacing. Numbers 32:23 reminds us: "And you may be sure that your sin will find you out."

Our sin surfaces in multiple ways—through actions, attitudes, countenance, guilt, bitterness, relationship problems, words, finances, and even health problems. Sometimes it silently sizzles, other times it surfaces with the force of a USS Greenville, with a Wham!—surfacing, colliding with the lies we have led others to believe about us, and sinking us. Sin brings death—not necessarily physical death, but certainly the death of peace and true joy in our lives.

And sin, when it is full-grown, gives birth to death.

—James 1:15

Are you wondering if you will ever get to the point in your struggle with your thought life that you will be able to finally deal with—and know success in avoiding—the sin to which you have sunk? Receiving the intervening help of God begins with the simple confession . . .

Help! I've Fallen and I Can't Get Up!

Do you remember the commercial showing an older woman who has fallen and is crying out into a tiny remote transmitter that she's wearing: "Help! I've fallen and I can't get up!"? You then see her successful rescue by the swift response of the Life Alert Medical and Security Emergency Response System people. Too often we believe the lie promoted by Satan that leads us to believe that when we have fallen into sinful thoughts or actions, we can never recover.

Defeated by the false assertions of this master deceiver who delights in seeing us incapacitated by our seemingly helpless plight, we seem to be crying out . . .

- "Help! I've fallen into sexual lust and I can't get up."
- "Help! I've fallen into temptation and I can't get up."
- "Help! I've fallen into a lie and I can't get up."
- "Help! I've fallen into bitterness and I can't get up."
- "Help! I've fallen into fear and I can't get up."
- "Help! I've fallen into worry and I can't get up."
- "Help! I've fallen into guilt and I can't get up."

As we were working on this chapter, the counselor on staff at my church informed me of a heart-breaking case where a church leader was arrested in another city in an undercover sting operation. This well-known, married man had been struggling with homosexuality and living a double life. After Charles was arrested for lewd and lascivious behavior, he expressed relief in finally being caught. He said that he hated the way he had been living but could not find a way out on his own. This disgraced-in-the-public's-eye man explained how he had prayed, not long before his arrest, that God would intervene and do whatever it took to bring an end to his misery. Broken, a fallen Charles received the help he was offered as a gift from God. Healing and restoration has now occurred in his life, marriage, and relationship to God.

You are probably familiar with the fall of televangelist Jim Bakker, who fell hard and in plain view of his adoring public. By the mid-1980s, Bakker and his wife, Tammy Faye, had built a multimillion-dollar religious empire that grew out of his PTL Club television ministry aired on hundreds of stations worldwide. His empire also included the Inspiration Network and Heritage USA. Everything Bakker touched seemed to have the "Midas touch." Pride had its claws tightly wrapped around the televangelist. But as Proverbs 29:23 warns, "A man's pride brings him low."

Enter Jessica Hahn, one-time church secretary. On March 19, 1987, Bakker resigned from his ministry. His sin had been found out— an extramarital affair with Jessica Hahn had occurred over six years previously. A sensation erupted when Bakker confessed to committing adultery.[2] In the aftermath a grand jury found evidence that Bakker had skimmed millions of dollars donated by his followers. On December 5, 1988, he was indicted and shortly thereafter convicted of conspiracy and fraud. He was sentenced to forty-five years in prison, but the sentence was later commuted after he had served only five of those years.[3] But, thank our gracious Lord, the story doesn't end with Bakker's fall.

I heard Jim Bakker share his testimony via a live church service radio broadcast not long after he was released from prison. I sat transfixed as he shared his heart with the audience. What came across was not a prideful man who was full of himself, but a broken man who had genuinely repented of his fallen ways.

The title of his book speaks volumes: I Was Wrong. In subsequent interviews, Jim Bakker has not cast blame on anyone else or made excuses. He took responsibility for his own downfall that ended up costing him everything. However, since Bakker died to self while in that prison cell,[4] he has become a forgiven man, a restored man, a humble man, and a now useful man for carrying out God's kingdom work on earth. Not only is Bakker's story a powerful reminder to Christians everywhere that no one is immune from falling into sin, but it is an encouragement to all of us that no matter how hard the fall and deep the pit, with Christ's help we can get up again.

> What power there is in the confession, "Help, Lord! I've fallen and I can't get up on my own. I need your help." Help is only a prayer and repentant heart away.

What power there is in the confession, "Help, Lord! I've fallen and I can't get up on my own. I need your help." Help is only a prayer and repentant heart away. No, we don't need Life Alert to cry out for this kind of help. We have something better—a heavenly Father on whom we can call any time and anywhere.

> Come near to God and he will come near to you. Wash your hands, you sinners, and purify your hearts, you double-minded. Grieve, mourn and wail. Change your laughter to mourning and your joy to gloom. Humble yourselves before the Lord, and he will lift you up.
>
> —James 4:8–10

Like David, who had fallen into—but then repented of—an adulterous relationship, both Charles and Jim Bakker experienced God's forgiveness and the restoration of a clean and pure heart.[5] These men may have fallen hard, but by God's grace both have gotten up again and are being used by God in powerful ways. This is good news for all of us fallen creatures! Your thought life can be restored to purity once again—and the light that illumines a mind focused on God can shine again.

This Little Light of Mine

My wife sometimes just does not get it. I am in here working on this chapter—doing really important spiritual stuff—and she dares to interrupt this high and holy time with my computer and God Almighty by expecting me to be a useful, contributing member of this household. My peaceful solitude was just shattered by the shrill and multiple-syllabic calling out of my name: "Ja-a-ay!" Doesn't Ang know that breaks my concentration? Oh, I can't believe it. Now she has the audacity to break into the sacredness of this moment by "politely shouting" a mundane question like: "Are you ever going to fix the living room lamp?"

Okay, this takes serious focus and a redirection of my energy. I'll feign trance-like concentration, and maybe she'll leave me alone while I rush to complete this section. Oh, no! She's not buying into this—not even for a moment! "Jay Dennis, I know you can hear me. Answer me. Are you going to fix the lamp? We have company coming over in a few hours, and you promised to do have this lamp working before they arrived. Ja-a-ay, stop with your writing and do something helpful!" Ouch! That got my attention. I'll get back to you in a little while . . .

I'm back. And frustrated. No, not with Angie. She was right in asking me to do what I should have done earlier—as I had promised. I should have helped out without her having to ask me. I feel badly about that. I do tend to get sidetracked with the things I most enjoy doing. About my frustration . . . I am really ticked about not being able to fix that stupid lamp! This should be a piece of cake. I am a fairly intelligent guy. This shouldn't be hard.

This is the deal. Maybe you can help me with it. We have this pretty lamp in our living room that "beautifies" the whole room. There's only one problem with that lovely lamp: It won't work—no way, no how. Oh, I've tried to fix it. A few weeks ago, I got in my car and went to my favorite store, Home Depot, and did the obvious: purchased some light bulbs. Surely, that was all it was. I don't know why Angie had not thought of that herself. Then, like Tim "The Toolman" Taylor on *Home Improvement*, I "ar-ar-arded" as I strutted into the living room and screwed that bulb into its socket. And voila! No light. (I'm so glad Ang was walking out the back door as I was coming in. But then, there's no disgrace in trying. Right?)

I've been "studying the problem" since then. It must be the wiring . . . or the switch . . . maybe the plug. That brings you up to today. So, after unplugging the lamp, removing the shade, lifting the lamp in the air, and examining it thoroughly for loose or burned out parts or wires, I was able to determine that the lamp is broken! When Ang came in there while I was doing this inspection, I told her that I was probably going to have to pull out the wires from inside the lamp so that I could better evaluate the situation. It was then that my beloved reminded me that God called me to preach and not to be Watty Watt the electrician.

To appease her concerns—which are completely unfounded, I might add—I opted for a less intrusive approach. I went after my trusty, no-fail flashlight so I could peer into that sucker. And you guessed it! I turned on the flashlight and nothing happened. No flash. No light. Nada.

So, feeling completely defeated by that frou-frou appliance, I just sulked back in here to my study. I have a lamp and a flashlight that are not doing what they were designed to do—that is, to shine. When it comes to our living room, we Dennises are still in the dark.

You and I are created to spiritually shine in a dark world.

> Let your light shine before men, that they may see your good deeds and praise your Father in heaven.
>
> —Matthew 5:16

However, through wrong choices, our light goes out, and we stumble in the darkness. The good news is, even if the light has gone out in our lives, for whatever reason, shining is possible again. We have the choice to let our light shine brightly again.

> The good news is, even if the light has gone out in our lives, for whatever reason, shining is possible again.

Hearing Billy Graham sing a trio with Bev Shea and Cliff Barrows at the recent Jacksonville crusade was something I will never forget. So, you may ask, "What song did Mr. Graham choose to sing?" He chose *This Little Light of Mine*—the same song many of us sung as children. It was a precious moment for those of us at Altell Stadium as we heard this giant of the faith sing with childlike humility and exuberance that he wanted his light to shine for Christ—and did not want Satan to extinguish it. Tears rolled down my cheeks as I prayed that God would indeed preserve this saint's light for many generations to come. Oh, that I would possess the same resolve to see Christ's light shine brightly in me!

American pastor Paul W. Quillian told the story of three rays of sunlight that decided not to fulfill their intended purposes. As it left the sun on its journey earthward, one ray of light said, "I don't make any difference. I am going where I please and do what I please. There are so many other rays that I will never be missed." The second ray agreed and said, "I'll go with you." The third ray said, "So will I. We're free to do as we please."

As the story goes, the three rays of light decided not to shine in the way in which they were intended to shine and this led to dark consequences. A young man, when he held a diamond to the sunlight to check for flaws before he purchased it for his soon-to-be fiancée, was deceived into thinking the stone was flawless, because the first ray of light was absent, and there was a momentary blur in his vision.

A surgeon performing an emergency, on-location, delicate eye surgery cut too deeply and blinded a young child, because the second ray of light had not shown up at the most critical moment in the surgical procedure.

Two young pilots experiencing instrument failure on their airplane and needing to fly through thick fog using only visual navigation crashed and died as they were about to land, because ray number three was elsewhere when they most needed to see where they were heading.[6]

Over the years as I have thought about that imaginary story, I have been prompted by God's Spirit to wonder how many times in reality have I been a rebellious ray of light—doing what pleased me instead of fulfilling God's intended design for my light. Too many times I have dimmed or shut off what should be my light for Christ shining at maximum wattage because I have allowed the darkness of sin in my life. I'm embarrassed to admit that, much too often, I have allowed pride, worry, and trying to please people to reduce the wattage in my spiritual light bulb. I have allowed anger, at times, to make some question if I even had the light.

God has been gracious by causing me to feel sorrow and true guilt for my sin—and when needed, by disciplining me to the point of breaking me of a sin habit. I cannot imagine what would have happened if his Spirit chose to leave me alone in my darkness instead of leading me back out into the light.

There's an inherent danger in our growing accustomed to the darkness of sin. I liken it to going into a dark movie theatre. For the first moments, it's impossible to see where to walk or sit. But after being in the darkness for a while, your eyes adjust and get used to it. Soon it becomes comfortable and doesn't seem so dark any more. Sin does just that. The more we allow it in our lives, the less it seems so dark or bad. We become comfortable with our sin choices. If we do not seek to be led out into the light, we can get stuck in a cycle of dark thoughts and actions that can extinguish our light.

Will the Cycle Be Broken?

Most of us are all familiar with the song "Will the Circle Be Unbroken?" I have another song of mine to share with you. It's my rip-off version of the circle song—à la Weird Al Yankovic—that goes: *Will the cycle be broken, my, oh my Lord, my, oh my. I keep running and a spinning, in this vicious cycle of my life.* I know, I know. I am a song-writing genus. And in those infamous words of Elvis let me say to you, "Thank you, thank you very much."

All kidding aside, the sin cycle is a serious problem that we all have to deal with. Sin is a vicious cycle that, unless broken, will eventually destroy the joy and peace that God so wants to give us. Too easily we find ourselves caught up in cycles of . . .

- life . . . running nowhere on life's treadmill because of compromise and disobedience to God's will
- lust . . . being held captive by the stronghold of wanting what lies outside of God's will
- lying . . . living with a lie that's eating us up with guilt
- losing . . . letting feelings of defeat keep us down and make us feel like losers

Is there anything that will break these sin cycles? Yes. It is *total confession of sin.* True confession always involves repentance. Here is how it works. When we contrast our sinfulness with Christ's holiness, we will feel the heavy burden of that sin, and it reveals our need to repent. The biblical word for confession means "to say the same thing as another—that is, to agree with, assent." Further, it conveys the idea of conceding, not denying, instead to admit or declare one's self guilty.[7]

Confession, as it applies to our sins, means that we bring our sins out into the light and agree with God about the darkness of it. We concede we are wrong and are totally responsible for our sin. We don't argue with God about it or attempt to excuse the sin. Biblical confession not only includes admitting it but a resolve to quit it. That's where repentance comes in.

> Sin is a vicious cycle that, unless broken, will eventually destroy the joy and peace that God so wants to give us.

Our sin cycles will lead to a downward spiral unless there is a God-intervention that we seek through our genuine repentance. Without repentance nothing ever changes, just the usual back-in-the-same-old-rut mess. What is genuine repentance?

First, let me share with you what it is not. Repentance is not . . .

> just being sorry you got caught
>> feeling badly because you did it
>>> regretting terribly what you did
>>> a tearful emotional experience
>>> turning over a new leaf
>>>> getting "religious"

While some of these things may precede repentance, they are not genuine repentance and will not break sin's cycle.

Now let me share with you a description of genuine repentance. It is a moment in time when God, the Holy Spirit, convicts you to truly change the direction you're going.

- It is a turning point—a "You-turn"—where you turn to God and away from your sin.
- It is letting go of sin and embracing of God's will.
- It is a change of mind that leads to a change of action.

> Repent, for the kingdom of heaven is near. . . . Produce fruit in keeping with repentance.
>
> —Matthew 3:2, 8

Intellectually speaking, you recognize your sin as being destructive in your life and contrary to God's will. Emotionally speaking, you experience an overwhelming sense of sorrow for what you have done. Behaviorally speaking, you vow no longer to do that which God has revealed as sin in your life.

True repentance leads to change. When the apostle Paul addressed King Agrippa, he said, "I preached that they should repent and turn to God and prove their repentance by their deeds" (Acts 26:20). With true repentance, there will be a change in your desires, devotion, direction, and decisions.

How do you, as a Christian, deal with sin and truly repent? The process of repentance includes:

- *recognition:* You have an acute awareness that you have sinned.
- *responsibility:* You blame no one else for your choices and actions.
- *release:* You confess your specific sins to God.
- *request:* You ask God to forgive you.
- *remove:* You must distance yourself from that which causes you to fall into sin.
- *return:* You once again strive to do only the will of God.
- *rejoice:* You can know victory and freedom from sin and guilt.

One of the greatest—and most comforting—promises in the Bible is found in 1 John 1:9: "If we confess our sins, he is faithful and just and will forgive us our sins and purify us from all unrighteousness."

Wisk Away the Sin

According to the findings of a recent Soap and Detergent Association National Cleaning Survey, 46 percent of all couples who live together argue about cleaning. Women claim they do 79 percent of the cleaning in their household, while men admit they only do 35 percent. The arguments run the gamut from who should do the cleaning (27%), to how often the cleaning should be done (24%), to the best way to clean (17%).

- Fifty-one percent say their partner's biggest cleaning weakness is that they don't clean often enough.

- Forty-one percent complain that their partner vacuums and dusts around items instead of moving them.
- Thirty-nine percent of respondents are annoyed by their partner's failure to clean up after using the kitchen.
- Thirty-eight percent mention bathroom cleanup or the lack there of as a source of contention.[8]

When I stop by the grocery store to pick up some things Angie has asked me to get on my way home from work, I always find myself in a dilemma when I go down the cleaning products aisle. Wow! It's more than I can handle. If Angie didn't tell me exactly what to buy—and what color container it's in—I would be incapable of deciding between all these "new and improved" products with their claims of removing tough stains and killing germs with a lemon-fresh scent while being milder on the hands. As sure as I would find great *Cheer,* experience sheer *Joy,* or know *Fab*-ulous *Gain* by enlisting the help of *Mr. Clean,* I would be *Wisk*-ed away by a *Breeze* or carried away by the *Tide* of the *Surf* and *All* my troubles would just begin!

So, are some laundry detergents better than others? All detergents, including soap, are "surfactants"—that is, organic chemicals that change the properties of water. By lowering the surface tension of water, surfactants enable the cleaning solution to wet a surface more quickly, so soil can be readily loosened and removed. Most dirt adheres to our skin, clothing, dishes, and cars by means of a sticky, oily film. All a detergent has to do is coax the film into the water and the "glue" will be removed that has adhered dirt to the objects. Surfactants do just that. They emulsify oily soils and keep them dispersed and suspended so they don't settle back on the surface. Many cleaning products include two or more surfactants in their formula to aid in this process.[9]

So, what's the difference between all those products at the gro-store?

> As sure as I would find great *Cheer,* experience sheer *Joy,* or know *Fab*-ulous *Gain* by enlisting the help of *Mr. Clean,* I would be *Wisk*-ed away by a *Breeze* or carried away by the *Tide* of the *Surf* and *All* my troubles would just begin!

Scientists have added other chemicals besides surfactants to their cleaning products to substantiate the manufacturers' claims, including acids and alkalis, antimicrobial agents, bleaches, builders, corrosion inhibitors, enzymes, fabric softening agents, fragrances, optical brighteners, preservatives, solvents, and suds-control agents. And, of course, don't forget the most expensive ingredient: advertising![10] Doing the laundry has never been this complicated before.

We need to go to God's Laundromat daily for the cleansing that comes through the daily confession of sin. Boyce Mouton has pointed out a biblical precedence for this need to be cleansed[11]:

- "Wash me!" was the anguished prayer of King David.
- "Wash!" was the message of John the Baptist.
- "Unless I wash you, you have no part with me," said the towel-draped Jesus to Peter.

Mouton adds, "Without our being washed clean, we all die from the contamination of sin. For God's sake, wash."

Isabella of Spain bragged that she had had only two baths in her life—one when she was born and the other when she married Ferdinand. She was given a third bath when she died.[12] Sometimes we can be like Isabella, bragging of God's washing away our sins at the time of our salvation but failing to seek daily cleansing of our sin-stained lives. Unless we bathe in the forgiveness of our Lord—using the best cleaning product ever marketed: the blood of Jesus Christ—we allow unconfessed sin in our lives to form more than stubborn rings around the collar. We build up a caked-on hardness of our soul.

We must daily confess the since-salvation sins in our lives, ask for God's cleansing forgiveness for these acts of weakness and disobedience, and seek to live in true repentance by the power of God's Spirit in us. Being washed daily by the blood of Christ cleanses us from all the world's dirt and mind pollution, as well as removes all hindrances to a deep, abiding relationship with the One who shed his blood for us.

> But if we walk in the light, as he is in the light, we have fellowship with one another, and the blood of Jesus, his Son, purifies us from all sin.
>
> —1 John 1:7

I read of an experiment whose results I questioned. The hypothesis was that when looking at the color red through red one sees white. To skeptical me, seeing was believing. Sure enough, as I looked at a piece of red clothing through red-tinted glass, it looked pure white. Our sins, in Scripture, are often portrayed as scarlet, a shade of red. Obviously, the color of blood is red. Jesus Christ shed his blood for our sin. When we accept that God-provision personally and apply it to our lives, as God looks at our scarlet sin through the blood of Jesus Christ, he sees us as white—no longer sin-stained, but pure and forgiven.

> "Come now, let us reason together," says the LORD. "Though your sins are like scarlet, they shall be as white as snow; though they are red as crimson, they shall be like wool."
>
> —Isaiah 1:18

Are you ready to stop sinful thoughts and actions? The first step in the S.T.O.P. method is essential to breaking the cycle of sin. Sinful thoughts must be confessed, and in that confession repentance must be at the core of it: "If we confess our sins, he is faithful and just and will forgive us our sins and purify us from all unrighteousness" (1 John 1:9).

A faithful church member wanted to know which word in the English language is the most difficult to say. His pastor suggested a few tongue twisters, but each time the old gentleman shook his head. Finally, the man answered his own question by spelling out the word *w-r-o-n-g*.[13]

1. **Sinful thoughts confessed**
   1 John 1:9
2. **T**hink on these things
   Philippians 4:8
3. **O**rder every thought
   2 Corinthians 10:5
4. **P**ursue Christ-mindedness
   Collossians 3:2

Once we admit we're wrong and seek God's forgiveness, the next step is to . . .

T. Think on These Things

I WANTED TO SEE for myself what the big deal was all about. I thought it would be a safe thing to experience in the privacy of my home study when no one was around. Dressed in my gym shorts and T-shirt, relaxed and stretched out from an afternoon run, I seized the opportunity to give it a try. I thought to myself, *Here's goes nothing!* as I placed my left foot on my right thigh. That was easy enough. But getting the right foot over my left thigh took a little doing! Looking a lot like one of those inflatable toy punching-bag people, going back and forth and side to side, I rolled around and around trying to force my foot to overlap my other leg. When I finally was able to stabilize myself, I was proud that I had assumed the full-lotus position that was pictured in the research I had downloaded.

I sat there for a few moments trying to ignore the shooting pains up the backs of my legs and to get in a meditative mindset. I understand now why people are coached to clear their minds. Wild were my thoughts of never being able to walk again and of trying to explain to my congregation on Sunday why I was not going to be able to stand up to preach. I know you are thinking this guy is just not sophisticated enough for this. You may be right. If this was supposed to get me in touch with my inner self, it didn't work. And if it was supposed to help me relax, it sure didn't do that either.

I might as well go ahead and confess what happened next. While in that position of supposed "higher consciousness," I got stuck. Really. My legs went numb. I couldn't uncross them, and I couldn't get up. I truly was the frozen chosen! I had heard Angie return home a few minutes earlier, but I didn't answer when she had called out for me. (I let her assume I was still out jogging.) I now had a choice: I could either start chanting mantras and humming "om-m-m," or I could swallow my pride and holler at the top of my lungs for my beloved.

The latter choice proved to be the one that got me in touch, not with myself, but with a wife who, unmercifully, laughed so hard she cried. After she had her fun, she helped un-pretzel me from that position. Humiliated, I bought her secrecy with a promised shopping excursion. Only after a hot bath could I manage to walk in an upright position.

That experience taught me two things: (1) Don't let your spouse catch you doing dumb things, as you may have to pay big time; (2) meditation is not about a physical posture, rather a heart posture. Before you question my thinking on this, you need to know that I have never considered incorporating Eastern mysticism techniques into my devotional practices. But a lot of folks have—including many professing Christians. And when I encourage Christians to meditate, I have to clarify what I am suggesting.

More than Mantras, Lotus, or Incense

East moved West in the last few decades as Eastern religious thought has taken up residence in the good ol' USA. These teachings are not just being propagated at the local Buddhist temple or Hindu mosque, but they are also being presented in training conferences for Fortune 500 companies, in school curricula, music, video games, medicine, best-selling books, movies, and television shows.

The book *Yoga for Dummies*, which has sold over fifty million copies,[1] shares the basics of Eastern thought concerning the mind/body connection. Americans are buying into these practices—literally. The companion book, *Meditation for Dummies*—which provides simplified meditation practices for novices, plus offers advice on a variety of sitting positions: chair, cushion, bench, and floor—encourages readers to shut the book, close their eyes, and head inward.[2] So, what's the problem with this advice?

Eastern meditation practices include "mind-sitting" or keeping a nonmoving mind. One technique used to accomplish this is keeping a "hwa tou" question to help give the practitioner a don't-know, before-thinking, questioning mind. Using a mantra to calm the mind and strengthen the center is another technique used. The usual technique is to recite the mantra constantly, focus on it, and allow all other thinking to drop away. A commonly used mantra for beginners, which is used in conjunction with a breathing exercise, is the repetition of the words "clear mind" and "dooooooonnn't knnnoooooow." There are other mantras for other purposes that come with the recommendation of repeating them three to ten thousand times in a day.[3]

> Unlike Eastern meditation, biblical meditation empties the mind of wrong thoughts so that it can be filled with what is right and true according to God's Word.

The problem with such meditation exercises is that these practices empty the mind so that something else can fill it. The danger is that it opens the mind up to fleshly or satanic influences. Unlike Eastern meditation, biblical meditation empties the mind of wrong thoughts so that it can be filled with what is right and true according to God's Word. It is objective and has a definite focus (God, his Word, his works, etc.),[4] not subjective with the detached purpose of letting "go of all thinking, opinions, and desires."[5]

We are instructed in Scripture to meditate: "Tremble, and do not sin; Meditate in your heart upon your bed, and be still" (Psalm 4:4 NASB). What is Christian meditation? It is the practice of focusing one's thoughts on God. Christian meditation consists of reflective thinking or contemplation on the things of God to discern their meaning, significance, or God-guided plan of action. The goal of Christian meditation is to internalize and personalize God's Word so that its truth can affect how we think and how we live. Worship, instruction, motivation, and transformation are some of the objectives of meditation.[6] Properly practiced, biblical meditation can bring about an inner peace of mind and a change of life.

Scripture instructs us to meditate on . . .

- God's Word

> Do not let this Book of the Law depart from your mouth; meditate on it day and night, so that you may be careful to do everything written in it. Then you will be prosperous and successful.
>
> —Joshua 1:8

> I will meditate on your precepts.
>
> —Psalm 119:78

This meditation practice is the exercise of reading, dwelling on, pouring over, and continually thinking about revealed truth—God's written revelation, the Bible.

- God's wonders

> I will meditate on your wonders.
>
> —Psalm 119:27

This exercise involves thoughts of God himself and the things that turn our minds toward him. It's thinking about things that only a God who is all-present, all-knowing, and all-powerful could do. It's the idea reflected by the words of the hymn "How Great Thou Art": "O Lord, my God, when I in awesome wonder, consider all the worlds thy hands have made. . . ."

- God's works

> They will speak of the glorious splendor of your majesty, and I will meditate on your wonderful works.
>
> —Psalm 145:5

Biblical meditation is recalling and thinking about the things that God has done in the past—the great biblical accounts of the acts of God in saving his people as well as the gracious acts of God in our lives (especially our own salvation and the ongoing work of the Holy Spirit within us to make us more like Christ).

It should be our goal to make meditation a regular practice in our lives. There are some practical tools that can help us in the discipline of meditation. Some find Scripture memory cards to be great primers for meditation as they aid in focusing on and memorizing Bible passages. These can be easily carried and taken out any time of the day for review. Others prefer to tear out a page of a Bible, fold it up, and pull it out throughout the day. Listening to audio tapes or CDs of Scripture or worship/praise music is another way of meditating on God's Word. Devotional guides—books or magazines—are helpful in providing inspirational and instructional material for contemplation. I often use a hymnal to reflect on the awesome works of God. The key in using these tools is to be alone in a quiet place with no interruptions so you can turn off the world, think about God, and focus on what he would say to you through his Word.

Marilyn has often shared with me about her "dates with God"— where she retreats to peaceful surroundings to spend an entire morning or afternoon alone with God. These dates—which she regularly takes about every three or four weeks—are a time for her to "catch up" on her relationship with God. It is a much-cherished time, where she can be quiet and hear from God. She may meditate on Scripture, pray, or just take a walk with God. And it is a time when she can reflect on what God is doing in and through her life.

Chew on This

Modern gum chewing began in 1869 when a ton of chicle was brought into the United States by exiled Mexican former president and general, Antonio Lopez de Santa Anna (of the infamous Alamo victory), who was living in New Jersey. Santa Anna persuaded Thomas Adams of Staten Island, New York, to buy the Mexican chicle. Adams tried to use the chicle as a rubber substitute, but failed. Noticing that Santa Anna enjoyed chewing the chicle, Adams boiled a small batch of chicle in his kitchen to create a chewing gum. He had hit on a successful creation. In 1871 Adams patented a gum machine so larger quantities could be made and marketed. He added a licorice flavoring to the chewing gum and called it Black Jack. Again, he was very successful.[7]

Scientific studies such as *The Psycho-Dynamics of Chewing* by Dr. H. L. Hollingsworth of Columbia University show how chewing relaxes people while they are working, reduces muscular tension, and helps people feel more at ease. Since chewing gum is acknowledged for helping a person keep alert and wide awake while it eases tension, the Armed Forces supplied chewing gum to the fighting men in World War I, World War II, the Korean War, and the Vietnam War. Today it is included in field and combat rations.[8]

Did you realize that the biblical word for *meditate* reflects the idea of chewing? I'm not talking about chewing your favorite brand of gum. Rather, it is idea of "chew on this." The booklet *A Primer on Meditation* addresses the idea of meditation as chewing. It does this by painting a graphic picture of a cow and her process of mastication, the regurgitation of previously digested food for renewed grinding and its preparation for assimilation. Meditation is "thought digestion"—that is, chewing on various thoughts deliberately and thoroughly, and mulling them over in the mind and heart. It is the processing of mental food. "What metabolism is to the physical body of a cow, meditation is to your mental and spiritual life."[9]

A recent *Psychology Today* focused on the work of Herbert Benson, M.D., the Mind/Body Medical Institute Associate Professor of Medicine at Harvard Medical School. It delineated some of the profound physiological effects of meditation on the body: "Studies have shown that, among other benefits, meditation can help reverse heart disease, the number-one killer in the U.S. It can reduce pain and enhance the body's immune system, enabling it to better fight disease."[10]

Meditation is so vital to the life of a child of God, that the psalmist declared its benefits:

> Blessed is the man
>   who does not walk in the counsel of the wicked
> or stand in the way of sinners
>   or sit in the seat of mockers.
> But his delight is in the law of the LORD,
>   and on his law he meditates day and night.

He is like a tree planted by streams of water,
which yields its fruit in season
and whose leaf does not wither.
Whatever he does prospers.

—Psalm 1:1–3

When he was emperor, Napoleon would sometimes stretch out on the settee near the fireplace and appear to be dozing. His aides soon learned, however, that he was meditating. Napoleon explained to them, "If I always seem to be ready for everything, to face up to anything, it is because I never undertake anything at all without first having meditated for a long time and foreseen what might happen. It is not a genie, but meditation, that suddenly reveals to me in secret, what I must say or do under circumstances not anticipated by others."[11]

> The benefits of meditation include an alertness to God and a heightened awareness of how to deal with sinful thoughts when they come.

We, too, need to meditate on the inevitable thought attacks and how we will handle them when they come. The benefits of meditation include an alertness to God and a heightened awareness of how to deal with sinful thoughts when they come. It helps us to un-cage our sinful thoughts and hold on to God-thoughts. How do we go about doing this? The story of Cindy illustrates this solution and perhaps will encourage you in your struggles.

Caged Fear

Cindy is a lovely, godly, and wise woman—formerly a pharmacist, now a full-time homemaker—who is a dear friend, as well as prayer partner, to Marilyn. She is married to a physician and has one teenage daughter—all of whom love the Lord. Cindy has been battling health problems off and on—mostly on—for more than eleven years. It was through her battle with chronic fatigue syndrome (CFS) and viral pancreatitis—a complication of the CFS—that God began showing Cindy how fear had permeated her life.

Cindy allowed Marilyn to read through the pages of her private journal for us to better understand what someone—a strong believer—goes through when faced with debilitating health challenges year after year. I was greatly moved by her articulate and honest description of her struggles with her thought-life during suffering:

> Worry and fear were inbred in my family and were passed down to me. I grew up thinking that worry was normal and that everyone worried about one thing or the other. In fact, I was deceived into thinking that if I worried enough about a given problem, then that concern would never come to pass. I falsely believed worrying was a way to control my situation.
>
> It was not until I came down with CFS that the Lord began to show me insights into those dark places in my heart where worry and fear lived freely and operated uncontrollably. Physical exhaustion took me off the fast track of endless volunteering. Sidelined—with plenty of time to evaluate my life—I began to realize that at the root of my busy-ness was the fear of rejection or not being accepted. This had been the driving force in my life for years of pouring myself out through endless "Yes, I can help do that" or "I'd be glad to lend a hand." I began to see that I had failed to set sensible, healthy boundaries in my life because of my deep need to please other people. This kind of lifestyle also robbed me of intimacy with God because I was too busy with so many "good" activities and "worthy" causes that I ignored my health and family time.
>
> During the years I suffered with chronic fatigue, my thinking dramatically changed. Knowing God became my passion and being with my family became a new priority. Realizing peace—the fruit of abiding and trusting in God instead of worrying and being fearful—transformed my motives for serving others. Life began to take on new meaning—and so did my prayer life. Christ's presence became more of a reality in my

daily life and prayer became an ongoing conversation with him throughout the day—and the sustaining force in my life. I began to truly understand that my worth was based on whose I am rather than in my performance. What a relief to know that, with my having CFS and so little energy!

God blessed me with four years of renewed strength and energy following my five-year bout with CFS. However, the freedom of improved health came to an abrupt halt one day when my mouth was over-stretched in a root cleaning procedure, and one of my TMJ discs was permanently dislodged. It was the beginning of a still ongoing battle with TMJ, which has ensued for more than two years, and after a year, turned into chronic facial myofacial pain or fibromyalgia, which now affects my whole body. I couldn't believe it when I was injured in this way. Why would God allow this to happen? What was it that I was supposed to learn this time? When was I going to be pain-free again? Again, worry and fear surfaced in my life.

This new health crisis has been tough—on me, my husband, and my teenage daughter. To keep from disturbing my husband with my getting up and down all night to handle the pain, I moved into the guest bedroom. Once again I battle worry about how this is going to affect our marriage. Kissing has been difficult—as has been laughing too hard, talking on the phone, singing, doing anything that touches the temporal area of my head or scalp. I have not been able to chew anything but mush since my jaw locked three months after the TMJ began. Because I have grown so disabled, I am not able to go to many of my daughter's school functions and do many of the mother-daughter things I would love to do with her. My husband has had to assume household chores that I formerly was able to do. I have not been able to go to church for many months. And my family doesn't want to go without me.

I am again struggling with fear—the fear of how my illness will impact our family. The battle of my thoughts continues to rage: Will my husband get tired of it all and abandon me? Will my daughter resent my not being able to do more for—and with—her? Will my friends desert me since I am getting worse instead of better? Will my parents understand because I can no longer make the long journey to visit them out-of-state? I am angry with you, God, for allowing all of this to happen. If I can't trust you, Lord, to take care of me, whom can I trust? My innermost being screams for your help and healing.

Suffering has brought me face to face with fear and its source: Satan. I have been learning how to replace his lies with God's truths. Satan wants me to doubt God's goodness, love, and faithfulness. I must fight my true adversary, Satan, with God's Word. God does not give me this spirit of fear, but rather he offers me a spirit of love and a sound mind. I must thank God that he will never leave or forsake me—and that he will meet my every need according to the glorious riches in Christ.

And truly God has been faithful through the pain! He has taken me to greater levels of spiritual intimacy with him. He has transformed my worship into warm, peaceful retreats into his presence. Now I sense his presence with me wherever I go. Through deeper worship, God's amazing love and grace toward me have been made more glorious and overwhelming than ever before! I am able to look at these many years of incapacitating health problems as a season of repose with a divine purpose that—although I do not understand the "why" of it all right now—is preparing me for God's ultimate use of my life. As I am being renewed in my thinking, I am beginning to sense God's call on my life to impact others through the careful and deliberate stewardship of these experiences.

> Each of us needs to ask the question, "What wrong thinking have I kept caged inside of me that I must now release?"

Cindy's uncaging her fearful thoughts was necessary to her taking those first steps toward victory over these destructive thoughts. As difficult as that was for her, it became the key to her getting on with her life and becoming empowered to deal with any future fear. Her uncaging action has changed her perspective from being inward-focused to being ministry-focused. Each of us needs to ask the question, "What wrong thinking have I kept caged inside of me that I must now release?"

Uncaging Your Thoughts

While conducting a revival, I was asked by the host pastor to accompany him on a visit to share the gospel with a couple who weren't Christians. As we approached their house, he warned me, "Jay, they have two big birds. One is very friendly and the other is very mean. Let's pray that the mean one is caged."

When we arrived at the home, we realized that the pastor's worst fear had come to pass: The mean bird was out. In a matter of moments, the evil bird flew over, landed on my pastor friend's shoulder, and began pecking the back of his head with his beak. This fowl-feathered fiend was no Tweety bird. I could see all of this out of the corner of my eye, and I had to bite my tongue to keep from bursting into laughter. I began praying that God would send a mean ol' "putty-tat" before that malevolent bird got to me!

As we left the house, my friend was in pain and the back of his head bleeding. When we got in the car, I asked him why he didn't say anything to the couple about their sinister bird. He said that he didn't want to say anything as it might offend the couple. While that couple didn't make a profession of Christian faith that day, I'm sure they were impressed that this man of God could keep smiling even while being attacked by their demonic bird.

Unlike that mean bird that, when uncaged, wreaked havoc, our sinful and wrong thoughts must be uncaged in order to bring us peace of mind. Releasing them is a necessary first step in getting them out in the light so God can help us to overcome them. The earlier in life that we can start cleaning out our caged thoughts, the better.

Quinton, a high school junior, was quite open about his thought life when interviewed for this book. Like many teens, he has struggled with thoughts of insecurity: "I never wanted people to know who I really was, because I was scared they'd reject who I was." At some point in the previous year, Quinton had come to the realization about his peers: "They're just as insecure as me." Tearing down the façade he had been constructing since middle school years, he determined no longer to live a life of "fakeness" and that from here on out he was "gonna make it" just being himself.

When asked about present thought challenges, Quinton said that he struggled with the typical guy sexual temptations. While he strives to live a disciplined Christian life, he says, "I will have just prayed five minutes earlier—no, two seconds earlier—that I would overcome an image in my mind and not dwell on it, and then I go there! It's so tough." When asked how that impacted his relationship with God, Quinton replied, "When I give in, I feel nasty on the inside. Fellowship with God is usually disrupted for a while."

I can relate to this young Christian man. I have fought the same thought battles since my teen years—with the issue of acceptance continuing to plague me. To be real transparent with you, I think a lot about what people think about me and what they will say about me. I struggle with thoughts that I am inadequate, unqualified, and unable to lead. At times, I battle thoughts of doubt and disappointment with God. There are times I feel my mind is in a boxing ring where bitter thoughts, depressing thoughts, and negative thoughts are winning that round.

If I were to let you see inside my caged thoughts, you'd see that I struggle with thoughts of how I am showing my love and devotion to my family: *Am I spending enough time with my family? Am I being the husband I need to be, when I can't seem to leave work at work? Am I so consumed with my ministry that I miss the little things at home?*

And if I were comfortable enough to show you around the cage, you'd see that I personally battle the thoughts: *How can I as a man of God—who is passionately committed to the Word of God and who is in it for hours each day—think such godless and evil thoughts? How could I even entertain such impure things in my mind? Why did I allow that thought to stay in my mind, when I should have immediately confessed it to God and dealt with it? Why did I enjoy that sinful thought?*

What thoughts do you have caged up? Are they thoughts about a sin stronghold in your life? Your career? Personal doubts and fears? Family issues? Financial worries? A survey of 1,500 men attending a Promise Keepers gathering indicated the following:

- Almost three-quarters reported that their sexual thoughts concern them.
- Half fantasize about having sex with women other than their wives.
- Half struggle with masturbation.
- A third reported enjoyment in looking regularly at sexually oriented material, including videos and magazines.
- Fifteen percent reported they were sexually unfaithful to their spouse.[12]

If we were to uncage our thoughts, what would fly out? Would our family and friends be shocked at what is caged up inside of our mind? Until we are willing to release those thoughts—wrong, negative, lustful, condemning, fearful, worrisome thoughts—nothing is going to change. Will it be painful? No doubt. Will it happen overnight? No way. It is a learned, lifelong process. To attempt to fill our mind with the right thoughts while hanging on to sinful thoughts is like trying to pump fresh water into a sewer. Pure and defiled thoughts cannot live peaceably in the same mind cage. "A double minded man is unstable in all his ways" (James 1:8 KJV). Don't you think it's time to clean out the cage? How? Let's address that next.

Replacement Thought Therapy

Once the cage has been opened and the "mean birds"—that is, sinful thoughts—have been uncaged, we must immediately seek to replace them with "good birds" or right thoughts. To simply leave the cage empty guarantees that the sinful thoughts will return.

This process, which we call "replacement thought therapy," is outlined and advised in Scripture:

Finally, brethren, whatsoever things are true, whatsoever things *are* honest, whatsoever things *are* just, whatsoever things *are* pure, whatsoever things *are* lovely, whatsoever things *are* of good report, if *there be* any virtue and if there be any praise, think on these things.

—Philippians 4:8 KJV

When you read that phrase *"Think on these things,"* do you think to yourself, "Sure. But first tell me how to rid my mind of all these other things that I have to think about just to survive my week"? How can you think on these things instead of less desirable thoughts? You must first decide what kind of thoughts you want to occupy your thought life. And then resolve to do it—with God's help.

In his commentary on this passage of Scripture, William Barclay writes:

> The human mind will always set itself on something and Paul wished to be quite sure that the Philippians would set their minds on the right things. This is something of the utmost importance, because it is a law of life that, *if a man thinks of something often enough, he will come to the stage when he cannot stop thinking about it* [italics mine]. His thoughts will be quite literally in a groove out of which he cannot jerk them. It is therefore, of the first importance that a man should set his thoughts upon the fine things and here Paul makes a list of them.[13]

Paul doesn't just tell us to quit thinking about wrong things, he shows us how to replace them with the right thoughts. Consider how this replacement thought therapy prescribed by "Dr. Paul" might work for you:

Replacement Thought Therapy

Instead of thinking about things that are . . .	*Replace them with things that are . . .*
Not true, deceptive, illusory	"True": genuine, authentic
Flippant, cheap, dishonest	"Honest": valuable, worthy of our time and not a waste of it
Wrong, immoral, unjust	"Just": encourage moral or right living
Impure, evil	"Pure": make us more kind, attractive, and loving

Filled with bitterness or lead to vengeance	"Lovely": admirable qualities, attractive, kind, winsome, sympathetic
Unfit for a Christian to say	"Of good report": evoke words you wouldn't mind God hearing
Immoral, vice-inviting	"Virtuous": lead to moral courage, integrity, and character
Worthless and fail to commend those who need to be affirmed and encouraged	"Praiseworthy": prompt us to affirm and encourage those who are doing something praiseworthy

The result of trying replacement thought therapy can be an incomparable peace of mind, a mind filled with thoughts that produce right living and true joy in the Lord.

Let me offer an example. Suppose someone does something that offends or hurts you. Such an experience could easily lead to bitterness in your heart or a desire for vengeance. Rather than acting on your pain, you decide to give this replacement thought therapy a try. You first have to deal with any feelings of unforgiveness in your own heart. Once you have done that, you have a choice: act on feelings or choose right actions.

As a rule, following one's feelings doesn't lead to doing the right thing, but right actions usually lead to right feelings.

As a rule, following one's feelings doesn't lead to doing the right thing, but right actions usually lead to right feelings. Instead of harboring anger or hurt—or choosing to retaliate—you try praying for that person for however long it takes for God to work on your heart and prompt you to act in a Christ-like way toward that person. When you are ready for right action, you do the unexpected. It might be to write the "offender" a note of encouragement or do something kind for that person. Rather than getting even, sincerely try to see that individual as Christ would see him or her—genuinely look to find something positive to appreciate.

I have discovered that given time and the right motives, this replacement method works. It may not always work on that other person (although most often it does), but it always does on me, helping me to become more like Christ.

Fill 'Er Up!

Abner Doble built the ultimate steam car in the early 1900s. These Doble locomobiles could reach full steam from cold in under 90 seconds, could run up to 1,500 miles on only 24 gallons of water, and had an efficient four-cylinder 75-bhp steam engine. The problem was the cost: $8,000 for a car in 1917 was too much. A less expensive but still exceptional $2,000 model was released in 1924—but it still was too much to pay when a gasoline engine car could be purchased for less than $1,000.[14]

The energy "shortfall" our nation is experiencing may push us to consider all kinds of solutions for our fuel pump blues. BMW is committing a lot of engineering resources to see if hydrogen, the simplest and most abundant element in the universe, might be the answer to our energy and clean air concerns. The German auto giant has developed a hydrogen vehicle that reportedly feels and operates like a normal car.

While these hydrogen sedans are not on the market yet, these cars can run on either liquefied hydrogen or gasoline. While hydrogen is the lightest element, it has some tricky characteristics. It only becomes liquid at dramatically low temperatures: minus 423 degrees Fahrenheit. To keep the fuel that cold, fuel tanks in the BMW are made of seventy layers of fiberglass and aluminum. Experts claim that fueling with hydrogen, the fuel of both the Hindenburg and the Challenger, is no more a risk than fueling with conventional automobile fuels.[15]

Okay, if that sounds too risky for you, have you considered the veggie car, the world's first sports car that runs on rotting vegetables? The car, known as the Advantage R, goes from 0 to 60 mph in under six seconds and can reach a top speed of 130 mph. Tests have shown that 220 pounds of smelly garbage will power this car for 62 miles. Developed by a Swiss manufacturer, the car runs on two sources of power: conventional gasoline and kompagas—a renewable fuel source made from rotting greenery.[16]

Finding the best fuel source is important—for automobiles and individuals. If we choose to fill our spiritual tanks with the rotting garbage that the world offers, we will quickly end up in a place where God never intended for us to go. In fact, he continually warns us in Scripture to carefully avoid those things that lead to wrong thoughts, which in turn lead to wrong actions. Those who desire to experience God cannot run on sinful thoughts and go forward spiritually.

We need to pull up to God's filling station every day and say through our obedience to his Word, "Fill 'er up!"

We live in a world where we continually have to make the choice whether to fill up at the world's or God's filling station. Choosing or not choosing high-octane spiritual fuel determines whether or not we are able to go the distance for Christ. Many seem to be flirting with an empty tank spiritually and are running on the fumes of past spiritual experiences. Some are filling up with the cheap substitutes of the latest spiritual fad or the newest program, yet they miss the fuel that God promises will allow them to run the race of life with maximum effectiveness. What is this high-octane spiritual fuel?

> Being filled with the Holy Spirit
> Being filled with the Word of God
> Being filled with faith in God
> Being filled with the joy of God
> Being filled with the peace of God
> Being filled with the love of God
> Being filled with the power of God
> Being filled with unceasing prayer

God's filling station must be continually visited. Waiting until the gauge is on -3/4, -1/2, -1/4—or especially if it's on "E"—is a dangerous thing. Only when the mind is filled—or occupied—with the things of God do we have any chance to rid ourselves of those thoughts not of

God. We need to pull up to God's filling station every day and say through our obedience to his Word, "Fill 'er up!"

God's filling station is open 24/7—even on holidays. The nearest location is a close as pulling up to an open Bible—reading, meditating on, studying, memorizing, and applying it. Furthermore, you will want the special additive of prayer added to your tank.

God has also located filling stations in the local church, the Body of Christ, where God's Word is faithfully taught. At this full-service station, you can refill your tank in corporate worship and Bible study. This station also has rest facilities for the tired and needy, as well as spiritual concessions for the hungry and thirsty. You will further be trained in the how-to's of self-service.

So, what fuel do you select? The Bible instructs us that we should be "filled with the Holy Spirit" (Ephesians 5:18) to operate with maximum efficiency. This holy Attendant seeks to service our vehicle from the inside out by draining us of our plans, desires, and ways, and then of filling us up with himself—a never-to-be-exhausted, premium-grade fuel supply. In being filled by and with the Holy Spirit, we will enjoy a smoother ride and better mileage in our Christian journey. And all we have to do is say, "Fill 'er up!"

The second step in the S.T.O.P. method of *Taming Your Private Thoughts* has been introduced: *Think on these things.* God's Word tells us, "Whatever is true, whatever is noble, whatever is right, whatever is pure, whatever is lovely, whatever is admirable—if anything is excellent or praiseworthy—think about such things" (Philippians 4:8).

So often in life, we are simply told *Stop!, Quit!,* or *Don't!* regarding something that is sinful. While the S.T.O.P. strategy encourages you to stop sinful thoughts, it doesn't leave you there with just your hand slapped. It guides you to a better way to

1. **S**inful thoughts confessed
   1 John 1:9
2. **T**hink on these things
   Philippians 4:8
3. **O**rder every thought
   2 Corinthians 10:5
4. **P**ursue Christ-mindedness
   Collossians 3:2

know success in the thought battle and provides the tools to replace wrong thinking with godly thinking.

It has been said, "We can't choose our relatives, but we can choose our thoughts, which influence us much more."[17] Once sinful thoughts are exchanged for God-honoring thoughts, the next principle in this method is to . . .

O. Order Every Thought

Since we began this book, my wife has put me on the Weight Watchers point system. The number of points—equaling how much food a Weight Watcher can eat—is determined by a person's weight. *Great!* I reasoned early on. *If I gain more weight, then I could have more points. And more points means more food.* When I shared this stroke of genius with my wife-slash-personal-diet-counselor, she quickly burst that bubble. "Sure," she said, "go ahead, dear, but remember you will lose points with me." I quickly decided against this ingenious plan.

Soon I learned to survive on my allotted points. One of the best things I do is to bank a few extra points for my Sunday night, after-church pig-out. My indulgence routine goes something like this: Return from preaching my fourth service of the day; put on my worn-out red and white athletic shorts that I've dug out of the trash more than once and my 1998 Master's Golf Tournament T-shirt; sit in my comfortable recliner; turn on *Touched by an Angel;* and wait for the Pizza Hut delivery person to make my day by ringing my doorbell.

One Sunday night not long ago, my mouth was salivating over just the thoughts of devouring those delicious extra points when the doorbell rang. I sprang to my feet and nearly tripped over the dog as I rushed to the front door. The money-for-food exchange was made, and alas! Heaven-in-a-box was now in my possession and pizza aroma was within my smell-zone.

As I tore into the box, I could not believe my eyes. Was this some kind of sick joke? I ordered pepperoni pizza with green peppers and onions, but what I got was anchovies and mushrooms. Oh, you need to understand I hate anchovies and mushrooms—no, not with a mild hatred, but with an enthusiastic passion. You might be able to guess where my thought life went from there. "Praise the Lord" or "Hallelujah" did not cross my mind at that point. And I most definitely failed to "count it all joy."

While messing up my pizza order was only a temporary—albeit painful to me—irritation, screwing up other orders could have profound, if not deadly consequences. If a police commander's orders were garbled by a poor radio transmission, and instead of "Hold your fire!" being heard by an officer, only the partial order "Fire!" was heard, the results could be tragic. If a physician's orders were improperly read and the wrong medication given to someone, a critical health crisis could arise. It is important that orders be carefully given and followed.

Giving or receiving wrong orders can greatly impact an outcome. We have been taught in church that we are to order our thoughts. How this is carried out affects everything we do—our actions, our words, our attitude, and our relationship to Christ. Just how are we supposed to order our thoughts? The apostle Paul instructs us that we are to give orders to our thoughts by holding every thought prisoner and making each thought submit to Christ:

> The weapons we fight with are not the weapons of the world. On the contrary, they have divine power to demolish strongholds. We demolish arguments and every pretension that sets itself against the knowledge of God, and we take captive every thought to make it obedient to Christ.
>
> —2 Corinthians 10:4–5

Battles with wrong thinking are won or lost in the mind. The thought battle is not a war that can be fought with M–16s, F–15s, tanks, or even Smart bombs. It is not a physical war, but a powerful, unseen, spiritual war. Victory or defeat will follow what we do with our thoughts. The Holy Spirit has supplied divinely powerful weapons for the destruction of the strongholds in our life: truth, righteousness, evangelism, faith, salvation, the Word of God, and prayer (Ephesians 6:14ff).[1]

Paul employs a number of military metaphors in 2 Corinthians 10:4–5. The "strongholds" that are being fought belong to the realm of will and intellect. "Argument" refers to reasoning that opposes godly thinking. This kind of argument is based on a purely human perspective. "Pretension" is an allegation that opposes God's viewpoint. Hence, Christian warfare is aimed at fighting thinking that elevates human reason devoid of the truths of God. Biblical scholar Philip Hughes writes, "To the Greek of Paul's day, who epitomized the worshipper of human wisdom, the word of the Cross was mere foolishness."[2] And this is not a one-time military action. The tense of the Greek verb indicates an ongoing process, a daily battle where the battlefield is our thought life.

> **Battles with wrong thinking are won or lost in the mind.**

We are told to "take captive every thought to make it obedient to Christ" (v. 5). The military imagery paints a picture of not only destroying the enemy's strongholds, but also of taking prisoners of war. These prisoners are the thoughts that are not on the side of godly thinking. They are the thoughts that the enemy would have infiltrate the ranks of pure, Christ-mindedness. In fact, the word "thought" in this verse is the same Greek word translated as "schemes" in 2 Corinthians 2:11 and is used of Satan's tactical warfare against us: ". . . in order that Satan might not outwit us. For we are not unaware of his schemes." This word means a device, a purpose, a design. Our thoughts can become devices—when not under the control of Christ—that assist Satan in strengthening his grip on our lives. That's precisely why Satan targets the mind. Consider the following example of arguments opposing biblical thinking.

Turner Thought Around

While addressing the United Nations World Peace Summit, American media mogul Ted Turner denounced his own childhood Christian faith.

To the approval of a thousand whooping delegates, Turner remarked in his off-the-cuff speech, "I turned away from Christianity when I discovered it was intolerant, because it taught we were the only ones going to heaven. That confused the devil out of me since that would have left heaven a very empty place." To the cheering approval of the audience, Turner praised "indigenous" religious faiths. He said that he realized that there was one God but multiple ways God manifests himself, and that it makes little difference which way to God is chosen.[3]

Turner's words provide us with a vivid example of a pretentious argument set up in opposition to sound biblical thinking. Although many praised him for what he said, his words were an attack on all faiths that profess an exclusive component, like Christianity and Islam.[4] This is not a new stance for Turner, who late in 1989 told the *Dallas Morning News* that "Christianity is a religion for losers." He went on to say in that interview that Christ shouldn't have bothered to die on the cross: "I don't want anybody to die for me. I've had a few drinks and a few girlfriends, and if that's gonna put me in hell, then so be it."[5] In the minds of many in our country and around the world, Turner's success in building a media empire qualifies him as a voice of authority. The problem is that his voice—which sounds a lot like the voice of the Greeks of Paul's day—speaks contrary to the Word of God.

> We are to deliberately place every thought under the control of Christ, not by request or suggestion but by command.

Whatever the sinful or wrong thoughts, we are to take immediate action to counter those thoughts, to turn them around. Our actions have nothing to do with feelings but with the exercise of the will to do what God has told us to do. We are to deliberately place every thought under the control of Christ, not by request or suggestion but by command. We are to refuse to allow any thought that is not of God to remain without an assault on our part. Those thoughts are to be bound, dragged away, and executed.[6]

That's where the S.T.O.P. method breaks up the sinful thought process. It involves action: our honestly saying to God, "This thought I am having is sinful and wrong. It violates what your Word says about my keeping a pure mind. I confess it now to you and seek your intervention as I place this thought under Christ's authority." This is not a once-and-for-all prayer. It is a daily, sometimes hourly, even minute-by-minute prayer.

Recently, while I was on an out-of-town trip to a denominational conference center, my mind was bombarded with negative, jealous, and unforgiving thoughts. I could feel my entire body tense up as I battled this assault on my thought life. Out of nowhere, I was being confronted with personal, unresolved issues that went back many years where I had not dealt with painful feelings about certain people and situations within my denomination. These feelings, when stirred up again inside of me, made me feel insecure and lonely. I could tell God was earnestly attempting to get me to face these issues and deal with them.

Late that night I went out for an extended run, something I often do when I need to do specific business with God. While running, I told God that I was ready to stop the thoughts. I asked him to help me apply the S.T.O.P. method to my problem. Right then . . .

1. I confessed my sinful thoughts to God—no excuses, no argument, and no blame.
2. I began to think on the things that God had given to me rather than think about what I didn't have or what people weren't doing for me.
3. I ordered these wrong thoughts to get under the control of Christ and made them submit to his authority.
4. I asked God to help me be Christ-minded regarding these issues and allow me to think about this situation the way Christ would think about it.

For me to tell you that it no longer entered my mind or bothered me would be wrong. However, I will tell you that since that run with God, I have had an undeniable freedom over this stronghold.

The consequences of our not ordering every thought is alluded to by Paul in 2 Corinthians 10:4, where he uses the term "stronghold": "On the contrary, they have divine power to demolish strongholds." When we fail to order our thoughts, a stronghold or sin habit can develop in areas we once formerly had under control. However, when we allow sinful thoughts to remain without a God-intervention and fail to order them to line up under Christ's authority, they begin to control us.

Multitudes of people—including Christians—live in the grips of sin habits because they have not learned to shackle those thoughts. Freedom is realized through replacing sinful thoughts with God-thoughts and learning to live in the grip of God's grace.

Bottomless Grace

Everything was going great in his ministry when the bottom fell out of Larry McFadden's life.[7] The previous year had been a tough one for this forty-something-year-old minister. Larry recounted, "It was one of the most hellacious times I have ever lived through—with one high-level stressor after another, one big deal ministry event every month. I was never at peace. I began to ask myself, 'Is this it? Am I to spend the rest of my life doing this?'"

While he loved his church, the people, and his ministry position, Larry had come to the crossroads that many his age approach and asked, "Is there more for me?" Larry explained, "I struggled with every decision. I no longer was able to clearly know God's will for my life. My relationship with God was very strained. All of these factors also contributed to some rocky times in my marriage, as well."

Restless and vulnerable, physically exhausted and emotionally drained—the worst time to make an important decision—Larry accepted a call to be minister of music at a church in another state, which he soon began to question.

> When we were cleaning the house after the movers had all the furniture out, I stood there in the family room and broke down in tears. I was scared to death about going. Had I not been concerned about Teresa's [his wife's] reaction, I would have backed out. Teresa had no idea of the turmoil going on inside of me. I talked to no one about it. I thought I could handle it. It never crossed my mind that I needed to open up and tell someone—especially her—what I was feeling.

Almost immediately upon arrival, my life began to crumble. As soon as I took the hitch off my van at the U-Haul place, I sat on the steps and said to myself, "What in the world have I done? What am I doing here?" I had this sinking feeling inside that I had failed God and my family. I had missed God's will—in a big way—and I was never again going to have an effective ministry. I had blown it.

It was that "thought tape" that played over and over in Larry's mind that day and in the coming days.

We had been in Teresa's "dream house" for only a few days when I got up one morning and struggled to go into the office. I stayed at the church for only five minutes before I turned around and went back home. When I got there, I asked Teresa to come into the family room where I was pacing back and forth like a caged animal. As soon as she entered the room, I blurted out, "We've made a grave mistake. We're going back to Orlando."

She looked at me as if I had lost my mind and said, "No, we are not going back. We are going to deal with whatever this is."

I listened to Teresa. We stayed and sought godly counsel from two of the pastors in my former church. I didn't feel I could talk to anyone else—especially the folks at my new church. I also went to a professional counselor a few weeks later, who informed me I was in clinical depression. That explained a lot as I didn't understand the person I had become. Not only was I totally confused about what was going on inside of me, my wife didn't understand what had happened to her husband, my children to their father, and my parents to their son. Without a doubt, it was the darkest time of my life.

I stayed near or in tears all the time. I was sullen and withdrawn—which is the opposite of my normal personality. I experienced sleepless nights, weight loss, and reoccurring physical problems—including the loss of my voice, which was devastating to me as it was an essential instrument of my ministry. I felt spiritually abandoned. I couldn't pray. I couldn't study God's Word. I had no spiritual sensitivity whatsoever. I was devastated at the thought that I had missed God's will. Gripped with fear, I overreacted to my regret and remorse of uprooting my family and making this move by throwing an internal temper tantrum. Downward I spiraled to depths of emotional, physical, and spiritual depression that I had never before known. The person I had known as Larry was gone.

I suffered for ten agonizing months. Finally, one day during my "quiet time" with God, I cried out *Where are you, God, in all of this?* God the Holy Spirit spoke to my heart and said, "Larry, I am right where I have always been. I am standing right next to the Refiner's fire controlling the heat and the amount of time you are to undergo the purification process." Oh, I cannot tell you the difference this realization made in my thinking! The Lord further assured me, "You have not missed my will, you're right in the middle of it. And, I have a plan for you."

> As sure as God puts His children in the furnace of affliction, He will be with them in it.
>
> —C.H. SPURGEON

This was the turning point in my recovery. I was finally able to stop the incessant playing of the "I have failed God" tape in my mind. I began to see a ray of hope, and the healing process had begun. While I did not receive an instantaneous healing, I did receive enough day-by-day strength to be able to trust in God's Word and begin the climb up from the bottom of the pit I had been in for so long. Hopelessness and worthlessness in my thinking began to be replaced with affirming thoughts. I had not been suffering from the consequences of my sin or my failure to make a choice God wanted me to make. Rather, it was because of the mysterious ways God was working in me to ultimately bring him greater glory in and through my life and ministry. By God's grace, I was freed of depression's hold on my life and allowed to enjoy a fullness in my relationship to Christ, in my life, in my marriage, and in my ministry as I had never known before.

Don't Go There

"Don't go there!" is a popular phrase many of us use when we want to avoid having someone say something we don't want to hear. Uncomfortable and unpleasant conversations aren't the only places which can be declared off-limits. There are, literally, some geographic locations we are warned not to go.

An ABC News special report featured Robert Pelton, lead writer and publisher of *Fielding's The World's Most Dangerous Places*. Pelton shares his frenetically typed diaries with ABC News as he travels to places listed on the State Department's travel warnings list. His goal "in going there" is to get to the real truth about why those places are considered so dangerous. "When I am interested in something, I don't trust journalists and politicians to explain it for me." His passport has stamps from Afghanistan, Albania, India, Iran, Iraq, Israel, North Korea, Pakistan, Rwanda, Sudan, Somalia, Turkey, and Uganda, among other countries.[8]

I found it of particular interest to read Pelton's rating of places Europeans regard as dangerous.[9]

Europeans' Most Dangerous Places

Florida	42%
North Africa	9%
Turkey	7%
California	7%
Kenya	7%

I doubt few Americans would have listed the same places. And I know that I as a Florida resident would not agree with the thinking of the Europeans. From my perspective, Florida is a safe place to go and live. For those who have heard scattered reports of the victimization of tourists at times in our state, Florida, I'm sure, seems like a dangerous place to go. And so it is with our perception of what are the dangerous places for us to go in our thought lives.

How do we decide what is truly dangerous for us or not? For someone who is trying to cultivate a pure thought life, there are some dangerous places that God has told us to stay away from. To go and investigate for ourselves, like Pelton on his find-out-for-myself visits, would be dangerous in itself, because it would threaten pure thoughts. We simply must accept God's Word as the truth about that sin location. These spiritually dangerous hot spots must be avoided. We must not pack our bags and go— physically or mentally—to any place that invites sinful thoughts or attacks pure thoughts.

> We must not pack our bags and go—physically or mentally—to any place that invites sinful thoughts or attacks pure thoughts.

Do you remember the children's song with the words "Oh, be careful little eyes what you see"? We men especially have to guard what we see or our eyes will quickly take us on a dangerous trip. I have developed my own personal list of dangerous thought places for men:

- gazing at women to whom you are not married—because of their physical features or the way they are dressed
- perusing catalogs or advertisements that are provocative, such as Victoria's Secret ads featuring scantily clad women
- ogling pornographic magazines
- looking at websites featuring celebrity hot pics or graphic sexual material
- viewing television shows with sexual content, such as late-night programming, scrambled-yet-clear-enough-to-see adult premium channels, three-minute promos for "mature audiences only" movies on cable and satellite, and pay-per-view in motels away from home
- watching movies and videos with sexual content

- checking out any place where you can more easily be bombarded with sinful thoughts, such as parties where inhibitions are lowered

In interviewing Dr. David Clarke,[10] a popular speaker and outstanding Christian psychologist in Tampa, Marilyn and I asked him what was the Number One problem for which men sought his help. Without hesitation he responded, "Issues related to sex. I constantly see men who are struggling with sexual fantasy, physical aspects of sex, visual traps such as the Internet, as well as the ability to focus exclusively on their wives during sex. In this sex-drenched society, men are being bombarded with sex. It's overwhelming."

When we asked Dr. Clarke for practical counsel regarding men who have abused the Internet, he offered this recommendation: "First the man must stay off the computer for six months. He must be accountable to someone—his wife, if he is married—to have the password and not allow him access until then. Thereafter, his spouse or accountability partner should regularly check this man's computer history to make sure he is not accessing inappropriate sites. Also, he must confess his sin by telling his wife and accountability partner all he has done on the Internet—not the gory details, just a basic sketch: the kind of sites or chat rooms accessed, the times spent visiting those sites, and the length of time online."

In their book *Every Man's Battle*, Stephen Arterburn and Fred Stoeker give helpful counsel for all men—young and old—on how to stay away from the day-in-day-out "dangerous places" that accost the eyes. Their advice is to bounce and starve the eyes: "You can win this battle by training your eyes to bounce away from sights of pretty women and sensual images. If you 'bounce' your eyes for six weeks, you can win this war. When your eyes bounce toward a woman, they must bounce away immediately." Starving the eyes means you refuse to look at that which would produce impure thoughts, such as attractions that threaten everything you hold dear.[11]

I can attest to the fact that when followed, this advise works. Case in point: My son, Will, and I enjoyed great seats at a thrilling Texas Rangers' baseball game. Nolan Ryan was pitching. As I was sitting there, I thought, "You know, it just doesn't get any better than this." But then enter a minor-, I mean major-, league distraction into that idyllic scene.

A man who was connected with an adult dance establishment in the area brought one of his female employees with him as his escort to the game. Given her attire—or lack thereof—me thinks she must have thought she was still at the club instead of at the ballgame. The couple sat right in front of us—which was kind of a distraction. But then she kept getting up and parading up and down the steps. Did I say that this was a major distraction? Oh, this wanting-to-stay-pure-in-thoughts dad activated his bounce and starve system immediately! Then I looked at my son—who was no longer focused on the ballgame—and reacted by putting my hands over his eyes at key times. As I sat there, I kept thinking of that Bible verse: "If your right eye causes you to sin gouge it out and throw it away" (Matthew 5:29)—and I didn't intend for either one of us to leave the ball park at Arlington blind!

When I e-mailed Marilyn this section of the chapter and asked if she thought I should also list dangerous places for women, she immediately e-responded with the less-than-exuding-confidence-in-my-ability response: "Sure, Jay, that would be awesome. I would love to see your list! (Tee-hee-hee-hee.) Do it without any Angie-input. Let's see if you have us gals figured out yet. Give it your best shot. And don't cheat!" If she weren't my dear sister in Christ and my please-be-honest-with-me writing partner, I might have taken offense at her comments.

The pressure was on. I had something to prove to that cocky-in-this, I-dare-you-to-try-to-figure-us-out woman. Where are the dangerous places for women's thoughts? I then remembered the second verse of that children's song which goes, "Oh, be careful little ears what you hear." I'm not suggesting that women cannot be affected by what they see. Of course they can. There is no doubt that women whose eyes are unguarded can fantasize over what they see. However, often it's what goes in the ears that affects their thought life. What a woman hears can take her on a trip to a dangerous place. While this list specifically targets married women, it can easily be adapted to singles:

- engaging in inappropriate flirtation with the opposite sex
- viewing soap operas, talk shows, and movies that condone affairs or improper sexual activity
- reading trashy romance novels or women's magazine articles that cause impure thoughts
- e-chatting with men to whom you are not married via Internet chat rooms
- enjoying compliments, flattery, and understanding words from someone to whom you are not married
- talking intimately with a man who is not your husband about problems in your marriage or listening to problems about his marriage

When I e-mailed this list to Marilyn, she remained e-silent for about a day, before she e-mailed me back with the "affirming" words: "Jay, you obviously cheated. What women's books did you read to come up with this list? This is it—especially for married women. But how did you know?"

To which I responded, "Well, Marilyn, contrary to what you and Angie think, I actually do listen to what you women say. Even though I am often guilty of being caught up with my guy preoccupations, I have been studying you females for decades with the tiniest hope that I might one day understand the way you think. Remember this the next time you want to tell me that I just don't get it."

Please don't tell Marilyn, but I did cheat ... but only a little. You see, I knew this stuff from my experience, as we guys struggle with many of these same things—but to a varying degree. The "don't go there" zones for both men and women contain much mutual turf. We all struggle with temptations to the eyes and the ears that impact our mind and our heart. Both men and women need to recognize and avoid the dangerous places in our lives so that we have a fighting chance to withstand Satan's schemes.

Spiritual War-Wear

Mr. Blackwell either loves what a celebrity wears or he hates it—and he doesn't mind letting the world know what he thinks about their attire. Of how he got started in this fashion commentary, Blackwell explains, "Since 1960, the annual worst dressed list has been something of a cause celèbre among fashion victims, Seventh Avenue, the American public, and the world at large. It began quite innocently. In 1960 I was asked by *American Weekly*, an insert magazine in Sunday newspapers across the country, to write a piece on Hollywood's worst and best dressed—never expecting the public explosion that followed."[12] Today, Blackwell's lists are synonymous with fashion faux pas and très chic style.

> Fashion-conscious Christians need only to don this Designer war-wear each day to make a fashion statement that Satan cannot ignore.

Would you make God's spiritually best-dressed list, or would you be on his worst-dressed list? Oh, I don't mean based on your fashion attire, but on the spiritual-wear you are donning. In Ephesians 6:13–17, we are given a description of Designer spiritual war-wear that always lands its wearers on God's best-dressed list.

> Therefore put on the full armor of God, so that when the day of evil comes, you may be able to stand your ground, and after you have done everything, to stand. Stand firm then, with the belt of truth buckled around your waist, with the breastplate of righteousness in place, and with your feet fitted with the readiness that comes from the gospel of peace. In addition to all this, take up the shield of faith, with which you can extinguish all the flaming arrows of the evil one. Take the helmet of salvation and the sword of the Spirit, which is the word of God.
>
> —Ephesians 6:13–17

The good news is that anyone can make God's best-dressed list. Fashion-conscious Christians need only to don this Designer war-wear each day to make a fashion statement that Satan cannot ignore.

You see, for our spiritual battles, which have their onset in our thought life, we are provided protection—this spiritual war-wear—from Satan and his unseen army's attacks. Since this book focuses on the thought life, we should note that although God has a distinct purpose for each piece of our spiritual war-ware, he has specifically designed one part of the fashion ensemble to protect the head with its mind: "Take the helmet of salvation. . ." (v. 17).

A helmet is designed to protect the head. The head area is one of the most vulnerable parts of the body. That's why soldiers, construction workers, football and baseball players, along with motorcycle riders and bicyclists wear helmets. God has designed a spiritual helmet to protect the mind. So many things can injure our minds:

confusion
    discouragement
        impurity
            doubt
                arrogance
                    negativism
                        fear
                        worry
                    guilt
                condemnation
            selfishness
        success
    false doctrine
avoidance of God's Word

Satan knows that if he can attack our minds and cripple our thought lives, he can gain control of us. However, there is a way to stop Satan from getting into our minds. When a person comes to Christ, he or she can put on the helmet of salvation to protect the mind. Each person who has experienced salvation possesses this helmet, even though some choose not to wear it. However, like a motorcyclist, we must put on the helmet so that we can be protected from injury and survive even the hardest hits on our thought life. We need

to wear it every day as we navigate the heavy and spiritually dangerous traffic of the world.

How does this helmet work? The helmet of salvation gives us the
wisdom to . . .

- see through Satan's schemes
- understand God's Word
- discern truth from error
- determine, "Is this from God or Satan?"
- know God's will

For those of us who are daily striving to place our thought life under
Christ's control, we really aren't concerned whether we make Mr.
Blackwell's worst-dressed list or *People's* best-dressed list. We, however, are
vitally interested in making God's best-dressed list in order to overcome
the assaults on our mind. As we seek a better wardrobe to fight our
thought battles, we may need to ask God to tailor and adjust our thoughts
for a better fit. Consider the following parallel in the physical world.

Make the Thought-Adjustment

The Kansai International Airport, Japan's first twenty-four-hour airport,
opened on September 4, 1994, in Osaka Bay, south of the center of
Osaka City. An offshore location was deemed the best option because
of the scale of the facility and the desired location. But what a chal-
lenging first-time civil engineering feat to reclaim land on the soft
seabed in the deep sea! An airport island seawall had to be constructed
before the reclamation of land could begin. Construction of the passenger terminal building commenced a year-and-a-half later when the
island was complete.

I was fascinated when I watched a television special on the construction of the island and the terminal. It took thirty-eight months and
six to ten thousand workers to build the Osaka City Air Terminal. The
facility houses tourist information facilities, a world travel information
station, governmental tourist offices for several countries, major airlines, travel agencies, and other commercial facilities. Yet there is one
problem with this ultra-modern facility: It is built on sinking sand.

But this is no newsflash to the planners and builders of this island and terminal. They knew from the start the island would settle—and little by little sink as it "packs down." To compensate, building designers built a supporting structure of over one thousand pillars, which go down through about sixty-six feet of seawater and sixty-six feet of mud to finally be driven into bedrock a little over 130 feet below. Each pillar is equipped with a special sensor that detects when settling has exceeded the maximum permitted tolerance (ten millimeters or about a third of an inch). The pillar also has a powerful hydraulic jack. Computers monitor these sensors, and when they indicate excessive settling, the pillar is "jacked up" to raise the building at that location, and then locked into the new position. The computers have the capacity to evaluate if the integrity of an area is being threatened and how much adjustment in its foundational support is needed. They plan for these adjustments to continue for ten years before the jacks will permanently be locked into place.[13]

> As you stand firm for Christ in a deep sea of shifting tides of opinions and challenges to your faith, you must constantly make thought adjustments to ensure that you don't sink to the lower depths.

When being sensitive to the Holy Spirit, your spiritual "computer"—that is, your internal belief system—will detect a shift in your life away from pure thoughts and pose a threat to your integrity. You must monitor every thought that would compromise your faith. As you stand firm for Christ in a deep sea of shifting tides of opinions and challenges to your faith, you must constantly make thought adjustments to ensure that you don't sink to the lower depths.

You can accomplish this by adjusting your thought life to make it support your Christian beliefs. This is done by daily aligning your thought life with God's standards found in Scripture. Because our tendency is to drift away from God, not toward him, we must daily align our thinking—and our actions—to his Word. Second Timothy 3:16

teaches, "Every part of Scripture is God-breathed and useful one way or another—showing us truth, exposing our rebellion, correcting our mistakes, training us to live God's way" (THE MESSAGE).

There is no shortcut. We must study and apply God's Word to our lives. Only by conforming our ways to God's way—by the blueprint found in Scripture—can we correct any shift away from God. His Word is like a solid rock in the midst of a culture that often bases its decisions on the sinking sand of relativism and constantly-changing public opinion.

1. **S**inful thoughts confessed
   1 John 1:9
2. **T**hink on these things
   Philippians 4:8
3. **O**rder every thought
   2 Corinthians 10:5
4. **P**ursue Christ-mindedness
   Collossians 3:2

"Take captive every thought to make it obedient to Christ" (2 Corinthians 10:5) is a moment-by-moment commitment and practice since our enemy Satan and the flesh—our unholy want-to—never let up. Thomas à Kempis wisely said, "The devil does not sleep, nor is the flesh yet dead; therefore, you must never cease your preparation for battle, because on the right and on the left are enemies who never rest."

Ordering every thought—putting all of our thoughts under Christ's control—is necessary before we can move to the final step in the S.T.O.P. method. Once our sinful thoughts are confessed, we commence thinking about the things of God, and we begin to order every thought captive, we will be better able to . . .

12

P. Pursue Christ-Mindedness

Pursued by dozens of emergency vehicles, a driverless, runaway freight train carrying thousands of gallons of hazardous chemicals rolled for more than sixty-five miles through northwestern Ohio and defied all attempts to stop it until a daring railroad employee grabbed a handrail, swung aboard, and slammed on the brakes. Jon Hosfield, the thirty-one-year railroad veteran who jumped onto the moving train, discovered that the locomotive cab was empty. Both the engineer and conductor had climbed off the train at its last stop, leaving no one aboard. Although the locomotive's breaks were set, the train rolled out of the busy switching yard near Toledo.

The engineer sprinted to tell yard supervisors, who immediately began calling area law enforcement agencies. The train was soon moving at forty-six miles per hour, according to a state trooper's radar gun. Rail officials attempted to derail the train, but their efforts failed. The train was moving too fast to be stopped. After the train had been on the loose for about an hour, two locomotives chased the forty-seven-car train, hooked onto its last car, and applied their brakes—slowing it enough for Hosfield to jump onboard.[1] He then shut the engines down and hit the brakes. The train came to a halt about a quarter of a mile down the track.[2]

As I watched the news footage of this dramatic maneuver, I reflected on how our thoughts are like this runaway train when they get out of control. Full speed ahead, our thoughts pull away and leave our heavenly Engineer behind. Unless we pursue those sinful thoughts, jump on them, and apply the brakes, they can derail or even destroy us. It is essential to the pursuit of Christ-mindedness that we get our thoughts under control and back on a spiritual track. How do we do that? We intend to show you in this final chapter as we consider the "P" in our S.T.O.P. acrostic: Pursue Christ-mindedness.

In the process of pursuing Christ-mindedness, there are some things that simply have to go. Sometimes it can be a painful process as we continuously review our life and ask God, "What needs to be edited out?"

Film Editing—The Life Version

Filmmaker Walt Disney was reportedly ruthless in his editing of films. It is reported that he would cut away at anything that got in the way of the flow of a story. Walt Kimball, one of the animators for *Snow White*, recalls working 240 days on a four-and-one-half minute comical film sequence in which the dwarfs make some soup for Snow White and almost destroy the kitchen in the process. While Disney thought the scene was funny, he decided it interrupted the flow of the picture and cut the scene.[3]

What are those things in your life that need to be eliminated— edited out so that they do not interrupt the flow of your progress in growing as a Christian? There may be other things that, although not considered sinful, stand in the way of your making the spiritual progress in your life. Perhaps you are . . .

too preoccupied with your work
too tired to practice those disciplines that help you to think purely
too quick in drawing conclusions before having the facts
too concerned about what other people will think
too grieved or feeling too guilty over your past

Have you heard the story of a man who built some crates for the clothes his church was sending to an orphanage in China? When the job was complete, the elderly gentleman headed home. En route, he reached is his shirt pocket to discover that his glasses were gone. He clearly remembered putting them in his pocket that morning.

He returned to the church to search for his glasses, but this proved futile. When he mentally replayed his day, he realized what had happened: His glasses had to have slipped out of his pocket unnoticed and fallen into one of the crates, which were now headed to China.

This was during the Great Depression. This man had spent twenty dollars for his glasses that very morning. He was upset at the prospect of having to buy another pair. "It's not fair," he told God, "I've been faithful in giving my time and money to your work, and now this."

Several months later the director of the Chinese orphanage was on furlough in the States. He came to speak one Sunday night at that gentleman's church. The missionary thanked the people for their faithfulness and generosity in supporting the orphanage.

Then he added, "But most of all, I must thank you for the glasses you sent last year. You see, the Communists had just swept through the orphanage, destroying everything, including my glasses. Even if I had the money, there was no way to replace those glasses. Along with not being able to see, I was experiencing headaches every day. My coworkers and I were much in prayer about this. Then your crates arrived and my staff removed the covers, they found a pair of glasses lying on the top. When I tried them on, it was as if they had been made for me!"

The people in the church were confused. They had sent no glasses to him. But sitting in the back of the church, with tears streaming down his face, the grandfather realized that the Master Carpenter had used him in an extraordinary way.[4]

Haven't you experienced something that you thought was a failure, only later to discover that what happened was the very thing God used to make a difference in your life and in the lives of others through your influence on them? God reserves the right to edit our lives for them to fit his program and for us to be able to participate in what he is doing. Sometimes that editing is painful and not understandable. At the time we don't comprehend what God is up to in our lives, but as we cooperate with him, he makes us more like Christ and causes us to grow spiritually.

> "For my thoughts are not your thoughts, neither are my ways your ways," declares the LORD. "As the heavens are higher than the earth, so are my ways higher than your ways and my thoughts than your thoughts.
>
> —Isaiah 55:8–9

We can rest assured that whatever God chooses to edit out of our lives, it is for our spiritual growth. The editing process begins with exercising the desire to change our minds.

Mind over Matters

The phrase "mind over matter" intrigues me. Does it mean that if I look outside at my grass—which needs mowing right now—and direct my energy toward mentally cutting the grass, I can have my mind mow the lawn? Does it mean that if I jump in a lake here in Florida and an alligator swims towards me, I can mentally cause him to do a U-turn and not have my arm as his snack? Or is it like *The Little Engine That Could*, where no matter what I'm facing, all I have to do is keep thinking, "I think I can, I think I can, I think I can"? You know, that kind of wishful thinking never took out the trash for me.

Psychologists at Manchester Metropolitan University came out with a study that is every couch potato's dream. They claim that just thinking about exercise stimulates your muscles just like twenty minutes on a Stairmaster. In a four-week study, one group of eighteen male students was asked to perform a series of hand and finger exercises. Another group simply imagined performing the same movements for the same amount of time. The results? The researchers claim that those who actually exercised their hands were thirty percent more fit. The mental exercisers improved by sixteen percent. They claim just visualizing going to the weight room can strengthen your muscles.[5]

When I read that, I thought, "That's great if it's your hand that's out of shape, but what if your . . . " Well, we won't go there. This study, I'm certain, will be challenged. However, there is one thing that is irrefutably true. Our lives will be improved by dramatic results by daily exercising the mind—that is, through applying the mind of Christ.

When Paul wrote to the Christians in the church at Corinth, he said to them, "But we have the mind of Christ" (1 Corinthians 2:16 NASB). What did he mean by that statement? One way to express it is to say that WWJT—that is, *What would Jesus think?*—should precede WWJD—*What would Jesus do?* We should consider how we should think or behave in a given situation. Thinking like Jesus is what God has in mind for each of us as we seek to have the mind of Christ.

> WWJT—that is, *What would Jesus think?*—should precede WWJD—*What would Jesus do?*

"Let this mind be in you, which was also in Christ Jesus" (Philippians 2:5 KJV). The word "mind" refers to one's attitude. How one thinks affects one's attitude about things. In the context, it refers to Christ's humility. Humility is possessing a right perspective of who we are and who God is. What does having the mind of Christ mean for us practically? It simply means we can think like Jesus thinks.

How does Jesus think? We can gain some insight by observing his earthly life. We know that he thinks thoughts of . . .

- love . . . even when others didn't love him back
- peace . . . even when circumstances threatened him
- forgiveness . . . even when people did him wrong
- compassion . . . even when others neglected him
- joy . . . reflecting his relationship with the Father
- obedience . . . applying and obeying God's Word
- faith . . . looking up and not around
- commitment . . . determining to fulfill his mission

Have You Changed Your Mind?

You may be saying, "That works for Jesus, but I'm not Jesus. So, what do I do on a daily basis? How can my mind overcome the matters I confront in my life?" Let's consider the kind of mind we need.

- *We need a mind that has been changed because of a personal relationship with God through faith in Jesus Christ.*

  When asked, "Can a person truly change his or her thought patterns?" psychologist David Clarke responds, "Only if the person knows Jesus can his or her thought life be changed." We cannot think the way God wants us to think without including God in our lives. Those without God don't have the capacity to understand spiritual things:

  > The god of this age has blinded the minds of unbelievers, so that they cannot see the light of the gospel of the glory of Christ, who is the image of God.
  >
  > —2 Corinthians 4:4

  > The man without the Spirit does not accept the things that come from the Spirit of God, for they are foolishness to him, and he cannot understand them, because they are spiritually discerned.
  >
  > —1 Corinthians 2:14

  When a person comes to faith in Christ, he or she is given the potential of understanding spiritual things.

- *We need a mind that is being renewed daily.*

  The beliefs, behaviors, and philosophies of this world can easily influence Christians. The daily barrage of news, advertisements, and entertainment takes its toll on the mind by influencing the way we think, as well as our interaction with people who don't include God in their lives.

  > Do not conform any longer to the pattern of this world, but be transformed by the renewing of your mind.
  >
  > —Romans 12:2

  Renewing the mind involves deliberately going back to God's Word and discovering his will and his perspective. Our mind is laundered through his Word. Doing these things transforms our minds—that is, changes our thinking and, therefore, changes our lives.

- *We need a mind that is consistently focused on the things of God.*

   We must constantly practice thinking about God-things.

   Set your minds on things above, not on earthly things.
   —Colossians 3:2

   In his teaching on Paul's writing, A. T. Robertson explained, "The Christian has to keep his feet upon the earth, but his head in the heavens. He must be heavenly-minded here on earth and so help to make earth like heaven."[6] How do we accomplish that? It involves a commitment to doing those things that keep our focus on God—like praying, reading Scripture, and worshiping and studying with other believers.

- *We need a mind that is disciplined.*

   It is essential to train our minds to think the right thoughts. That doesn't just happen. It requires the daily discipline of a mind that is under the control of the Holy Spirit:

   The mind of sinful man is death, but the mind controlled by the Spirit is life and peace.
   —Romans 8:6

   We are also told in Scripture to "be filled with the Spirit" (Ephesians 5:18). To be Spirit-controlled or Spirit-filled means that daily we empty ourselves of sin—through confession and repentance—and surrender our wills to the Holy Spirit. This Person of the Trinity is the One that initiates God-thoughts in our minds and warns us of thoughts not from God that enter our mind. A thought life that is bordered by God's will brings peace of mind.

A Subtle Dance with Printed Romance

When she sat across from Marilyn to begin her second interview for this book, Jean began the session by proudly proclaiming, "I have known such incredible victory over temptation since we last met! And it feels so good!" Jean was grinning from ear to ear, and her eyes sparkled as she radiated God's gracious love and mercy in her life.

When we asked Jean to contribute to this book, Marilyn and I had something totally different in mind than what we are about to share with you. This tends to happen when God is a dynamic part of the writing process. On a number of occasions, as we have gotten to better know the people whom we have used as our case studies, the interviews have more resembled counseling sessions than fact-finding, question-and-answer sessions. Jean shocked us with her refreshing candor and complete vulnerability in the first meeting. We were both anxious to hear what she would share in her second session:

> I went to WalMart the other day and God gave me the strength to walk past the book aisle. I had picked up a few things I needed, and instead of doing what I normally do— heading to the section with the romance novels—I turned my cart and went in another direction. Later, I passed by the aisle again. It was a struggle, I admit, but I kept on walking past the books. When I got into my car after going through the checkout line, I gripped the steering wheel, closed my eyes, and said, "Thank you, Lord, for helping me overcome this temptation. Lord, you know I feel terrible when I am weak. Thank you for giving me your strength just then."

Jean loves the Lord, and seeks to obey and serve him in all that she does. But some days she struggles, feeling lonely and longing to be loved. And sometimes romantic fantasies are the relief she feels she needs in those vulnerable moments. Her impure thoughts may be launched by the explicit sex scenes vividly described in her romance novels or a love scene on television. Then she spins a romantic scenario in her mind that gives her the momentary high and the gratification she craves. Afterwards, however, this romantic intoxication leaves Jean feeling hungover with guilt and shame.

Did I mention that Jean is a widow? And that she is in her seventies? Are you shocked to read that senior saints still struggle with lustful thoughts? I must admit I was taken aback the first time an elderly widower came to me for counsel about church women who were offering him far more than hot casseroles to satisfy his needs! When Jean was asked if her friends talked to her about struggling with impure thoughts, she did not hesitate to respond, "Why, yes, indeed! I know church women in their eighties who have shared with me that they still fantasize and masturbate." Jean added, "When I asked one of my friends if she thought this was alright, she said, 'Sure! It's only a fantasy. It's not wrong. Besides it's not me in the fantasy—it's somebody else. It's a pretend world that helps make me feel better.'"

"And what do you think about it, Jean? Is it okay for you to do this?" Marilyn asked.

"I never really gave it much thought until after I was a widow. The more I was alone, the more I depended on God and spent time with him. He began to convict me that what I was doing was wrong. It's as if I am a small child that my heavenly Father is trying to restrain in the face of imminent danger by saying, 'No, Jean! Don't go there in your mind!'"

When Jean shared about her struggle with romantic fantasies, Marilyn asked Jean what she thinks and how she feels after she has sought relief through this means of comfort. Jean said that at first she rationalizes what she is doing. She thinks about the pain of loneliness she is trying to endure and uses that to justify her actions. This struggling saint shared that she always feels tremendous shame for not being strong enough to resist this temptation. Sometimes her actions leave her feeling more depressed than before.

She doesn't feel "clean enough" to approach God in prayer just after these times of weakness. She feels like a spiritual failure—as if she has let God down. When she finally feels distanced enough from her sin to pray, she gets on her knees and begs God to take away this temptation. Jean then promises God she will never do this again—but deep down inside, Jean fears that she is just days away from breaking her latest promise to God.

Hey, This Stuff Really Works!

Marilyn asked Jean if she presently had an accountability partner—or ever had one. Had she ever been mentored by a more mature Christian woman? She responded No on all counts. She said that she had never before spoken to anyone about her struggle in this sin area. She never opened up with her friends; in fact, she had even protected herself in conversations with those friends who were openly sharing about their struggles.

Marilyn suggested that Jean do the following four things in preparation for their next interview:

1. RECORD. Jean was asked to record her thoughts, memories, feelings, temptations, anything in the area of sexual temptation in a journal. Her writing would remain her private property—unless she wanted to share something with Marilyn.
2. REDIRECT. Jean was asked to redirect her energies from watching, buying, or reading anything that would feed her fantasies. If she began to have romantic fantasies, she was encouraged to stop that fantasy process by doing something that was a healthier choice for her—maybe calling one of her children or a friend—and meeting her emotional needs in this way.
3. REVEAL. She was to pray that God would reveal the secret things in her heart that needed healing or forgiving. She was to pray in the times of struggle—even though she may feel too impure to approach God at her weakest moments.
4. REPENT. Jean was to genuinely repent of those things that caused her shame so that she might truly know the peace and freedom of living in the reality of God's forgiveness and grace. (Review chapter 9 for a discussion of repentance.)

Jean wholeheartedly agreed to do these things. She said that she had been looking for this kind of sisterly support in her struggle. Because Jean desperately wanted to change her thoughts and behavior, she longed to be accountable to someone. She said she had never felt comfortable discussing these matters with anyone before, and it felt good to confess it to another Christian.

When Marilyn met with Jean the second time, it was obvious that God had worked in her life through this process. In journaling her thoughts and struggles, God revealed much to Jean. He allowed her to remember clearly—for the first time in many decades—the pain of not being shown love by her mother, her older brother's inappropriate sexual advances and comments, and having her privacy violated by her drunken father, who masturbated while he watched her bathe. She recalled escaping to a dream world as a young girl to escape the neglect, abuse, shame, and pain that were too prevalent in her real world.

Jean shared too that she had even rethought the reasons why, at age sixteen, she had married an older man. Was it that this man offered her the love she had never felt and the romance she dreamed of experiencing? If that were it, her marriage did not live up to her fantasy of what it would be like. In reality, Jean's marriage was far from the marriage of her dreams.

Her husband was not a Christian when they were first married. They had many tough years together before they experienced the joy and intimacy of a Christian marriage. During those rough times that preceded her husband's salvation—when her husband was drinking too heavily and gambling away their financial resources—Jean would again escape to the dream world she had invented with the perfect man with the model family living an ideal life full of happiness, love, and romance.

As she journaled these things, Jean asked God to help her with the anger, unforgiveness, bitterness, betrayal, and hurt she had experienced throughout her life. She begged God to forgive her for escaping to a fantasy world, instead of going to him with her loneliness and pain. "Only through confessing and praying and staying away from the temptation have I been able to handle things differently since I last met with you, Marilyn," Jean explained. "I was wondering if I would ever find a way to handle this temptation in my life."

The key for each of us is finding a person or a small group of believers with whom we can consistently meet and to whom we have given the freedom to ask us the hard questions about our thought life and actions. That's why . . .

Everyone Needs a Saint Ned

Who is the most visible evangelical to many Americans? Is it Billy Graham, Robert Schuller, Pat Robertson, or D. James Kennedy? No, for a large segment of the American population, it is the animated television character Ned Flanders. Each Sunday evening millions of Americans tune in to watch this amiable next-door neighbor, Ned, and what may be America's most recognizable dysfunctional family, *The Simpsons.*

A 1999 survey conducted by Roper Starch Worldwide found that 91 percent of American children between the ages of ten and seventeen and 84 percent of adults could identify members of the Simpson family.[7] You probably know at least two of the family members: Homer, the self-centered, hedonistic, beer-guzzling couch potato and his out-of-control, void-of-a-moral-compass son, Bart. So, how does their okily-dokily evangelical neighbor fit in their lifestyle?

Referred to by Homer as "Saint Flanders," "Charlie Church," and "Churchy La Femme," Ned is the perfect neighbor for the Simpson family. Ned was recently described in *Christianity Today* as an Oral Roberts University graduate who carries a big Bible and a piece of the "true Cross." Allowing his religious perspective to infiltrate every area of his life, Ned's doorbell chimes "A Mighty Fortress Is Our God" and his air horn blares out the "Hallelujah Chorus." Ned prays with his family at meals and at bedtime. He attends church three times a week and tithes his income, as well as contributes to seven other congregations.[8] He exemplifies the kind of guy any pastor would love to have as a church member.

While Ned's not the kind of neighbor that Homer Simpson wants, he is exactly the kind of neighbor Homer Simpson needs in order to keep him accountable and remind him that God is more than a vain name or someone he calls on only in times of trouble.

Each of us needs a Ned Flanders—that is, someone to whom to be accountable in our lives. It is wise for a Christian to have someone that holds him or her accountable for his or her thoughts, words, and behavior.

> And let us consider how we may spur one another on toward love and good deeds. Let us not give up meeting together, as some are in the habit of doing, but let us encourage one another—and all the more as you see the Day approaching.
>
> —Hebrews 10:24–25

Having an accountability partner means that you give that person permission on a regular basis to ask you the hard questions, such as . . .

- "Have you achieved the goals you set for Bible study and prayer?"
- "Have you had lust in your heart toward a person of the opposite sex?"
- "Have you viewed or read sexually explicit material?"
- "Have you been a person of character in all your financial dealings?"
- "Have you spent quality and quantity time with your spouse and family?"
- "Have you just lied about any of the above questions?"

An accountability partner or group provides us with one of the best deterrents to falling into sin.

Let me encourage you to find at least one person—or a small group of people—of the same sex who will commit to meet with you on a regular basis (weekly is preferable) as your accountability partner(s). As you meet face-to-face, you should mutually and honestly share what is going on in your lives—your struggles, temptations, and moral/spiritual setbacks. You should seek to apply biblical principles to your life as the basis to help you become more like Christ.[9] Having an accountability partner will cause you to examine your life in ways that you, perhaps, have never previously done, and to think twice about some of the things that you do or say. [Note: Teenagers need an accountability partner who is at least two years older than they. This may start out as a mentoring relationship but can evolve into an accountability partnership if honesty and trust are established from the outset.]

This has proven to be effective in my own life. I know that if I am going to have to face at least one person each week and give an account of my actions, it becomes a strong motivation for me not to do those things I have no business doing as one who desires to please God. At times I have looked so forward to those accountability meetings because I had been faithful to the commitment I made to my accountability partner. But other times, quite honestly, I have dreaded with a passion those meetings. I have gone so far as to hope for just a mild case of the flu so I wouldn't have to face his questions. However, I have found that accountability is an effective roadblock to sinful thoughts and actions that I constantly need.

> I have found that accountability is an effective roadblock to sinful thoughts and actions that I constantly need.

Isolation from those who would hold us accountable—what might be called the "Lone Ranger Syndrome"—gives our minds an opportunity to drift away from God. Who will be your Ned Flanders? Although Homer Simpson is hardly a role model for born-again Christians to emulate, the principle of having someone like "Saint Flanders" in our lives is invaluable in our pursuing Christ-mindedness. Whom will you allow God to use to help you see those things in your life that hinder your spiritual journey? I thank God for those who have held me accountable—especially as I have been working on this writing project, a task that has not been without an . . .

Assault on My Thought Life

The personal journey I have taken in writing *Taming Your Private Thoughts* has been interesting, to say the least, and at times difficult. In fact, if I could be so blunt, this book has been unbelievably tough to write. Why would I say that? It has nothing to do with the actual writing process or collaboration. That's a joy. I am talking about the personal attack on my thought life that Satan has waged against me as I have worked on this project. I have relived experientially what I always knew to be true in the back of my mind: that Satan has his greatest victories through the thought life.

Obviously, any time anyone attempts to expose his methods, this enemy attacks. Well, let me tell you that there has been an assault on my thought life as I had never before experienced! It has come in several different ways. There were increased thoughts of self-condemnation, such as: "Who am I to be writing on this subject?

Someone else would be much more qualified to deal with this subject. I'm a nobody . . . and it would be much better for a well-known somebody to write this book."

Then there were the negative thoughts that attempted to convince me that all is in vain—including my writing, my ministry, and my life. I constantly have had to battle thoughts of depression. It seemed like a cloud was hanging over my head. There were days while writing this book that it seemed as if there was no way out and no way through some of the problems I was facing—especially the challenges of pastoring a church that is growing so fast that there's never enough staff, infrastructure, or money to handle the challenges. Top that off with the problems and needs of the members.

I know I'm sounding like Eeyore in *Winnie the Pooh*, but that's just how Satan attacks the mind. Now that I look back on these past months, it's almost comical how tempting thoughts came at my mind. For example, late one night, after everyone else had gone to bed, I went to the front door to check the lock before going to bed. When I did, I saw something lying on our front porch. I couldn't make out what it was, so I opened the door. To my amazement, someone had strategically placed a pornographic magazine in plain view. In shock, I did a double-take.

Satan attacks the mind fast and hard. Was I tempted to look? Well, like any other red-blooded male, I did not have thoughts of just reading the articles. It would have been so easy to sneak a peak while disposing of this magazine in the trash. Then, another thought crossed my mind: *How does a pastor dispose of such a magazine?* First, I didn't even want to bring it into the house. Second, I could just envision the headline in the newspaper, "Trash collectors find pornographic magazine in pastor's garbage."

Well, I did trash that trash. And God gave me a victory over curious thoughts of what might be contained in its pages. While I was able to resist the temptation, I was reminded of the degree to which "Satan, the world, and the flesh" will go in combining their efforts to try to whip our thoughts into their submission.

So, how did I stop these runaway thoughts? I had to realize they were not from God, but from Satan, "the accuser of our brothers"

(Revelation 12:10). In his assault on my thought life I began standing on what God said in his Word instead of trusting in my own feelings. Simply, I chose to believe God over what Satan was whispering in my ear.

In Revelation we are given a glimpse of the once-and-for-all victory over all of Satan's assaults that will be ours as believers "because of the blood of the Lamb and because of the word of their testimony" (Revelation 12:11 NASB). In this passage, "the blood of the Lamb" refers to Christ's finished work on the cross that secured our salvation. The devil cannot undo what Christ did at the cross and in my life as a result of my placing my faith in him. I reminded Satan of the absolute victory of Jesus over him, over sin, over death, over my sinful thoughts.

> As Satan took me back and reminded me of my past—the skeletons in my closet—I simply reminded him of his future!

The phrase "the word of their testimony" refers to a confession of faith that demonstrates not only in word, but also in lifestyle, that Christ has changed their lives. As Satan took me back and reminded me of my past—the skeletons in my closet—I simply reminded him of his future!

We must understand that Satan cannot make us act on our thoughts. He can plant them, but we choose either to stop them or act on them. There are times I say aloud, "Stop the thought"—as Dr. Arch Hart suggested—to interrupt the progression of temptation to sin. I have learned that it is better to confess immediately those sinful thoughts and seek God's forgiveness then, right in the middle of the thought battle.

I have also taken some practical measures in protecting my thought life, such as imposing a self-rule while using the Internet: an open-door-at-all-times-while-on-the-Internet policy. In fact, we have made that a standing rule for the whole Dennis family.

There are some other practical guidelines for our family's thought protection that we have initiated in our home. But my purpose in mentioning this is certainly not to advocate a rule-bound atmosphere in our homes, since I think a principle-driven atmosphere is far more successful in helping each family member to grow more fully in his or her Christian walk. I believe each person, each couple, and each family must decide how they will incorporate in their thinking and conduct within their home those things that will help create an environment where Christ-mindedness can be passionately pursued out of loving, mutual respect.

Staying on Track

In one of the final interviews for the book, Marilyn and I met with Dwight Bain,[10] a nationally known certified counselor, motivational speaker, and executive coach from Orlando. Dwight offered tremendous insight into the thought life, explaining to us the importance of our perception and perspective of things—that is, how we interpret what happens to us—in determining the success or failure of how we handle challenges and Satan's assaults on our thought life. Our perception is affected by our beliefs and the way we were raised. As Christians, our beliefs are shaped by the hearing and doing of God's Word. We have the resurrection power of Jesus Christ within us to deal with those things from our past that continue to haunt us.

> Consider the possibility that there may be a better way to have the life you want.
>
> —DWIGHT BAIN

Dwight also pointed out that our thought life begins to change when we develop a positive support system along with healthy coping skills. The Christian life provides us not only with something true and life-transforming in which to believe, but it also connects us with other believers who will support us as we seek healthy, God-focused ways to cope with whatever comes into our lives.

Dwight told us that he likes to say to his patients, "Consider the possibility that there may be a better way to have the life you want."

We would like to also suggest that perhaps you should open your mind to the possibility that there may be a better way to have the thought life you want. The suggestions we have offered in *Taming Your Private Thoughts* line up well with Dwight's counsel, because they are not just untested theories. Rather, they are biblical principles that will work in your life. The S.T.O.P. method will provide you with healthy coping skills that can radically change the way you handle your thoughts, your temptations, and your challenges.

Dwight concluded our interview with the statement, "You always have options." And you most certainly do—even if your life has stayed in the same old rut for years, even if you see no way to handle all that is on your mind and heart, even if you have tried a hundred times before and failed. There is a way that will work.

Like that runaway train, our thoughts can get out of control. It's time that each of us "allows" God to be the engineer of our thought life—the One in control of our train. There is good news for those of us who have gotten off track: We can get back on track! This can be accomplished by disciplining our minds daily to think the kind of thoughts that lead to pure living and bring us victory over wrong thinking. By doing so, we can successfully stop sin where it starts and thus stay spiritually on track. Keep in mind that this is a process, not an instant rescue-us-in-the-middle-of-thought-derailment. The more we practice God's S.T.O.P. method, the more on-track our thoughts will stay as we pursue Christ-mindedness: "Set your mind on things above, not on earthly things" (Colossians 3:2).

1. **S**inful thoughts confessed
   1 John 1:9
2. **T**hink on these things
   Philippians 4:8
3. **O**rder every thought
   2 Corinthians 10:5
4. **P**ursue Christ-mindedness
   Colossians 3:2

Will this method work for you? Yes! You can S.T.O.P. sin where it starts—in your thought life.

Questions for Individual or Group Study

Chapter 1

1. Think through a scenario of the consequences that would follow your falling into moral sin. If time allows, write down this rehearsal.
2. In this chapter the expression *Thought Genesis* is used. Explain what you think is meant by that expression.
3. Based on the Genesis 3 account, how does Satan plant thoughts that eventually grow into sin?
4. How could Eve and Adam have prevented their sin?
5. Why is it dangerous to say, "I can handle it!" when it comes to temptation?
6. List at least five differences in how men and women think.

Chapter 2

1. Write three original "pick-up lines" that Satan could use to lead someone into sin. Would any of these work on you?
2. Explain what you think is meant by the sentence: "Our minds are the doorkeepers—the gatekeepers—to what we eventually do."
3. Describe the inner braking system that each Christian possesses that can stop temptation in its tracks.
4. At what point in the story of King David's affair with Bathsheba did he entertain sin? At what point could he have stopped sin in its tracks?
5. List at least three ways in which we fertilize our wrong thoughts with Satan's "Miracle Grow."
6. Give three examples of how our culture is becoming desensitized to sin.

Chapter 3

1. Write an appealing ad that Satan might use to creatively market sin in our society.
2. List two ways in which our minds are like a circus.
3. What is something you hold dear in your life that presently is being threatened by sinful runaway thoughts? Discuss.
4. What would the enemy use as bait to lure you into wrong thinking?
5. How has Satan been guilty of attempted rape in your spiritual life?
6. What does Satan have "Behind Door #1" that he would have you trade for your pure thoughts?

Chapter 4

1. Offer a brief explanation of how the following stages in the birth process compare to the development of a specific sin in your life:
   a. Conception
   b. First Trimester
   c. Second Trimester
   d. Third Trimester
   e. Labor and Delivery
2. Are you a "dumpster diver" when it comes to your thought life? Explain.
3. If Satan played a tape of your past in order to keep you feeling defeated, to what event would he rewind and play over and over?
4. Describe how skelephobia has affected you in the past.

Chapter 5

1. Compare your thought wars with military battles. In what ways are they similar?
2. In your life experience, what losses has Satan used to make you believe you are a failure or are finished?
3. In the wrestling match of your thought life who is winning? Explain why.
4. List some "nails" that Satan uses in order to seal the coffin that contains your pure thoughts.
5. What one thing would a man most hate to lose? What one thing would a woman most hate to lose? Explain.

Chapter 6

1. When's the last time you caught a "whether report" for your life? What was the forecast?
2. How does Satan try to convince us that God's laws are dumb laws?
3. What benefits will observing God's laws bring to you?
4. Compare two of God's laws with Satan's whopper lies.
5. Describe a time when you thought, "How could I have allowed myself to fall for this?"
6. List four ways Satan tries to bully us to get us to stray from God.

Chapter 7

1. Consider the testimony of the Marlboro Man. What do you think his story teaches us about the consequences of wrong thoughts?
2. Give a personal example of a specific time in your life when you thought, "I never thought it would lead to this."
3. How can compromise in the little things get you off course in a big way in your thought life?
4. What are some potential landmines that could blow up in your life? What could you do to diffuse them?
5. What in your life would cause you to have a time-out in the sin bin?
6. Why is it that many who start out strong in the Christian life morally crash and burn somewhere along the way?

Chapter 8

1. What are some links in the "sin chain" that Satan uses to lead you away from God and keep you in bondage?
2. How might the H.A.L.T. principle be effective in your life as you are faced with making important choices?
3. Why is the frog-in-the-kettle syndrome dangerous for a Christian in today's culture?
4. What are some parallels between corporate Israel's Old Testament sin history and this country's sin profile?
5. What are three possible suggestions Satan might give for dealing with difficult situations? Contrast those with what God's Word might advise.

Chapter 9

1. Give an example of how Numbers 32:23 ("Be sure your sin will find you out") has proven true in your life.
2. What do you think it will be like when you stand before the Lord to give an accounting of your life? Describe how you think you might feel.
3. List and briefly explain the four steps discussed in this chapter for overcoming a sinful fantasy. Do you think this process might be helpful for you?
4. How can crying out to God, "Help! I've fallen and I can't get up!" be the beginning of pure-thought recovery?
5. How would you define repentance? List those steps necessary for forgiveness.

Chapter 10

1. Compare and contrast Eastern and Christian meditation. Have you ever practiced either form of meditation? Explain.
2. List three things on which God wants you to meditate.
3. What was the turning point in Cindy's battle with fear? Explain why this was the defining moment in the beginning of her road to recovery.
4. Why is it vital that we uncage our sinful thoughts?
5. How might replacement thought therapy transform your thinking?
6. What spiritual fuel do we need to keep us running on "Full" instead of "Empty" daily?

Chapter 11

1. How might taking captive every thought in order to make it obedient to Christ change your life?
2. What part did grace play in Larry's dealing with his depression? As with Larry, how might God's bottomless grace help you deal with life's struggles?
3. List those places where men and women should not go in order to protect their thought life. What specific place gives you the most problems in protecting yours?
4. Explain how the helmet of salvation could be used to protect your thought life. When was the last time you put it on?

5. When sinking spiritually, what adjustments could be made in your thought life to elevate it to higher ground?

Chapter 12

1. Why is it important to have accountability built into your Christian walk? Do you presently have an accountability system? Explain.
2. What are some things in your life that—although they are not considered sinful—might be impeding your Christian growth?
3. How would the way you approach things change if you applied the "mind of Christ" to your thinking? Give a specific example.
4. According to psychologist Dwight Bain, our thought life begins to change when two things happen. What are those two things, and how does Christianity provide us with those?
5. How can having a positive support system and healthy coping skills help your thought life to change?

Scripture for Applying the S.T.O.P. Method

Step 1: S. Sinful Thoughts Confessed

1 John 1:7–9

But if we walk in the light, as he is in the light, we have fellowship with one another, and the blood of Jesus, his Son, purifies us from all sin. If we claim to be without sin, we deceive ourselves and the truth is not in us. If we confess our sins, he is faithful and just and will forgive us our sins and purify us from all unrighteousness.

James 4:6–10

But he gives us more grace. That is why Scripture says: "God opposes the proud but gives grace to the humble." Submit yourselves, then, to God. Resist the devil, and he will flee from you. Come near to God and he will come near to you. Wash your hands, you sinners, and purify your hearts, you double-minded. Grieve, mourn and wail. Change your laughter to mourning and your joy to gloom. Humble yourselves before the Lord, and he will lift you up.

James 5:16

Therefore confess your sins to each other and pray for each other so that you may be healed. The prayer of a righteous man is powerful and effective.

Numbers 32:23

And you may be sure that your sin will find you out.

1 Corinthians 6:11

And that is what some of you were. But you were washed, you were sanctified, you were justified in the name of the Lord Jesus Christ and by the Spirit of our God.

Ecclesiastes 12:14

For God will bring every deed into judgment, including every hidden thing, whether it is good or evil.

Luke 12:2–3

There is nothing concealed that will not be disclosed, or hidden that will not be made known. What you have said in the dark will be heard in the daylight, and what you have whispered in the ear in the inner rooms will be proclaimed from the roofs.

2 Corinthians 5:10

For we must all appear before the judgment seat of Christ, that each one may receive what is due him for the things done while in the body, whether good or bad.

James 1:15

And sin, when it is full-grown, gives birth to death.

Matthew 5:16

Let your light shine before men, that they may see your good deeds and praise your Father in heaven.

Matthew 3:2, 8

Repent, for the kingdom of heaven is near. . . . Produce fruit in keeping with repentance.

Isaiah 1:18

"Come now, let us reason together," says the LORD. "Though your sins are like scarlet, they shall be as white as snow, though they are red as crimson, they shall be like wool."

Step 2: T. Think on These Things

Joshua 1:8

Do not let this Book of the Law depart from your mouth; meditate on it day and night, so that you may be careful to do everything written in it. Then you will be prosperous and successful.

Psalm 119:27, 78

Let me understand the teaching of your precepts; then I will meditate on your wonders. . . . I will meditate on your precepts.

Psalm 145:5

They will speak of the glorious splendor of your majesty, and I will meditate on your wonderful works.

Psalm 1:1–3

Blessed is the man who does not walk in the counsel of the wicked or stand in the way of sinners or sit in the seat of mockers. But his delight is in the law of the LORD, and on his law he meditates day and night. He is like a tree planted by streams of water, which yields its fruit in season and whose leaf does not wither. Whatever he does prospers.

James 1:8

He is a double-minded man, unstable in all his ways.

Ephesians 3:20

Now to him who is able to do immeasurably more than all we ask or imagine, according to his power that is at work within us,

Colossians 3:1–2

Since, then, you have been raised with Christ, set your hearts on things above, where Christ is seated at the right hand of God. Set your minds on things above, not on earthly things.

Philippians 4:8

Finally, brothers, whatever is true, whatever is noble, whatever is right, whatever is pure, whatever is lovely, whatever is admirable—if anything is excellent or praiseworthy—think about such things.

Proverbs 16:18

Pride goes before destruction, a haughty spirit before a fall.

Psalm 71:20

Though you have made me see troubles, many and bitter, you will restore my life again; from the depths of the earth you will again bring me up.

Romans 15:4, 13

For everything that was written in the past was written to teach us, so that through endurance and the encouragement of the Scriptures we might have hope. . . . May the God of hope fill you with all joy and peace as you trust in him, so that you may overflow with hope by the power of the Holy Spirit.

Isaiah 1:16b – 17a
Stop doing wrong, learn to do right.

Step 3: O. Order Every Thought

2 Corinthians 10:4–5
The weapons we fight with are not the weapons of the world. On the contrary, they have divine power to demolish strongholds. We demolish arguments and every pretension that sets itself up against the knowledge of God, and we take captive every thought to make it obedient to Christ.

2 Corinthians 2:11
. . . in order that Satan might not outwit us. For we are not unaware of his schemes.

Matthew 12:34, 36–37
For out of the overflow of the heart the mouth speaks. . . . But I tell you that men will have to give account on the day of judgment for every careless word they have spoken. For by your words you will be acquitted, and by your words you will be condemned.

1 Corinthians 15:33
Do not be misled: "Bad company corrupts good character."

Matthew 15:19
For out of the heart come evil thoughts, murder, adultery, sexual immorality, theft, false testimony, slander.

Ephesians 4:25–32
Therefore each of you must put off falsehood and speak truthfully to his neighbor, for we are all members of one body. "In your anger do not sin": Do not let the sun go down while you are still angry, and do not give the devil a foothold. He who has been stealing must steal no longer, but must work, doing something useful with his own hands, that he may have something to share with those in need. Do not let any unwholesome talk come out of your mouths, but only what is helpful for building others up according to their needs, that it may benefit those who listen. And do not grieve the Holy Spirit of God, with

whom you were sealed for the day of redemption. Get rid of all bitterness, rage and anger, brawling and slander, along with every form of malice. Be kind and compassionate to one another, forgiving each other, just as in Christ God forgave you.

Ephesians 6:10–18

Finally, be strong in the Lord and in his mighty power. Put on the full armor of God so that you can take your stand against the devil's schemes. For our struggle is not against flesh and blood, but against the rulers, against the authorities, against the powers of this dark world and against the spiritual forces of evil in the heavenly realms. Therefore put on the full armor of God, so that when the day of evil comes, you may be able to stand your ground, and after you have done everything, to stand. Stand firm then, with the belt of truth buckled around your waist, with the breastplate of righteousness in place, and with your feet fitted with the readiness that comes from the gospel of peace. In addition to all this, take up the shield of faith, with which you can extinguish all the flaming arrows of the evil one. Take the helmet of salvation and the sword of the Spirit, which is the word of God. And pray in the Spirit on all occasions with all kinds of prayers and requests. With this in mind, be alert and always keep on praying for all the saints.

Luke 1:37

For nothing is impossible with God.

1 Corinthians 16:13

Be on your guard; stand firm in the faith; be men of courage; be strong.

1 Timothy 6:12

Fight the good fight of the faith. Take hold of the eternal life to which you were called when you made your good confession in the presence of many witnesses.

Proverbs 4:23

Above all else, guard your heart, for it is the wellspring of life.

1 Corinthians 6:18

Flee from sexual immorality. All other sins a man commits are outside his body, but he who sins sexually sins against his own body.

James 1:22

Do not merely listen to the word, and so deceive yourselves. Do what it says.

Matthew 7:7

Ask and it will be given to you; seek and you will find; knock and the door will be opened to you.

1 Peter 4:7

The end of all things is near. Therefore be clear minded and self-controlled so that you can pray.

2 Timothy 3:16

All Scripture is God-breathed and is useful for teaching, rebuking, correcting and training in righteousness.

Step 4: P. Pursue Christ-Mindedness

Psalm 119:37

Turn my eyes away from worthless things; preserve my life according to your word.

Hebrews 12:2

Let us fix our eyes on Jesus, the author and perfecter of our faith, who for the joy set before him endured the cross, scorning its shame, and sat down at the right hand of the throne of God.

Job 31:1

I made a covenant with my eyes not to look lustfully at a girl.

Matthew 5:28

But I tell you that anyone who looks at a woman lustfully has already committed adultery with her in his heart.

Romans 12:1–2

Therefore, I urge you, brothers, in view of God's mercy, to offer your bodies as living sacrifices, holy and pleasing to God—this is your spiritual act of worship. Do not conform any longer to the pattern of this world, but be transformed by the renewing of your mind. Then you will be able to test and approve what God's will is—his good, pleasing and perfect will.

Isaiah 55:8–9

"For my thoughts are not your thoughts, neither are your ways my ways," declares the LORD. "As the heavens are higher than the earth, so are my ways higher than your ways and my thoughts than your thoughts."

Romans 8:6–7

The mind of sinful man is death, but the mind controlled by the Spirit is life and peace; the sinful mind is hostile to God. It does not submit to God's law, nor can it do so.

Ephesians 5:18–21

Do not get drunk on wine, which leads to debauchery. Instead, be filled with the Spirit. Speak to one another with psalms, hymns and spiritual songs. Sing and make music in your heart to the Lord, always giving thanks to God the Father for everything, in the name of our Lord Jesus Christ. Submit to one another out of reverence for Christ.

James 1:13–16

When tempted, no one should say, "God is tempting me." For God cannot be tempted by evil, nor does he tempt anyone; but each one is tempted when, by his own evil desire, he is dragged away and enticed. Then, after desire has conceived, it gives birth to sin; and sin, when it is full-grown, gives birth to death. Don't be deceived, my dear brothers.

1 Thessalonians 5:16–22

Be joyful always; pray continually; give thanks in all circumstances, for this is God's will for you in Christ Jesus. Do not put out the Spirit's fire; do not treat prophecies with contempt. Test everything. Hold on to the good. Avoid every kind of evil.

1 Corinthians 10:31

So whether you eat or drink or whatever you do, do it all for the glory of God.

1 Corinthians 2:14

The man without the Spirit does not accept the things that come from the Spirit of God, for they are foolishness to him, and he cannot understand them, because they are spiritually discerned.

Matthew 5:8

Blessed are the pure in heart, for they will see God.

2 Chronicles 16:9

For the eyes of the LORD range throughout the earth to strengthen those whose hearts are fully committed to him. You have done a foolish thing, and from now on you will be at war.

Proverbs 3:5–6

Trust in the LORD with all your heart and lean not on your own understanding; in all your ways acknowledge him, and he will make your paths straight.

1 John 2:15–17

Do not love the world or anything in the world. If anyone loves the world, the love of the Father is not in him. For everything in the world—the cravings of sinful man, the lust of his eyes and the boasting of what he has and does—comes not from the Father but from the world. The world and its desires pass away, but the man who does the will of God lives forever.

Philippians 2:5

Your attitude should be the same as that of Christ Jesus.

1 Corinthians 2:16

"For who has known the mind of the Lord that he may instruct him?" But we have the mind of Christ.

2 Corinthians 5:7

We live by faith, not by sight.

Hebrews 10:24–25

And let us consider how we may spur one another on toward love and good deeds. Let us not give up meeting together, as some are in the habit of doing, but let us encourage one another—and all the more as you see the Day approaching.

Ecclesiastes 4:9–12

Two are better than one, because they have a good return for their work: if one falls down, his friend can help him up. But pity the man who falls and has no one to help him up! Also, if two lie down together, they will keep warm. But how can one keep warm alone? Though one may be overpowered, two can defend themselves. A cord of three strands is not quickly broken.

2 Thessalonians 3:2

And pray that we may be delivered from wicked and evil men, for not everyone has faith.

Hebrews 11:6, 33

And without faith it is impossible to please God, because anyone who comes to him must believe that he exists and that he rewards those who earnestly seek him.... Who through faith conquered kingdoms, administered justice, and gained what was promised; who shut the mouths of lions.

Revelation 12:11

They overcame him by the blood of the Lamb and by the word of their testimony.

Galatians 5:1

It is for freedom that Christ has set us free. Stand firm, then, and do not let yourselves be burdened again by a yoke of slavery.

Romans 12:11

Never be lacking in zeal, but keep your spiritual fervor, serving the Lord.

1 Corinthians 10:8

We should not commit sexual immorality, as some of them did—and in one day twenty-three thousand of them died.

Ephesians 5:3

But among you there must not be even a hint of sexual immorality, or of any kind of impurity, or of greed, because these are improper for God's holy people.

Romans 8:1, 5–6

Therefore, there is now no condemnation for those who are in Christ Jesus.... Those who live according to the sinful nature have their minds set on what that nature desires; but those who live in accordance with the Spirit have their minds set on what the Spirit desires. The mind of sinful man is death, but the mind controlled by the Spirit is life and peace.

Mark 12:30

Love the Lord your God with all your heart and with all your soul and with all your mind and with all your strength.

Scriptures may be accessed through www.zondervanbibles.com/home.asp

Notes

Chapter 1: It Began Just as a Thought

1. J. Oswald Sanders, *A Spiritual Clinic* (Chicago: Moody, 1961), page unknown.

2. After a year-and-a-half estrangement from God following the disclosure of his sin, Jack sought reconciliation with the Lord. He married "the other woman" after his divorce became final—and after she made a life-changing profession of faith in Christ. He has sought the forgiveness of those whom he harmed through his actions. He has also been able to restore his relationship to his children.

3. The English title, *Genesis*, is Greek in origin and comes from the word *genesis*—which can mean "birth," "genealogy," or "history of origin"—which appears in the Greek translation (called the Septuagint) of Genesis 2:4; 5:1. In both its Hebrew and Greek forms, then, the title of Genesis appropriately describes its contents, since it is primarily a book of beginnings.

4. "Genesis: Introduction," *NASB Study Bible* (Grand Rapids: Zondervan, 1999), 1.

5. Paul Lee Tan, *Encyclopedia of 15,000 Illustrations* (Dallas: Bible Communications, 1998), 2960.

6. Leslie Flynn, as quoted by Robert J. Morgan, *Stories, Illustrations, and Quotes* (Nashville: Thomas Nelson, 2000), 554.

7. "Snake Charmers Now Fighting for Their Survival," *ANI* (New Delhi, Nov. 19, 2000).

8. Author unknown, *The Snake* website, 5–6.

9. Joe Brogan, *Palm Beach Post* (April 5, 2000).

10. Lynn Vincent, *World Magazine* (Nov., 2000), 18.

11. You need to understand that we wrote this chapter prior to my wife's putting me on Weight Watchers (see ch. 11). Oh, how I long for the good ol' days!

12. Erwin Lutzer, "Those Sins That Won't Budge," *Moody* (March 1978), 48.

Chapter 2: Flirting with Desire

1. "Playboy Enterprises, Inc.," Hoover's, Inc. website, Jan., 2001, 1.

2. Statistics compiled from *Publishers Weekly*, Ingram, The Book Industry Study Group, ABA, and Harlequin Ent. Ltd. Published online as "Facts & Figures About the Romance Genre," Central New York Romance Writers website (Liverpool, N.Y.: Jan. 19, 2001), 1.

3. The 1998–1999 remake of this series did not grab my attention like the original "Fantasy Island."

4. Many thanks to Celia Reeder, Randall James, and the other awesome staff members of The First Foundation as well as Sue Price, Jerry Montgomery, Vickie Sovel, and the incomparable Faith Hall staff, who have welcomed us time and again to work in your wonderful facilities. You are dear friends and always make us feel so comfortable when we are in your midst!

5. Associated Press, "Have Your Chocolate—and Soak In It, Too," *Orlando Sentinel* (Jan. 20, 2001), B9.

6. D. Edmond Hiebert, *The Epistle of James* (Chicago: Moody, 1979), 105.

7. Michelle McKinney Hammond, *The Genius of Temptation* (Eugene, Ore.: Harvest House, 1998), 199.

8. "Rash of U.S. Train Wrecks Preventable, Paper Says," Nando.net and Reuter Information Service, 1996, 1.

9. Ibid., 1.

10. "Stalking & Stalkers," *The Antistalking Web Site* (Jan., 2001), 1.

11. Patricia Tjaden and Nancy Thoennes, "Stalking in America: Findings from the National Violence Against Women Survey," U.S. Department of Justice Office of Justice Programs and the National Institute of Justice Centers for Disease Control and Prevention website (April, 1998), 3.

12. "Company Info: History," The Scott Company website, Winter 2000–2001, 2.

Chapter 3: Behind Closed Door #1: Lust

1. "Top Ten Slogans of the Century," *Advertising Age* website, 2001, 1.

2. It was founded in 1870.

3. John E. Shepler, "Golden Age of the Circus," *A Positive Light* website, 1999–2001, 1–2.

4. "Cirque du Soleil's 'O' Defies Reality with the Help of Working Model Motion," *Customer Success Stories, MSC Software* website, 2000, 1.

5. "Six Escaped Circus Lions Cause Panic in Brazil," *Excite News* online, August 7, 2000, 1.

6. "Circus Lions Eat Boy in Brazil," fr. the *Electronic Telegraph* (London: April 5, 2000) and published on the *Igorilla* website, 1.

7. "Amazon Fishing Adventure," *Explorations, Inc.* website, 2001, 1.

8. "Amazon Peacock Bass Fishing in Manaus Brazil," *Des Peres Travel* website, 2001, 2–3.

9. This number is accurate at the time of writing this book. Larry Larsen owns and operates a business called Larsen's Outdoor Publishing, Lakeland, Florida.

10. Nathan Hamilton, "Introduction," *Theories of Persuasive Communication and Consumer Decision Making* (Univ. of Texas at Austin website, Nov. 25, 1998), 1.

11. Nathan Hamilton, "Lust," *Theories of Persuasive Communication and Consumer Decision Making* (Univ. of Texas at Austin website, Nov. 25, 1998, 1–2.

12. Nathan Hamilton, "Conclusion," *Theories of Persuasive Communication and Consumer Decision Making* (Univ. of Texas at Austin website, Nov. 25, 1998), 1.

13. "Discussion about Rape," *AARDVARC* website, 2001, 1.

14. "What Is Acquaintance Rape?" *SAFE: Sexual Assault Education* website, 2001, 1.

15. "Discussion about Rape," 2.

16. Note: Proabortion used in this context has nothing to do with aborting the life of a child. It is used figuratively here to mean terminating a sinful thought.

17. "Decisions, Decisions, Decisions!," *Let's Make a Deal* website, 1999–2001, 1–2.

Chapter 4: Peeking Behind the Skeleton Door . . . Sin

1. "Top 100 Names of 2000," *The Baby Zone* website, 2001, 1.

2. Source unknown.

3. Source unknown.

4. "Dumpster Diving," *The Jargon Dictionary* online, 2001, 1.

5. Sheldon Miller, "Dumpster Diving: Treasure and Trash," *University of Notre Dame* website, 2001, 2.

6. Ibid.

7. "Hewitt says 'I Still Know' Scarier than the First," *CNN Entertainment Weekly* online, November 12, 1998, 1–2.

8. Geoffrey Brewer, "Snakes Top List of Americans' Fears," *The Gallup News Service* online, March 19, 2001, 1.

9. Fred Culbertson, *The Phobia List* online, March 7, 2001, 1–14.

10. Author unknown, fr. *FunnyStuff Mailing List*, Apr. 24, 2001, 1.

Chapter 5: Death of Pure Thoughts

1. Don Henley and B. R. Hornsby, *The End of the Innocence*, Cass Country Music/Zappa Music ASCAP, 1987.

2. Don Holloway, "Stealth Secrets of the F–117 Nighthawk," *The History Net* website, March, 1996, 1–8.

3. The Associated Press, "Razorbacks Lose Then Get Lost," *Gator Sports* online, March 29, 1997.

4. "Property Identification and Recovery System," *Lost and Found International* website, 2001, 1.

5. "A Pastor's Good News and Bad News for a Pastor," *Cybercheeze* online, Yes Interactive AS, 1997–1999, 1.

6. Source unknown.

7. R. Kent Hughes, *Ephesians: The Mystery of the Body of Christ* (Wheaton: Crossway, 1990), 214.

8. "Stats," *The Rock* website, World Wrestling Federation, Inc., 2001, 2.

9. "Frequently Asked Questions," *Direct Casket* online, 2001, 1.

10. "Facts for Consumers from the Federal Trade Commission: Caskets and Burial Vaults," *Consumer Law Page* online, August, 1992, 1.

11. Freddie Mercury, *Bohemian Rhapsody*.

Chapter 6: The Exhilaration of Deceptive Thoughts

1. Stephen Arteburn, *Addicted to "Love"* (Ann Arbor, Mich.: Vine Books, 1996), 27, 136–38.

2. "Deception," *Today in the Word* (July, 1995), 27.

3. Author unknown, "Dumb Laws: Big Government. Small Brains. Dumb Laws," *Dumb Laws* online, Bueno Technologies, 1998–2001.

4. Author unknown, "Phony Cigars," *Today in the Word* (December 16, 1992), n.p.

5. Keith C. Heidorn, "Mirages: A Primer," *Weather Phenomena and Elements, Islandnet* online, July 1, 1999.

6. Raymond McHenry, *Something to Think About* (Peabody, Mass.: Hendrickson, 1998), 65.

7. Brian Schmitz, "The Legend of Dale Earnhardt," *Orlando Sentinel* (Orlando, Fla.: Feb. 23, 2001), Section D, 3.

8. Lowell D. Streiker, *Big Book of Laughter* (Nashville: Thomas Nelson, 2000), 219–24.

Chapter 7: I Never Thought It Would Lead to This

1. Alan Landers, "Winston Man: Alan Lander's Bio", *WinstonMan* website, Part 1, 1–3; Part 2, 1.

2. "Cali, Colombia 757 Crash on Approach," *National Transportation Safety Board Report* online (Washington, D.C.: Dec. 28, 1995), 2–4.

3. Chris Johnson, ed., "Workshop on Human Error and Systems Development," Glasgow Accident Analysis Group (Dept. of Computing Science, Glasgow University, Scotland: Mar. 19–22, 1997), 4–10.

4. R. C. Sproul as quoted in *The New Encyclopedia of Christian Quotations* (Grand Rapids: Baker, 2000), 950.

5. John Chambliss, "Teen Comes Back Home," *The Ledger* (Lakeland, Fla.: Feb. 6, 2001), B1.

6. Julia Ferrrante, "Mom: Teen's Adventure Was 'Too Easy,'" *The Ledger* (Lakeland, Fla.: Feb. 17, 2001), A1.

7. Ibid.

8. Author unknown, "Acorns," from "Bits and Pieces," *Biblical Studies Foundation* website, 1990, 24.

9. Dirk Beveridge, "WWII-era Bombs Dredged Up at Hong Kong Disney Site," *The Associated Press* as published in the *Orlando Sentinel* online, Feb. 5, 2001, 1–2.

10. Mike Loftus, "Ice Hockey: Introduction," *Microsoft Encarta Online Encyclopedia*, 2001, 1.

11. Lloyd Freeberg, in an editorial review for his book, *In the Bin: Reckless & Rude Stories from the Penalty Boxes of the NHL*, for *Amazon.com*, Oct. 25, 1998, 1–2.

12. John A. Shaw, "Mir: About to Take a Dive?," *Science News from the Web, Web Science News* online, 2001, 1.

13. Simon Saradzhyan, "March 23rd:D-day for Mir," *Space.com*, Mar. 19, 2001, 1.

14. Lee Seats, "Free Tacos for All?" *Freebies, About.com*, Mar. 23, 2001, 1.

15. Michael Cabbage, "The Station Should Crash at Sea, but Russia Is Hedging Its Bets," *Orlando Sentinel* (Orlando, Fla.: Mar. 18, 2001), C1.

16. Justin Pritchard, "Once in Demand, Foreign Workers Among the Dot-com Fallout," The Associated Press, *Sun-Sentinel* online, 1.

17. David Kleinbard, "The $1.7 Trillion Dot.com Lesson," *CNNfn* online, Nov. 9, 2000, 2.

18. Julekha Dash, "Survey: CEOs Are the Sacrificial Lamb at Failing Dot-Coms," *Computer World* online, Nov. 6, 2000, 1.

19. J. Kenneth Kimberlin, as quoted in *The New Encyclopedia of Christian Quotations*, 949.

Chapter 8: Slave to Your Thoughts

1. David Wellington, "The Secret Room," *SOON Magazine* online, March 1999, 5, 13.

2. At the time of this writing, eight million pounds equals around $11.5 million.

3. "Corporate Information: History," *Sotheby's* online, 2001, 1.

4. "The Present and Future of the Auction Profession," *The Walton School of Auctioneering* website, 2–5.

5. Ibid., 2–3.

6. Dave Wilkinson quoting Thomas Costain, *The Three Edwards*, as published online by Biblical Studies Foundation, 2001, 3.

7. Patricia L. Maclay, M.D., P.A., appears frequently on television and radio. She often lectures and leads group seminars on her educational program, "Choosing Wellness." Office phone: (497) 299–2882.

8. Counselor Dwight Bain suggests adding an "S" to the formula for "Stressed" or "Sad."

9. Ellen Goodman, "Battling Our Culture Is Parents' Task," *Chicago Tribune* (August 18, 1993), n.p.

10. William J. Bennett, *The Index of Leading Cultural Indicators 2001, Empower.org*, 2001, 1–5.

11. Alex Cukan, "Bill Bennett's Index of Leading Cultural Indicators: Good News, Bad News," *UPI* (Albany, N.Y.: March 10, 2001), 1–2.

12. Robert P. Dugan Jr., *Winning the New Civil War* (Sisters, Ore.: Multnomah, 1991), 169.

13. See 1 Corinthians 10:1–7, especially verse 7.

14. George Barna, *Boiling Point* (Ventura, Calif.: Regal, 2001), 82.

15. Michael Esslinger, "Escape Attempts," *Alcatraz History* website, 2001, 1–2.

16. A quote by Hammarsten.

Chapter 9: S.—Sinful Thoughts Confessed

1. "Sub Tragedy: How Drill Turned to Disaster," *BBC News* online, Feb. 16, 2001, 1–4.

2. "Jim Bakker," *The Columbia Electronic Encyclopedia*, Columbia University Press, 1994, 2000, 1.

3. Phil Callaway, ed., "Jim Bakker Interview," *Servant* magazine online, Prairie Bible Institute, Winter, 1997, 1.

4. Ibid., 3.

5. Phil Callaway, ed., "Between the Lines," *Servant* magazine online, Prairie Bible Institute, Winter, 1997, 1.

6. Charles Allen, *The Sermon on the Mount* (Old Tappan, N.J.: Revell, 1966), 44–46.

7. "The KJV New Testament Greek Lexicon," *Crosswalk*.com, 1996–2000, 1.

8. "1999 SDA National Cleaning Survey," *The Soap and Detergent Association* website, 2001, 1–2.

9. "Soap Ingredients," *The Soap and Detergent Association* website, 2001, 1.

10. Robert L. Wolfe, *What Einstein Told His Barber* (New York: Dell, 2000), 194–96.

11. Source unknown.

12. Source unknown, "Cleansing," *Biblical Studies Foundation* website, 1995–2000, 1.

13. David F. Burgess, *Encyclopedia of Sermon Illustrations* (St. Louis: Concordia, 1988), 46–47.

Chapter 10: T.—Think on These Things

1. Barbara Bianco, "Venture Inward/Part One: Meditation for Dummies," *New Age* website, 2001, 1.

2. Ibid., 1–2.

3. "A Quick Guide to Sitting Meditation," *Kwan Um School of Zen* website, 2001, 1–2.

4. J. Hampton Keathley, "Biblical Meditation," *Biblical Studies Foundation* website, 2001, 2–3.

5. "A Quick Guide to Sitting Meditation," 1.

6. Keathley, "Biblical Meditation," 1–3.

7. Ricjk Kaczur, "Gum History: A Little Chewing Gum History," *AOL Members* website, 1997, 2.

8. "The Story of Chewing Gum: The Benefits of Chewing Gum," *Wm. Wrigley Jr. Co.* website, 2001, 1.

9. Author unknown, *A Primer on Meditation* (Colorado Springs, Colo.: Navigators, n.d.), 3.

10. Cary Barbor, "The Science of Meditation," *Psychology Today* (June, 2001), 58.

11. Robert J. Morgan, *Stories, Illustrations, and Quotes* (Nashville: Thomas Nelson, 2000), 547.

12. *New Man* (November/December 1994), 8.

13. William Barclay, *The Letters to the Philippians, Colossians, and Thessalonians* (Philadelphia: Westminster, 1975), 79.

14. Kevin Clements, "A Head of Steam," *European Car Magazine* (April, 2001), n.p.

15. Marsha Walton, "Could Hydrogen Be the Fuel of the Future?" *CNN Science and Technology* website, March 16, 2001, 1–3.

16. Author unknown, "Veggie Car Takes a Spin," *BBC News* website, May 3, 2001, 1–2.

17. Source unknown.

Chapter 11: O.—Order Every Thought

1. Philip E. Hughes, *The Second Epistle to the Corinthians* (New International Commentary on the New Testament, Grand Rapids: Eerdmans, 1962), 350–51.

2. Ibid., 351–52.

3. Austin Ruse, "Turner Attacks Christianity at U.N. 'Peace Summit,'" *NewsMax.com*, Aug. 30, 2000, 1–2.

4. Ibid., 2.

5. "Ted Turner Voices the Truth (Finally)," *HolySmoke* website, 2001, 1.

6. R. C. H. Lenski, *Interpretation of 1 and 2 Corinthians* (Minneapolis: Augsburg, 1937), 1209.

7. Evangelist Larry McFadden has written an effective booklet entitled *What to Do When the Bottom Falls Out!* which deals with his experiences with depression and offers helpful counsel to others who are dealing with this kind of pain. It is published by and available through Larry McFadden Ministries, P.O. Box 568545, Orlando, FL 32856 or at McFaddenMin@aol.com.

8. "Everyone Wants to Rule the World," *ABCNews.com Special Report*, ABC News and Starwave Corp., 1998, 1–3.

9. Robert Young Pelton, "What Danger Awaits the Weary Traveler?" *Robert Young Pelton's Dangerous Places, Comebackablive.com*, Fielding Worldwide, Inc., 1998, 1.

10. David Clarke, Ph.D., is the author of *A Marriage after God's Own Heart* (Portland: Multnomah, 2001). Dr. Clarke may be contacted at his practice, Marriage & Family Enrichment Center/Institutes, in Tampa, Florida, or via his website: www.davidclarkeseminars.com.

11. Stephen Arterburn and Fred Stoeker, *Every Man's Battle* (Colorado Springs: WaterBrook Press, 2000), 125, 133, 163.

12. Mr. Blackwell, "Mr. Blackwell's Wit and Wisdom," *Mr. Blackwell* website, 1997, 1.

13. Kevin Matthews, "Kansai Air Terminal: Introduction," *Renzo Piano Workshop Foundation* website, Artiface, Inc., 1994–2001, 1–2.

Chapter 12: P.—Pursue Christ-Mindedness

1. William Claiborne and Don Phillips, "Railroad Worker Jumps Into, Stops Runaway Train," *The Washington Post* (May 16, 2001), A03.

2. Eric Slater, "Runaway Freight Train Is Finally Halted," *Los Angeles Times* online, May 16, 2001, 1–3.

3. Author unknown, "Elimination," *Biblical Studies Foundation* website, 2001, 3–4.

4. Cheryl Walterman Stewart, "A Perfect Mistake," 1989, reprinted in *Christianity Today* 42 (March/April, 1998): 83.

5. Buck Wolf, "Mind over Matter," *The Wolf Files: News You Might Have Missed*, ABC News website, Dec. 17, 2000, 2.

6. A.T. Robertson, *The Epistles of Paul: Vol. IV, Word Pictures in the New Testament* (Nashville: Broadman, 1931), 500.

7. Mark I. Pinsky, "Saint Flanders," *Christianity Today* 45 (Feb. 5, 2001), 29.

8. Ibid., 29–30.

9. Jim Clayton, "Part One: Getting Ready," *Accountability: Pursuing Vital Relationships, Men of Integrity* website, 2001, 1–4.

10. For more information about Dwight Bain, visit his website: www.dwightbain.com.

If you are interested in having Jay Dennis or Marilyn Jeffcoat speak at your church, conference, retreat, or Christian event, please contact:

Interact: 1-800-370-9932

We want to hear from you. Please send your comments about this book to us in care of the address below. Thank you.

GRAND RAPIDS, MICHIGAN 49530

WWW.ZONDERVAN.COM